THE WHOLE30®
SLOW COOKER

THE WHOLE30®
SLOW COOKER

150 Totally Compliant
Prep-and-Go Recipes
for Your Whole30

MELISSA HARTWIG

Photography by Ghazalle Badiozamani

HOUGHTON MIFFLIN HARCOURT
Boston • New York • 2018

Copyright © 2018 by Thirty & Co., LLC

Whole30® is a registered trademark of Thirty & Co., LLC.

The Whole30 logo is a trademark of Thirty & Co., LLC.

Photography copyright © 2018 by Ghazalle Badiozamani

Prop styling by Paola Andrea

Food styling by Monica Pierini

www.hmhco.com

Library of Congress Cataloging-in-Publication Data
Names: Hartwig, Melissa, author. | Badiozamani, Ghazal photographer,
Title: The Whole30 slow cooker : 150 totally compliant prep-and-go recipes
for your Whole30 with Instant Pot recipes / Melissa Hartwig ;
photography by Ghazalle Badiozamani.
Description: Boston : Houghton Mifflin Harcourt, 2018. | Includes index.
Identifiers: LCCN 2018032711 (print) | LCCN 2018035447 (ebook) |
ISBN 9781328531087 (ebook) | ISBN 9781328531049 (paper over board)
Subjects: LCSH: Diet therapy—Popular works. | Nutrition—Popular works. |
Food habits—Popular works. | Self-care, Health—Popular works. |
Weight loss—Popular works. | Menus—Planning—Popular works. | Pressure cooking.
| Electric cooking, Slow. | LCGFT: Cookbooks.
Classification: LCC RA784 (ebook) | LCC RA784 .H37295 2018 (print) |
DDC 641.5/884—dc23
LC record available at https://lccn.loc.gov/2018032711

Book design by Vertigo Design NYC

Printed in USA DOC 10 9 8 7 6 5 4 3 2 1

To my mom, who just finished her first Whole30 and made me so proud

CONTENTS

ACKNOWLEDGMENTS

To Justin Schwartz, my editor at Houghton Mifflin Harcourt, somehow each book we do together gets better and better. For that, and you, I am grateful.

To Bruce Nichols, Ellen Archer, Marina Padakis, Claire Safran, Rebecca Liss, Brianna Yamashita, Breanne Sommer, Allison Chi, Rebecca Springer, and the entire Houghton Mifflin Harcourt team, you've helped me bring six (!) resources for my community to life. I am so happy to be part of the HMH family.

To Andrea Magyar and Tonia Addison at Penguin Canada, thank you for your continued faith in me and the Whole30, and for helping me serve my Canadian community.

To Christy Fletcher, I wouldn't want to do any of this without you. Thank you for being a friend, an advocate, and the best damn agent I could have hoped for.

To Grainne Fox, Melissa Chinchillo, Erin McFadden, Sarah Fuentes, Alyssa Taylor, and the Fletcher and Company team, you support my books, events, and speaking engagements so tirelessly. I am so lucky to have you all on my team.

To Ghazalle Badiozamani, how lucky am I to have you shoot two books? These photos are even more beautiful than the last, and I am grateful for your vision.

To Paola Andrea and Monica Pierini, your skills and creativity brought these meals to life. Thank you for sharing your talents with us.

To my Whole30 team: Kristen Crandall, Shanna Keller, Jen Kendall, Karyn Scott, Stephanie Greunke, Bill Ferrante, and Maggie Lopez, your passion for our program and community are unparalleled. You are Whole30.

To my team of Whole30 Certified Coaches, out there spreading the love in your local communities: you are the future of this program, and I am so grateful for you all.

To Sarah Steffens, our in-house recipe creative, thank you for sharing your best tips and tricks for this book. Your vision and execution were, as always, flawless.

To my mom, who not only took on the Whole30 this year but *rocked it* in a spectacular fashion . . . I'm thrilled, and honored, and so happy you had a great experience.

To my family and friends, I feel like you didn't even know I was working on this book, which is a really good sign that I took on just the right amount of work this year. Sweet. (And thank you for your ongoing love and support.)

To Dallas, thank you for your contributions to the Whole30 program so many years ago.

To my son, you are my whole world.

Finally, to YOU, my Whole30'ers. All of this is for you. It's always for you. My love for you and this program is fierce and undying. For you, I am grateful.

PREFACE

I bought my first Instant Pot in 2017, after hearing so many friends rave about how fast and easy it made meal prep. I'd been using my slow cooker a few times a week, adding ingredients in the morning to be ready for dinnertime. But it wasn't always easy to chop, brown, and measure while trying to get my son ready for the day, and more often than not I found myself doing the math around lunchtime: "If I start prepping now, we can eat at eight p.m. . . ." I was sure the Instant Pot was going to be the answer—all the same delicious meals in a fraction of the time.

When I took the thing out of the box, though, I immediately felt overwhelmed. So many buttons. A steam release valve with a danger warning. A timer that counts down, THEN BACK UP—what kind of wizardry is that? I Googled a little, then stuffed it back in the cabinet and went back to my trusty slow cooker.

Once I started seeing the Instant Pot recipes my team was creating for this book, though, I knew it was time to pull on my big-kid pants, dust the thing off, and give it another go. If so many of you could learn your way around an Instant Pot, so could I . . . especially if I wanted to taste-test these recipes for myself. I asked Whole30's in-house recipe creative, Sarah Steffens, for her best slow-cooker and Instant Pot tips. (You can find them on page xxi.) After reading through her helpful hints, I realized I was overthinking it.

It's like *two buttons*, Melissa. You can handle that.

Following the Instant Pot instructions in the sidebar, I made my first official Whole30 Instant Pot recipe—the Chicken, Lime, and Avocado Soup from guest contributor Alex Snodgrass (page 93). It was everything I'd hoped it would be. Delicious, hearty Whole30 ingredients dumped into one pot, magically transformed into a complete meal in under an hour . . . with very little hands-on time. A little chopping, a little measuring, and BOOM, we had soup.

What TOOK me so long?

Today, I'm seeing the Instant Pot *everywhere*, but whether you're in on the trend of pressure cooking or in a committed relationship with your slow cooker, these kitchen tools are mission-critical for your Whole30. Sure, the program itself is only 30 days, and you *could* cook everything by hand in the oven or on the stovetop for a month. But in a survey of nearly 5,000 Whole30 alumni, 72 percent of them said they had retained most of the healthy habits they learned during their Whole30 program more than a year after their program was over. That means you'll almost surely still be happily cooking mostly Whole30 meals a year from now! And a year-plus is a long time to cook everything by hand on demand.

Learning to incorporate a slow cooker or Instant Pot into your weekly routine will make mealtime—especially weeknight dinners and leftover lunches—fit seamlessly around work, kids, exercise, homework, laundry, and social events. You can prep in the morning and set for dinner, as I do, or prep the night before, taking two minutes to toss it all in the next day. (Or, prep in the evening and let it cook overnight*, waking up to the delicious smell of "what's for dinner tonight?" victory.)

And if slow cooking brings to mind the heavy, uniformly brown, sometimes tough stews your mom used to make . . . think twice. We've got salads, wraps, veggie "noodle" dishes, even fish and shellfish that can be prepared quickly and easily in your slow cooker or Instant Pot. Light, fresh, company-worthy dishes with a secret—you barely did any work at all to take them from ingredients to a complete meal. And many of the recipes make extra, because on the Whole30, leftovers are gold. Plain old eggs for breakfast take on new life when topped with leftover pork belly (Pork Belly Breakfast Bowl, page 141), and lunchtime is exciting again when you're bringing in Sesame Chicken Wraps (page 20). Just be prepared for "What kind of gourmet lunch are you eating today?" from your co-workers.

Before we dive into Sarah's best Instant Pot and slow cooker tips, and the more than 150 delicious all-new recipes in this book, I'll also give you a quick review the Whole30 program basics. Whether it's your first Whole30 or your fourth, it never hurts to refresh your memory on the rules or useful tips to help you prepare for Day 1. (For a detailed guide to everything you need to know to succeed with the program, see *The Whole30: The 30-Day Guide to Total Health and Food Freedom*.)

I hope the recipes and cooking techniques in this book help you enjoy this Whole30 experience more than any other, getting you out of the kitchen and enjoying all the benefits the program has to offer faster and easier than ever. Happy slow (or quick) Whole30 cooking!

Best in health,
Melissa

*Yes, I've seen that episode of *This Is Us*. I promise, today's slow cookers and Instant Pots have *many* features that make it perfectly safe to cook while you're at work or asleep.

WHAT IS THE WHOLE30?

Think of the Whole30 like pushing the reset button with your health, your habits, and your relationship with food. The premise is simple: certain food groups could be having a negative impact on your body composition, health, and quality of life without you even realizing it. Are your energy levels inconsistent or nonexistent? Do you have aches and pains that can't be explained by overuse or injury? Are you having a hard time losing weight no matter how hard you try? Do you have some sort of condition (like skin issues, digestive ailments, seasonal allergies, or chronic fatigue) that medication hasn't helped? These symptoms may be directly related to the foods you eat—even the "healthy" stuff.

So how do you know if (and how) these foods are affecting you? Eliminate them from your diet completely. Cut out all the psychologically unhealthy, hormone-unbalancing, gut-disrupting, inflammatory food groups for a full 30 days. Let your body heal and recover from whatever effects those foods may be causing. Push the "reset" button on your metabolism, systemic inflammation, and the downstream effects of the food choices you've been making. Learn once and for all how the foods you've been eating are actually affecting your day-to-day life and your long-term health.

HOW IT WORKS

For a full 30 days, you completely eliminate the foods that scientific literature and my clinical experience have deemed the most commonly problematic in one of four areas—your cravings, metabolism, digestion, and immune system. During the elimination period, you'll be completely eliminating these foods for a set period of time, experiencing what life is like without these commonly problematic triggers while paying careful attention to improvements in energy, sleep, digestion, mood, attention span, self-confidence, cravings, chronic pain or fatigue, athletic performance and recovery, and any number of other symptoms or medical conditions. This elimination period will give you a new "normal"—a healthy baseline where, in all likelihood, you will look, feel, and live better than you ever imagined you could.

At the end of the 30 days, you then carefully and systematically reintroduce those foods you've been missing, again paying attention to any changes in your experience. Do your two p.m. energy slumps return? Does your stomach bloat? Does your face break out, your joints swell, your pain return? Does your Sugar Dragon rear his ugly head? The reintroduction period teaches you how specific foods are having a negative impact on *you*, and exactly how these foods are making you look and feel less than your best.

Put it all together, and for the first time in your life, you'll be able to make educated decisions about when, how often, and in what amount you can include these "less healthy" foods in your daily diet in a way that feels balanced and sustainable, but still keeps you feeling as awesome as you now *know* you can feel.

THE RESULTS

We cannot possibly put enough emphasis on this simple fact—the next 30 days will change your life. They will change the way you think about food, they will change your tastes, they will change your habits and your cravings. They could, quite possibly, change the emotional relationship you have with food, and with your body. They have the potential to change the way you eat for the rest of your life. We know this because we did it, and hundreds of thousands of people have done it since, and it changed our lives (and their lives) in a very permanent fashion.

The physical benefits of the Whole30 are profound. A full 96 percent of participants lose weight and improve their body composition without counting or restricting calories. Also commonly reported? Consistently high energy levels, better sleep, improved focus and mental clarity, a return to healthy digestive function, improved athletic performance, and a sunnier disposition. (Yes, many Whole30 graduates say they felt "strangely happy" during and after their program.)

The psychological benefits of the Whole30 may be even more dramatic. Through the program, participants report effectively changing long-standing, unhealthy habits related to food, developing a healthier body image, and dramatically reducing or eliminating cravings, particularly for sugar and carbohydrates. The words so many Whole30 participants use to describe this place?

"Food freedom."

Finally, testimonials from thousands of Whole30 participants document the improvement or "curing" of any number of lifestyle-related diseases and conditions.

• high blood pressure •
high cholesterol • type 1 diabetes
• type 2 diabetes • asthma •
allergies • sinus infections • hives
• skin conditions • endometriosis
• PCOS • infertility • migraines
• depression • bipolar disorder
• heartburn • GERD • arthritis
• joint pain • ADHD • thyroid
dysfunction • Lyme disease •
fibromyalgia • chronic fatigue •
lupus • leaky gut syndrome •
Crohn's • IBS •
celiac disease • diverticulitis
• ulcerative colitis

THE WHOLE30 RULES

For the next 30 days, you'll be eating meat, seafood, and eggs; lots of vegetables and fruit; and natural, healthy fats—with no slips, cheats, or special occasions. Below are the program rules. (Please refer to *The Whole30: The 30-Day Guide to Total Health and Food Freedom* for a complete list of rules, and use that book to prepare for and succeed with your program.)

DO NOT CONSUME ADDED SUGAR OF ANY KIND, REAL OR ARTIFICIAL. No maple syrup, honey, agave nectar, coconut sugar, Splenda, Equal, Nutrasweet, xylitol, stevia, etc. Read your labels, because companies sneak sugar into products in ways you might not recognize.

DO NOT CONSUME ALCOHOL IN ANY FORM. No wine, beer, champagne, vodka, rum, whiskey, tequila, etc., whether consumed on its own or used as an ingredient—not even for cooking.

DO NOT EAT GRAINS. This includes wheat, rye, barley, oats, corn, rice, millet, bulgur, sorghum, sprouted grains, and all gluten-free pseudo-cereals like amaranth, buckwheat, or quinoa. This also includes all the ways we add wheat, corn, and rice into our foods in the form of bran, germ, starch, and so on. Again, read your labels.

DO NOT EAT LEGUMES. This includes beans of all kinds (black, red, pinto, navy, white, kidney, lima, fava, etc.), peas, chickpeas, lentils, and peanuts. This also includes all forms of soy—soy sauce, miso, tofu, tempeh, edamame, and all the ways we sneak soy into foods (like soybean oil or soy lecithin). No peanut butter, either. The only exceptions are green beans and snow/snap peas.

DO NOT EAT DAIRY. This includes cow's-, goat's-, or sheep's-milk products such as cream, cheese, kefir, yogurt, and sour cream. The only exceptions are clarified butter or ghee.

DO NOT CONSUME CARRAGEENAN, MSG, OR ADDED SULFITES. If these ingredients appear in any form in the ingredient list of your processed food or beverage, it's out for the Whole30.

DO NOT RE-CREATE BAKED GOODS, "TREATS," OR JUNK FOODS WITH APPROVED INGREDIENTS. No banana-egg pancakes, Paleo tortillas, or coconut milk ice cream. (See Let's Get Specific on page xv for more details.) Your cravings and habits won't change if you keep eating these foods, even if they are made with Whole30 ingredients.

DO NOT STEP ON THE SCALE OR TAKE MEASUREMENTS. Your reset is about so much more than just weight loss; focusing on your body composition means you'll miss out on the most dramatic and lifelong benefits this plan has to offer. So no weighing yourself, analyzing body fat, or breaking out the tape measure during your Whole30.

LET'S GET SPECIFIC

A few off-limits foods that fall under the "No baked goods, treats, or re-created junk foods" rule include pancakes, bread, tortillas, biscuits, crepes, muffins, cupcakes, cookies, pizza crust, waffles, cereal, store-bought chips of any kind, restaurant French fries, and that one recipe where eggs, date paste, and coconut milk are combined with prayers to create a thick, creamy concoction that can once again transform your undrinkable black coffee into sweet, dreamy caffeine. However, while this list of off-limits foods applies to everyone (even those who don't "have a problem" with bread or pancakes), you may decide your personal Off-limits List includes additional foods that you already know make you feel out of control. (See page 95 in *The Whole30* for guidance.)

THE FINE PRINT

These foods are exceptions to the rule and are allowed during your Whole30.

CLARIFIED BUTTER OR GHEE. Clarified butter (page 296) or ghee are the only sources of dairy allowed during your Whole30, as they've had their milk solids rendered out. Plain old butter is *not* allowed, as its milk proteins could impact the results of your program.

FRUIT JUICE AS A SWEETENER. Products or recipes that include orange, apple, or other fruit juices are permitted on the program, although we encourage you not to go overboard here.

GREEN BEANS AND SNOW/SNAP PEAS. While these are technically legumes, they are far more "pod" than "bean," and green plant matter is generally good for you.

VINEGAR. Most forms of vinegar, including distilled white, balsamic, apple cider, red wine, white wine, champagne, and rice, are allowed during your Whole30 program. The only exceptions are flavored vinegars with added sugar, or malt vinegar, which is thought to contain gluten.

COCONUT AMINOS. All brands of coconut aminos (a brewed and naturally fermented soy sauce substitute) are acceptable, even if you see the word "coconut nectar" in the ingredient list.

IODIZED SALT. All iodized salt contains a tiny amount of dextrose (sugar) as a stabilizer, but ruling out table salt would be unreasonable. This exception will not impact your Whole30 results in any way.

IT'S FOR YOUR OWN GOOD

Here comes the tough love, heavy on the love—perhaps the most famous part of the Whole30. This is for those of you who are considering taking on this life-changing month, but aren't sure you can actually pull it off, cheat-free, for a full 30 days. This is for people who have tried to make lifestyle changes but "slipped" or "fell off the wagon" or "just *had* to eat [fill in food here] because of this [fill in event here]."

IT IS NOT HARD. Don't you dare tell me this is hard. Beating cancer is hard. Birthing a baby is hard. Losing a parent is hard. Drinking your coffee black is. not. hard. You've done harder things than this, and you have no excuse not to complete the program as written. It's only 30 days, and it's for the most important health cause on earth: the only physical body you will ever have in this lifetime.

DON'T EVEN CONSIDER CHEATING. Unless you physically trip and your face lands in a box of doughnuts, there is no "slip." You make a choice to eat something unhealthy. It is always a choice, so do not phrase it as if you had an accident. Commit to the program 100 percent for the full 30 days. Don't give yourself an excuse to fail before you've even started.

YOU NEVER, EVER, EVER HAVE TO EAT ANY-THING YOU DON'T WANT TO EAT. You're all big boys and girls. Toughen up. Learn to say no (or make your mom proud and say, "No, thank you"). Learn to stick up for yourself. Just because it's your sister's birthday, or your best friend's wedding, or your company picnic does not mean you have to eat anything. It's always a choice, and we would hope that you stopped succumbing to peer pressure in seventh grade.

THIS DOES REQUIRE A BIT OF EFFORT. Grocery shopping, meal planning, dining out, explaining the program to friends and family, and dealing with stress will all prove challenging at some point during your program. We've given you all the tools, guidelines, and resources you'll need in our books and on our website, but you also have to take responsibility for your own plan. Improved health, fitness, and quality of life don't happen automatically just because you're now taking a pass on bread.

YOU *CAN* DO THIS. You've come too far to back out now. You want to do this. You need to do this. And we know that you can do this. So stop thinking about it, and start doing it. Right now, this very minute, commit to the Whole30.

I want you to participate. I want you to take this seriously and see amazing results in unexpected areas. Even if you don't believe this will actually change your life, if you're willing to give it 30 short days, *try it*. It is that important. I believe in it that much. It changed my life, and I want it to change yours, too.

Welcome to the Whole30.

GETTING STARTED WITH THE WHOLE30

Planning and preparation are the key to success on the Whole30. Here are some basic steps for getting your home and your head Whole30-ready. For a more detailed step-by-step plan for getting started with the program, see pages 17 to 31 in *The Whole30*.

STEP 1: CHOOSE YOUR START DATE

Start *as soon as you possibly can*, but plan carefully. If you've got a once-in-a-lifetime vacation, a planned trip to an unfamiliar location, or a wedding (especially your own!) in your immediate future, consider starting the Whole30 after those events. It's also important not to have your Whole30 end the day before a vacation, holiday, or special event. That portion of the program is just as critical as the 30-day elimination. Ideally, you'll allow a full 10 days after your Whole30 is done to go through the schedule as outlined, *then* enjoy your special event.

Finally, take a look at your calendar during the proposed 30-day period and see what business or personal commitments you have in place. If you've got a family dinner, a business lunch, or a bridal shower in your imminent future, excellent! Consider it an opportunity to take your Whole30 skills out on the town, and create a plan for how to handle it (see Step 4). You'll have to deal with lots of new situations during your program, so *don't* let them push your Whole30 off.

In summary, there will never be a "perfect" time to do the Whole30, so think about what you have coming up, choose a date, and circle it on your calendar in permanent marker. (Really—write it down. Habit research shows that putting your commitment on paper makes you more likely to succeed.)

STEP 2: BUILD YOUR SUPPORT TEAM

Finding the right support network will be critical to keeping you motivated, inspired, and accountable during your program. The first step is sharing a bit about the program, leading with the things you *will* be eating. Say something like, "For thirty days, I'll eat lots of whole, fresh, nutritious foods—no calorie counting at all! Breakfast could be a vegetable frittata, fresh fruit, and avocado; lunch is a spinach salad with grilled chicken, apples, pecans, and a raspberry-walnut vinaigrette; and dinner is pulled pork carnitas with roasted sweet potato and a cabbage slaw."

You should also share with those you care about *why* you are choosing to embark upon this journey. Make it personal. Share your current struggles, your goals, and all the ways you believe the program will make you healthier and happier. Try something like, "Every day at three p.m., I feel like I need a nap. I'm hoping the Whole30 will help me keep my energy up without my usual afternoon soda and candy bar."

Finally, don't forget to *ask* for their support. Saying very directly, "Can I count on you to support me for the next thirty days?" lets them know how important these efforts are to you and how much you'd value their encouragement and help.

Still, despite all your best efforts, family and friends may be less than supportive of your Whole30 plan. If you're having a hard time talking to friends and family about the Whole30 or are dealing with pushback during your conversations, read the Friends, Family, and Food section in *Food Freedom Forever* for guidance.

STEP 3: GET YOUR HOUSE READY

First, get all the stuff you won't be eating out of the house. It's time to clean out the pantry—be thorough; throw out the foods you won't be eating, give them to a neighbor for safekeeping, or (if you feel right about this) donate them to a local food bank.

If you're the only one at home doing the Whole30, dedicate one drawer in your fridge and one out-of-the-way cabinet for your family's off-plan items, so you don't have to reach around the Oreos every time you need a can of coconut milk.

Even if you're not the planning type, make a plan for what you'll eat for breakfast, lunch, and dinner for the first three to seven days of your Whole30. Then, go grocery shopping and buy everything you need for your first set of meals, plus Whole30 pantry staples. (See whole30.com/pdf-downloads for a detailed Shopping List.)

STEP 4: PLAN FOR SUCCESS

Think about the next 30 days, and write down every potentially stressful, difficult, or complicated situation you may encounter during your Whole30. These may include business lunches, family dinners, travel plans, a long day at work, birthday parties, holiday celebrations, office gatherings, family stress, job stress, financial stress . . . anything you think might derail your Whole30 train. Then, make a plan for how you'll handle it. Use if/then statements when crafting plans. Some examples might include:

BUSINESS LUNCH: If my coworkers pressure me to have a drink, then I'll say, "I'm doing this food experiment to see if I reduce my allergies—I'll just have a mineral water, please."

FAMILY DINNER: If Mom invites me out for dinner, then I'll remind her I'm doing the Whole30 and ask if I can cook for her instead.

TRAVEL DAY: If I get to the airport and my flight is delayed, then I'll snack on the EPIC bars, apples, carrot sticks, and individual-size packet of almond butter I brought in my carry-on.

Finally, plan three quick and easy "go-to" meals you can make in 10 minutes or less with foods you always have on hand. Write your list down and post it on your fridge so you'll always have a plan for nights when things just get crazy.

STEP 5: TOSS THAT SCALE

This is your last and final step in preparing for the Whole30—for the next 30 days, get rid of your scale. Put it in the garage, give it to a friend to "hold," or better yet, take it out back and introduce it to your sledgehammer in a nice little pre-Whole30 ritual.

We don't want you to ignore your body for the next 30 days—keep an eye on how your clothes are fitting, whether your stomach is flatter, your rings are looser, or your skin is clearer. You can also take before and after measurements; weigh yourself, take body measurements, and/or a photograph on Day 0, and then again on Day 31.

READY, SET, WHOLE30!

And with that (and perhaps a quick refresher of the program details, FAQs, and Whole30 Timeline in *The Whole30*), you're ready to dive into your Whole30 program . . . and these delicious meals you'll find in the seven recipe chapters. *Bon appétit!*

WHOLE30 AND SLOW COOKING

Slow cooking is one of our favorite ways to prepare delicious, nurturing, and hearty meals with little effort and big results. The ritual of filling your slow cooker with seasonal meats and veggies to enjoy after a long day is so satisfying. Whether you are prepping a slow-cooked meal to come home to after a busy weekday or enjoying the aromas of a pressure-cooked meal in your Instant Pot on a Sunday evening, slow cooking remains one of the easiest ways to prepare and savor Whole30 meals any day of the week.

SLOW COOKER TIPS

A slow cooker is one of the most cost-effective and useful Whole30 kitchen gadgets. It makes meal prep and clean-up a breeze, and does all the hard work of cooking for you, sometimes while you're not even home. To make the most out of your slow cooking, here are some best practices.

- Fill your slow cooker half to two-thirds full for best results.

- If using lots of different veggies, cut them the same size for uniform cooking times.

- Cheaper cuts of meat cook best in the slow cooker. Think brisket, chuck roasts, bone-in chicken, and pork shoulder. Leaner cuts such as chicken breast and pork loin tend to dry out more easily, so if using these meats, be generous with added fats such as ghee or coconut oil.

- Avoid using frozen foods in the slow cooker.

- It's not necessary to brown the meat you cook in the slow cooker, but if you have time, it will enhance the flavor of your meal.

- Don't peek and open the lid while slow cooking! It's tempting, but for every time you remove the lid, you'll need an extra 15 to 20 minutes of cooking time. Patience is a virtue.

- If you live in a high-altitude area, calculate an extra 30 minutes for each hour of cooking time suggested in recipes.

- If you find you have a lot of extra liquid in your slow cooker, transfer it to a sauce pan and simmer over medium heat for about 10 minutes, allowing it to thicken, for a flavorful sauce to serve with your dish.

- Salt your food at the *end* of cooking. Vegetables will release water as they cook, and the salt you add at the start of slow cooking will dissipate. Try salting to taste at the end of cooking for exceptional flavor.

- Fresh herbs such as parsley, scallions, cilantro, mint, and dill make any slow-cooked dish pop with color, so garnish liberally for a beautiful and delicious dish.

- Protect the ceramic insert from cracking by not placing it in cold water while it is still hot. This goes also for a cold insert that you have prepped in the fridge—allow it to come to room temperature before turning the slow cooker on.

WHOLE30 AND THE INSTANT POT

We can't help but think the Instant Pot was created *just* for the Whole30, and we're willing to bet that once you use it, it'll change your life, too. The Instant Pot is perfect for Whole30 meals that are rich in flavor, tender, and cook fast. From hearty stews and juicy roasts to quickly steamed veggies, hard boiled eggs, and bone broth, you will love preparing delicious Whole30 meals in your Instant Pot, even if you *aren't* short on time!

INSTANT POT TIPS

- The Instant Pot is safe to use for home cooks at all levels of experience; simply follow the recipe and wait to open the lid until the recipe suggests.

- Check your recipe to determine whether you set the venting knob to sealed or not.

- The cook time to which you set your Instant Pot is *not* the actual time it will take to cook. Your Instant Pot will need 10 to 15 minutes to heat up and build pressure. Once your timer reaches "0," recipes requiring steam to release naturally will need another 15 to 30 minutes to finish cooking.

- Always have at least ½ cup of liquid in the insert at all times, but do not fill with ingredients and liquid more than two-thirds full.

- Use cooking liquids such as bone broth, stocks, and coconut milk.

- Smaller cuts of meat will cook faster than larger cuts and whole roasts. If you are short on time, cube your meat in bite-size pieces to speed up cooking time!

- A splash of fresh citrus juice or apple cider vinegar will go a long way to tenderize your meats even more.

- When using quick release, allow 1 to 2 minutes for all of the steam to vent.

- You can easily steam veggies in your Instant Pot. Simply refer to the timing chart in your Instant Pot manual.

- You can also sauté foods in your Instant Pot. This is perfect for browning a cut of meat before setting it to pressure cook, as it will save an extra pan when it comes time to clean up.

- You can create delicious sauces with the liquid leftover in your insert after cooking by removing all the cooked pieces of food, transferring the liquid to a saucepan, and simmering over medium heat for about 10 minutes.

- As with slow cooking, salt your dishes to taste *after* they are finished cooking.

- Your Instant Pot will keep foods warm (and safe to eat) for 10 hours.

- You can remove the plastic sealer on your Instant Pot lid to clean it. A crumpled piece of aluminum foil can be used to clean the insert.

MAIN-DISH SALADS AND WRAPS

BEEF FAJITA SALAD

SERVES 6

PREP: 50 minutes

SLOW COOK: 6 hours (low) or
3 hours (high)

TOTAL: 6 hours 50 minutes

Lean and flavorful flank steaks are slow cooked with onions and peppers in a lime-shallot-garlic-paprika-cumin marinade. The long soak gives the meat amazing flavor before it's sliced and served on crisp romaine lettuce with a tomato-avocado salsa.

2 beef flank steaks (1 pound each)

¼ cup plus 1 tablespoon
fresh lime juice

¼ cup plus 1 tablespoon
avocado oil

¼ cup finely chopped shallots

2 cloves garlic, minced

1 teaspoon paprika

½ teaspoon ground cumin

1 medium red onion, cut into
½-inch-thick slices

3 medium red, green, or yellow
bell peppers, quartered

1 medium avocado, halved,
pitted, peeled, and chopped

¾ cup quartered cherry tomatoes
or chopped seeded tomatoes

¼ cup thinly sliced green
onion tops

⅛ teaspoon salt

⅛ teaspoon cayenne pepper

6 cups torn romaine lettuce

½ cup chopped fresh cilantro

USING a sharp knife, score the flank steaks on both sides with shallow diagonal cuts 1 inch apart. Place the steaks in a large shallow baking dish. In a small bowl, whisk together ¼ cup of the lime juice, ¼ cup of the oil, the shallots, garlic, paprika, and cumin. Pour over the steaks in the baking dish, turning to coat the steaks all over with the marinade. Cover and marinate at room temperature for 30 minutes, turning once. (For even more flavor, marinate the steaks, covered, in the refrigerator for up to 8 hours.)

PLACE the red onion slices in a 5- to 6-quart slow cooker. Top with the marinated steaks. Top the steaks with the peppers. Cover and cook on low for 6 to 7 hours or on high for 3 to 3½ hours.

IN a medium bowl, combine the remaining 1 tablespoon lime juice, remaining 1 tablespoon avocado oil, the avocado, tomatoes, green onion tops, salt, and cayenne.

USING a slotted spoon, transfer the peppers and onions to a cutting board; cut the peppers into thin strips. Transfer the steaks to the cutting board; thinly slice across the grain. Arrange the lettuce on six serving plates. Top with the beef, pepper strips, onion slices, guacamole, and cilantro.

CARNE ASADA STEAK SALAD

SERVES 4

PREP: 35 minutes

SLOW COOK: 4 hours (low) or 2 hours (high)

TOTAL: 4 hours 35 minutes

Tenting the meat with foil after it comes out of the cooker helps preserve some of the heat as it rests—and resting the meat is crucial to the tastiest results. As it sits, the juices are reabsorbed back into the meat, keeping it juicy and flavorful. Slice it too soon and all of those yummy juices end up on the cutting board.

FOR THE STEAK

1 cup fresh orange juice

¼ cup fresh lemon juice

¼ cup fresh lime juice

2 tablespoons olive oil

2 tablespoon minced jalapeño

6 cloves garlic, minced

1 tablespoon chopped fresh cilantro

¼ teaspoon salt

1 pound flank or sirloin steak

FOR THE SALAD DRESSING

1 avocado, halved, pitted, and peeled

3 tablespoons extra-virgin olive oil

1 tablespoon minced jalapeño

1 tablespoon fresh lime juice

2 tablespoons chopped fresh cilantro

⅛ teaspoon ground cumin

¼ teaspoon salt

½ cup water

FOR THE SALAD

6 cups mixed salad greens

¼ cup sliced radishes

1 cup halved grape or cherry tomatoes

½ cup coarsely chopped green bell pepper

¼ cup sliced green onions

MAKE THE STEAK: In a 4-quart slow cooker, combine the orange, lemon, and lime juices, olive oil, jalapeño, garlic, cilantro, and salt. Place the steak in the slow cooker; turn to coat both sides.

COVER and cook for 4 hours on low or 2 hours on high, turning the steak once halfway through cooking. Transfer the steak to a cutting board; tent with foil while preparing the salad dressing.

MAKE THE DRESSING: In a food processor, combine the avocado, olive oil, jalapeño, lime juice, cilantro, cumin, and salt. Process until smooth. Continue to process, slowly adding water until the dressing reaches the desired consistency.

ASSEMBLE THE SALAD: Arrange the salad greens, radishes, tomatoes, and bell pepper on four serving plates. Slice the steak thinly and add to the salads. Drizzle with the avocado dressing and top with sliced green onions.

CHICKEN TACO SALAD

SERVES 4

PREP: 15 minutes

SLOW COOK: 5 hours (low) or 2½ hours (high)

TOTAL: 5 hours 15 minutes

A mixture of lime zest, lime juice, cilantro, and salt provides the base for flavoring both the chicken and the dressing. Chili powder and cumin are added to the seasoning for the chicken—and a splash of olive oil is added to make the dressing.

1 tablespoon minced fresh cilantro

1 teaspoon grated lime zest

¼ cup fresh lime juice

½ teaspoon salt

1 medium onion, cut into wedges

1½ pounds bone-in chicken thighs, skin removed

1 tablespoon chili powder

1 teaspoon ground cumin

2 tablespoons extra-virgin olive oil

8 cups torn romaine lettuce

1 medium tomato, chopped

1 avocado, halved, pitted, peeled, and thinly sliced

Chopped fresh cilantro, for serving (optional)

IN a small bowl, combine the cilantro, lime zest, lime juice, and salt until well blended. Divide the lime juice mixture into two small bowls; set aside.

IN a 3½- to 4-quart slow cooker, layer the onion and chicken thighs. To one of the bowls of the lime juice mixture, add the chili powder and cumin and pour over the chicken and onions. Cover and refrigerate the remaining lime juice mixture for the dressing.

COVER and cook on low for 5 to 6 hours or on high for 2½ to 3 hours. Transfer the chicken and onions to a cutting board. Using two forks, pull the chicken apart into large shreds.

MEANWHILE, whisk the olive oil into the reserved lime juice mixture until well combined.

LAYER the lettuce, chicken, onions, tomato, and avocado on serving plates. Drizzle with the dressing and top with cilantro, if desired.

INSTANT POT VARIATION *Follow the directions using a 6-quart Instant Pot. Lock the lid in place. Select Manual and cook at high pressure for 15 minutes. Use natural release for 5 minutes, then quick release. Follow the remaining directions.*

CHIMICHURRI SHREDDED PORK AND CABBAGE SALAD

SERVES 6

PREP: 45 minutes

SLOW COOK: 9 hours (low) or 4½ hours (high)

TOTAL: 9 hours 45 minutes

Tender shredded pork shoulder is served on a crunchy and colorful riot of shredded cabbage, carrot, green onions, and golden raisins and drizzled with a chimichurri vinaigrette. Be sure to buy unsulfured golden raisins. They are sometimes referred to as sultanas and will be darker in color than sulfured golden raisins.

1 teaspoon salt

1 teaspoon garlic powder

1 teaspoon ground cumin

1 teaspoon black pepper

2½ to 3 pounds boneless pork shoulder, trimmed and cut into 3 pieces

1 cup packed fresh cilantro, large stems removed, plus extra for serving

1 cup packed fresh flat-leaf parsley, large stems removed, plus extra for serving

¼ cup chopped shallots

3 cloves garlic, chopped

¼ cup plus 3 tablespoons extra-virgin olive oil

3 tablespoons white wine vinegar

¼ teaspoon red pepper flakes

8 cups coarsely shredded cored savoy or green cabbage

1 cup purchased shredded carrots

½ cup thinly sliced green onion tops

½ cup unsulfured golden raisins

3 tablespoons fresh lemon juice

3 tablespoons extra-virgin olive oil

½ cup chopped walnuts or pecans, toasted (see Tip)

IN a small bowl, combine ½ teaspoon of the salt, the garlic powder, cumin, and pepper. Sprinkle all over the pork pieces; rub in with your fingers. Place the pork in a 4-quart slow cooker. Add ½ cup water.

COVER and cook on low for 9 to 10 hours or on high for 4½ to 5 hours. Transfer the pork to a cutting board; cool for about 10 minutes. Using two forks, coarsely shred the pork; transfer to a large bowl.

MEANWHILE, in a blender or food processor, combine the cilantro, parsley, shallots, garlic, ¼ cup of the olive oil, the vinegar, and red pepper flakes. Cover and blend or process until almost smooth. Pour over the shredded pork and stir to combine. Set aside.

IN a large bowl, toss together the cabbage, carrots, green onion tops, and raisins. In a small bowl, whisk together the remaining 3 tablespoons olive oil, remaining ½ teaspoon salt, and the lemon juice. Pour over the cabbage salad and toss to coat. Stir in the pork. Sprinkle with the walnuts and additional cilantro and/or parsley.

> **TIP** *To toast the walnuts or pecans, heat in a dry skillet over medium heat, stirring, until fragrant and lightly browned, about 2 minutes.*

> **INSTANT POT VARIATION** *Cut the pork into 6 pieces. Follow the directions in the first two steps using a 6-quart Instant Pot. Lock the lid in place. Select Manual and cook at high pressure for 30 minutes. Use natural release for 10 minutes, then quick release. Continue with the remaining directions.*

MEDITERRANEAN CHICKEN SALAD

SERVES 4

PREP: 15 minutes

SLOW COOK: 5 hours (low) or 2½ hours (high)

TOTAL: 5 hours 15 minutes

If you don't have Italian seasoning in your spice cabinet, you can make your own: In a container with an airtight lid, combine 1 tablespoon each dried oregano, basil, and thyme; and 1 teaspoon each dried rosemary and sage. Store in a cool, dry, dark place. Shake or stir before measuring and using.

FOR THE DRESSING
½ cup extra-virgin olive oil

¼ cup fresh lemon juice

2 cloves garlic, minced

2 teaspoons Whole30-compliant Italian seasoning

¼ teaspoon salt

FOR THE CHICKEN AND SALAD
1 pound bone-in, skinless chicken thighs

1 medium red onion, cut into wedges

8 cups torn romaine lettuce

1 red bell pepper, chopped

1 medium cucumber, chopped

¼ cup sliced pitted Whole30-compliant Kalamata olives

MAKE THE DRESSING: In a small bowl, combine the olive oil, lemon juice, garlic, Italian seasoning, and salt until well blended; set aside.

MAKE THE CHICKEN: In a 4-quart slow cooker, layer the chicken and onion. Pour half the dressing over the chicken and onions. Cover and refrigerate the remaining dressing.

COVER and cook on low for 5 to 6 hours or on high for 2½ to 3 hours. Transfer the chicken and onions to a cutting board. Using two forks, pull the chicken apart into large shreds.

ARRANGE the lettuce, chicken and onion, bell pepper, cucumber, and olives on serving plates. Drizzle with the reserved dressing.

INSTANT POT VARIATION *Follow the directions using a 6-quart Instant Pot. Lock the lid in place. Select Manual and cook at high pressure for 15 minutes. Use natural release for 5 minutes, then quick release. Follow the remaining directions.*

ORANGE-OREGANO CHICKEN AND KALE SALAD WITH PICKLED ONION DRESSING

SERVES 6

PREP: 20 minutes

SLOW COOK: 6 hours (low) or 3 hours (high)

TOTAL: 6 hours 20 minutes

With a cook time of 3 to 6 hours, there's plenty of time for the onions to get good and pickled for the dressing, which is both tangy and slightly sweet from the orange juice.

FOR THE CHICKEN
3 bone-in, skin-on chicken breast halves

3 sprigs fresh oregano

2 teaspoons grated orange zest

2 cloves garlic, minced

1½ teaspoons dried oregano

½ teaspoon salt

½ teaspoon black pepper

¼ cup fresh orange juice

2 tablespoons extra-virgin olive oil

FOR THE DRESSING
2 tablespoons red wine vinegar

1 tablespoon fresh orange juice

½ teaspoon salt

½ teaspoon black pepper

3 tablespoons extra-virgin olive oil

½ cup thinly sliced red onion

1 bunch kale, stems removed and torn into bite-size pieces

MAKE THE CHICKEN: Use your fingers to loosen the skin from the meat of the chicken but do not remove the skin. Place an oregano sprig underneath the skin of each breast half. In a small bowl, combine the orange zest, minced garlic, oregano, salt, and pepper; rub over the chicken. Place the chicken in a 3½- to 4-quart slow cooker. Drizzle with the orange juice, then the olive oil.

COVER and cook on low for 6 to 7 hours or on high for 3 to 3½ hours. Remove the chicken; let cool until easy to handle. Remove the chicken from the bones; discard the skin, bones, and herb sprigs. Use two forks to shred the chicken. Moisten the chicken with the cooking liquid.

MAKE THE DRESSING: Meanwhile, in a small bowl, combine the vinegar, orange juice, salt, and pepper. Whisk in the olive oil. Add the onion; cover and let stand for at least 1 hour.

PLACE the kale in a large bowl. Drizzle with the dressing and toss to coat. Add the chicken and toss to combine (the kale will wilt slightly).

INSTANT POT VARIATION *Follow the directions in the first two steps using a 6-quart Instant Pot. Lock the lid in place. Select Manual and cook at high pressure for 30 minutes. Use natural release for 10 minutes, then quick release. Follow the remaining directions.*

POLYNESIAN CHICKEN SALAD

SERVES 4

PREP: 20 minutes

SLOW COOK: 4 hours (low) or 2 hours (high)

TOTAL: 4 hours 20 minutes

The sweetness of the pineapple in this tropically inspired chicken salad helps balance out the earthy flavor of the chard. Be sure you buy pineapple that's packed in 100% juice, with no added sugar or syrup.

1½ pounds boneless, skinless chicken breasts

1 can (20 ounces) crushed pineapple in 100% pineapple juice, drained

1 green bell pepper, diced

1 red onion, finely chopped

1 clove garlic, minced

2 tablespoons coconut aminos

½ teaspoon salt

¼ teaspoon black pepper

8 chard leaves, stems removed and leaves sliced into ribbons

1 avocado, halved, pitted, peeled, and sliced

1 jalapeño, seeded, if desired, and sliced

Lime wedges

IN a 4-quart slow cooker, combine the chicken, pineapple, bell pepper, onion, garlic, coconut aminos, salt, and pepper. Turn the chicken to coat. Cover and cook on low for 4 to 5 hours or on high for 2 to 3 hours.

TRANSFER the chicken to a cutting board. Use two forks to shred the chicken, then return to the slow cooker and stir.

DIVIDE the chard among four bowls; top with the chicken mixture, avocado, and jalapeño. Serve with lime wedges.

INSTANT POT VARIATION *Cut the chicken crosswise into 1-inch-wide strips. Follow the directions in the first step using a 6-quart Instant Pot. Lock the lid in place. Select Manual and cook at high pressure for 8 minutes. Use natural release for 3 minutes, then quick release. Continue with the remaining directions.*

PORK CARNITAS LETTUCE WRAPS

SERVES 4
PREP: 20 minutes
SLOW COOK: 7 hours (low) or
3½ hours (high)
BROIL: 3 minutes
TOTAL: 7 hours 20 minutes

Prep for this popular Mexican-style dish could not be quicker or simpler—less than 15 minutes and you are on your way to the rest of your day, knowing that a healthful and wholesome dinner will be waiting for you when you get home.

1½ teaspoons ground cumin

1½ teaspoons salt

1 teaspoon black pepper

1 teaspoon chili powder

1 teaspoon dried oregano

½ teaspoon ancho chile powder

2 pounds boneless pork shoulder, trimmed and cut into 2-inch pieces

1 cup Whole30-compliant beef or chicken broth

1 onion, cut into large wedges

4 cloves garlic, minced

1 avocado, halved, pitted, peeled, and sliced

¼ cup chopped fresh cilantro

12 large Bibb lettuce leaves

1 lime, cut into wedges (optional)

IN a small bowl, combine the cumin, salt, pepper, chili powder, oregano, and ancho chile powder. Place the pork in a 4-quart slow cooker; sprinkle with the spice mixture and toss to coat. Add the broth, onion, and garlic. Cover and cook on low for 7 to 8 hours or on high for 3½ to 4 hours.

USING a slotted spoon, transfer the pork and onion to a cutting board. Use two forks to shred the pork. Preheat the broiler. Place the pork on a large rimmed baking pan. Broil until the pork is crisp, 3 to 4 minutes. Drizzle the pork with some of the cooking liquid to moisten.

DIVIDE the pork, onions, avocado, and cilantro among the lettuce leaves. Serve with lime wedges, if desired.

PORK SALAD WITH CILANTRO-LIME DRESSING

SERVES 4

PREP: 20 minutes

SLOW COOK: 5 hours (low) or 2½ hours (high)

TOTAL: 5 hours 20 minutes

Most commercial mayonnaise is made with soybean oil and preservatives—definitely not Whole30 compliant. The most common compliant mayo is made with avocado oil. It's mild-tasting enough that it doesn't interfere with the other flavors in the food that are supposed to be in the forefront—like the lime and cilantro in the dressing for this salad.

FOR THE PORK

2 teaspoons chili powder

½ teaspoon salt

¼ teaspoon ground cumin

¼ teaspoon black pepper

Dash cayenne pepper

1 Whole30-compliant pork tenderloin (about 1¼ pounds), trimmed

½ cup Whole30-compliant chicken broth or Chicken Bone Broth (page 294)

FOR THE SALAD

½ cup Whole30-compliant mayonnaise

½ teaspoon grated lime zest

1 tablespoon fresh lime juice

2 tablespoons chopped fresh cilantro

6 cups chopped butterhead lettuce

1 medium avocado, halved, pitted, peeled, and diced

1 cup grape tomatoes, halved

¼ cup sliced green onions

MAKE THE PORK: In a small bowl, combine the chili powder, salt, cumin, pepper, and cayenne; sprinkle over the pork. Add the pork to a 4-quart slow cooker. Pour the broth around the pork.

COVER and cook on low for 5 to 6 hours or on high for 2½ to 3 hours. Transfer the pork to a cutting board; cut into ½-inch slices. Discard the cooking liquid.

MAKE THE SALAD: In a small bowl, combine the mayonnaise, lime zest, lime juice, and cilantro. If the dressing is too thick, stir in water, 1 teaspoon at a time, to reach desired consistency. Arrange the lettuce on plates. Top with the pork, avocado, tomatoes, and green onions. Spoon the dressing on top. Season with additional pepper, if desired.

INSTANT POT VARIATION *Follow the directions in the first two steps using a 6-quart Instant Pot. Lock the lid in place. Select Manual and cook at high pressure for 15 minutes. Use natural release for 5 minutes, then quick release. Continue with the remaining directions.*

SESAME CHICKEN WRAPS

SERVES 4

PREP: 10 minutes

SLOW COOK: 5 hours (low) or 2½ hours (high)

TOTAL: 5 hours 10 minutes

Toasted sesame oil is delightfully powerful stuff—just a couple of teaspoons infuses the filling for these crunchy lettuce wraps with its distinctive nutty, toasty flavor.

¼ cup apple cider

¼ cup coconut aminos

2 teaspoons toasted sesame oil

2 cloves garlic, minced

½ teaspoon ground ginger

½ teaspoon red pepper flakes

1½ pounds boneless, skinless chicken thighs

12 leaves butterhead lettuce

¼ cup sliced green onions

4 teaspoons sesame seeds, toasted (see Tip)

IN a 3½- to 4-quart slow cooker, stir together the apple cider, coconut aminos, sesame oil, garlic, ginger, and red pepper flakes. Add the chicken and turn to coat the pieces.

COVER and cook on low for 5 to 6 hours or on high for 2½ to 3 hours. Transfer the chicken to a bowl. Use two forks to shred the chicken. Strain the cooking liquid. Add enough cooking liquid to the chicken to moisten. Serve the chicken in the lettuce leaves, sprinkled with the green onions and sesame seeds.

TIP *To toast sesame seeds, heat in a small dry skillet over medium heat, stirring frequently, until fragrant and light golden-brown, 3 to 5 minutes. To quickly cool, transfer the toasted seeds to a small plate.*

WARM CHICKEN SALAD

SERVES 4

PREP: 20 minutes

SLOW COOK: 4 hours (low) or
2 hours (high)

TOTAL: 4 hours 20 minutes

This is a fresh, updated, whole-foods take on an old-fashioned casserole—hot chicken salad—that's traditionally made with canned soup, cheese, and mayonnaise and topped with potato chips. This slow-cooked version has all of the same homey appeal as its retro namesake, but it won't weigh you down. (And the crunch comes from romaine lettuce, not potato chips!)

4 green onions

2½ pounds bone-in chicken thighs, skin removed (see Tip, page 169)

½ cup Whole30-compliant chicken broth or Chicken Bone Broth (page 294)

3 cloves garlic, minced

1 medium red bell pepper, diced

2 stalks celery, thinly sliced

1 tablespoon Whole30-compliant Dijon mustard

2 tablespoons cider vinegar

½ cup Whole30-compliant mayonnaise

1 package (16 ounces) hearts of romaine, chopped

THINLY slice the green onions; separate the white bottoms from the green tops. In a 4-quart slow cooker, combine the green onion whites, chicken, broth, and garlic.

COVER and cook on low for 4 hours or on high for 2 hours. Add the bell pepper and celery. Turn the slow cooker to high if using low setting. Cover and cook for 20 to 30 minutes, or until the pepper and celery are tender. Using a slotted spoon, transfer the chicken, pepper, and celery to a large bowl.

LET the chicken cool slightly. Remove the chicken from the bones; discard the bones. Use two forks to shred the chicken. Stir the mustard, vinegar, and mayonnaise into the shredded chicken.

ARRANGE the lettuce on four plates; top with the warm chicken salad. Sprinkle with the reserved sliced green onion tops.

INSTANT POT VARIATION *Follow the directions in the first two steps using a 6-quart Instant Pot. Lock the lid in place. Select Manual and cook at high pressure for 20 minutes. Use quick release. Add the bell pepper and celery to the pot. Lock the lid in place. Select Manual and cook at high pressure for 3 minutes. Use quick release. Follow the remaining directions.*

CHICKEN SHAWARMA SALAD WITH TAHINI DRESSING

FROM GRACE BRINTON OF TRU PROVISIONS

SERVES 4

PREP: 45 minutes

MARINATE: 1 hour

SLOW COOK: 6 hours (low) or 3 hours (high)

TOTAL: 7 hours 45 minutes

The best shawarma I ever had was in Europe, in a train station, for breakfast, while sitting on my suitcase. It doesn't get much better than warm spiced chicken served with a crunchy cold salad. The contrast of flavors and textures was so satisfying and the tang from onion and lemon gave it the perfect little kick. For this recipe, the longer the chicken marinates (up to 8 hours), the more it absorbs the flavors of the marinade. However, it is still delicious if you don't have time to marinate it very long. Prepare the salad just before the chicken is done cooking.

FOR THE CHICKEN

2 pounds boneless, skinless chicken thighs, cut into 2-inch pieces

3 cloves garlic, minced

2 tablespoons fresh lemon juice

2 tablespoons avocado oil

1 teaspoon ground cumin

¾ teaspoon dried thyme

¾ teaspoon paprika

¾ teaspoon chili powder

¼ teaspoon ground cinnamon

¾ teaspoon salt

¼ teaspoon black pepper

1 cup Whole30-compliant chicken broth or Chicken Bone Broth (page 294)

FOR THE TAHINI DRESSING

3 tablespoons tahini

Juice of 1 lemon

1 tablespoon cider vinegar

½ teaspoon garlic granules

¼ teaspoon ground cumin

¼ teaspoon salt

Pinch black pepper

(continued)

MAKE THE CHICKEN: In a medium bowl, combine the chicken, minced garlic, lemon juice, 1 tablespoon of the avocado oil, the cumin, thyme, paprika, chili powder, cinnamon, salt, and pepper. Toss to combine. Cover and marinate in the refrigerator for 1 hour or up to 8 hours.

IN a large skillet, heat the remaining 1 tablespoon avocado oil over medium heat. Add the chicken and cook until browned, about 5 minutes. Transfer the chicken to a 4-quart slow cooker. Add the chicken broth to the skillet and stir with a spatula, scraping up any brown bits; pour the broth over the chicken.

COVER and cook on low for 6 hours or on high for 3 hours.

MEANWHILE, MAKE THE DRESSING: In a small bowl, whisk together the tahini and lemon juice. Add 1 teaspoon water, the vinegar, garlic granules, cumin, salt, and pepper; whisk until smooth. Cover and refrigerate until serving.

WHEN the chicken is done, use a slotted spoon to transfer it to a bowl. Use two forks to break up the chicken into smaller pieces. Discard the cooking liquid.

(continued)

FOR THE SALAD

1 large cucumber, diced (2 cups)

1 cup cherry tomatoes, quartered

3 tablespoons finely chopped shallot or red onion

1½ tablespoons extra-virgin olive oil

2 teaspoons fresh lemon juice

Pinch salt and black pepper

1 small head iceberg lettuce (about 1 pound), thinly sliced

MAKE THE SALAD: In a medium bowl, combine the cucumber, tomatoes, shallot, olive oil, lemon juice, salt, and pepper.

ARRANGE the lettuce on a platter and top with the cucumber mixture. Spoon the chicken on top and drizzle with the dressing.

GRACE BRINTON, TRU PROVISIONS

Grace Brinton is the executive chef and founder of Tru Provisions, a Whole30 Approved meal delivery service based in Boston, MA. Her love for healthy cooking started as a child growing up on a farm in rural Maine. In 2012, as she began addressing some health issues, Grace discovered the Whole30 program. Not only did it lead to positive changes in her health, it also inspired her approach to running a health-focused business.

GERMAN POTATO SALAD WITH CHICKEN SAUSAGE AND SPINACH

SERVES 4

PREP: 20 minutes

SLOW COOK: 5 hours (low) or 2½ hours (high)

TOTAL: 5 hours 20 minutes

This hearty, warm salad features the flavors of classic German potato salad—tanginess from vinegar and smokiness from bacon—but has chicken-apple sausage and baby spinach added to make it a complete meal.

1½ pounds small red potatoes, sliced ¼-inch thick

1 small sweet onion, chopped

2 stalks celery, chopped

1 green bell pepper, chopped

2 slices Whole30-compliant bacon, chopped into 1-inch pieces

1 tablespoon olive oil

½ teaspoon salt

½ teaspoon black pepper

1½ packages (24 ounces total) Whole30-compliant chicken-apple sausage, halved

¼ cup Whole30-compliant chicken broth or Chicken Bone Broth (page 294)

3 tablespoons cider vinegar

¼ cup chopped Whole30-compliant dill pickles

3 tablespoons chopped fresh dill

6 cups baby spinach

IN a 4- to 5-quart slow cooker, combine the potatoes, onion, celery, bell pepper, bacon, olive oil, salt, and pepper. Add the sausages and broth. Cover and cook on low for 5 to 6 hours or on high for 2½ to 3 hours, until the potatoes are tender.

REMOVE the sausages from the slow cooker; cover to keep warm. Add the vinegar, pickles, and dill to the potato mixture in the cooker; toss to combine.

DIVIDE the spinach among four serving bowls; top each with some of the potato mixture and three sausage halves.

CHILE PORK WRAPS

SERVES 6

PREP: 25 minutes

SLOW COOK: 8 hours (low) or 4 hours (high)

TOTAL: 8 hours 25 minutes

If you can plan ahead just a bit, start soaking the cashews for the Cashew Cream the day before you plan to make the wraps. The longer they soak, the richer the flavor and texture of the finished cream. The jicama "tortillas" add a refreshing crunch to the rich pork filling and silky Cashew Cream.

FOR THE CASHEW CREAM

1 cup raw unsalted cashews, rinsed

1 teaspoon grated lime zest

⅛ teaspoon salt

FOR THE PORK

2 to 2½ pounds pork shoulder, trimmed and cut into 2-inch pieces

8 ounces tomatillos, husks removed and quartered

1 medium yellow onion, chopped

¼ cup Whole30-compliant chicken broth or Chicken Bone Broth (page 294)

1 poblano pepper, seeded and quartered

1 small jalapeño, seeded and quartered

2 cloves garlic, minced

1 teaspoon ground cumin

½ teaspoon dried oregano

½ teaspoon salt

¼ teaspoon black pepper

1 tablespoon fresh lime juice

1 jicama, sliced into 18 tortillas (see Tip, page 113)

Chopped fresh cilantro

MAKE THE CASHEW CREAM: Place the cashews in a bowl and add enough water to cover by 1 inch. Cover the bowl and let stand for 4 hours or up to overnight. Drain the cashews and rinse under cold water. Place the cashews and ¾ cup fresh water in a high-speed blender. Cover and blend until smooth. Add additional cold water, 1 tablespoon at a time, to reach drizzling consistency. Stir in the lime zest and salt.

MAKE THE PORK: In a 6-quart slow cooker, combine the pork, tomatillos, onion, broth, poblano pepper, jalapeño, garlic, cumin, oregano, salt, and pepper.

COVER and cook on low for 8 to 10 hours or on high for 4 to 5 hours. Stir in the lime juice. Transfer the pork to a bowl with a slotted spoon and use two forks to shred. Use an immersion blender to blend the cooking liquid until smooth. (Or transfer the cooking liquid to a blender, cover, and process until smooth.) Stir some sauce into the meat to moisten.

FOR the jicama tortillas, use a "Y" peeler to peel the jicama. Trim the edges to fit a mandoline. Set the mandoline to the thinnest setting and carefully slice the jicama. (One jicama yields about 18 rounds.)

SERVE the pork in the jicama tortillas. Drizzle with the cashew cream and top with chopped fresh cilantro.

TIP *Cashew cream is a silky-smooth dairy-free substitute for cream and sour cream. It can be made up to 1 week ahead; cover and store in an airtight container in the refrigerator.*

MEDITERRANEAN CHICKEN WRAPS

SERVES 4

PREP: 25 minutes

SLOW COOK: 2½ hours (high)

TOTAL: 3 hours

These wraps are aptly named—they're flavored with all kinds of hallmark ingredients from the Mediterranean, including olives, capers, roasted red peppers, lemon, garlic, and herbs.

---

1 medium onion, finely chopped

2 pounds boneless, skinless chicken breasts

1 teaspoon salt

½ teaspoon coarsely ground black pepper

1 jar (15 ounces) roasted red peppers, drained and roughly chopped

½ cup Whole30-compliant Kalamata olives

3 tablespoons Whole30-compliant capers, drained

2 tablespoons fresh lemon juice

1 tablespoon extra-virgin olive oil

2 large cloves garlic, minced

2 teaspoons Whole30-compliant Italian seasoning

16 Bibb lettuce leaves

Fresh chopped basil

PLACE the onion in a 4-quart slow cooker. Season the chicken with salt and pepper and place on the onion. Add the roasted red peppers, olives, and capers. In a small bowl, whisk together the lemon juice, olive oil, garlic, and Italian seasoning; pour over the chicken.

COVER and cook on high for 2½ to 3 hours.

USE a slotted spoon to transfer the chicken and vegetables to a bowl. Use two forks to shred the chicken; moisten with some of the cooking liquid. Serve the chicken and vegetables in the lettuce leaves, topped with basil.

MEXICAN PICADILLO
FROM ALEX SNODGRASS OF THE DEFINED DISH

SERVES 4

PREP: 25 minutes

SLOW COOK: 7 hours (low) or 3½ hours (high)

TOTAL: 7 hours 25 minutes

Take Taco Tuesday to the next level with this absolutely easy Mexican Picadillo recipe. Throwing all of the ingredients in a slow cooker and letting them stew all day lends itself to one flavorful combination. I like to serve mine in a bowl over cauliflower rice—or in lettuce cups, taco style!

1 pound extra-lean ground beef

1 medium russet potato, peeled and chopped into ½-inch cubes

1 cup diced yellow onion, plus more for serving

1 cup diced peeled carrot

½ medium green bell pepper, diced (¾ cup)

½ cup Whole 30-compliant salsa

4 cloves garlic, thinly sliced

1 jalapeño, seeded and diced

1 teaspoon chili powder

1 teaspoon salt

1 teaspoon ground cumin

½ teaspoon dried oregano

¼ teaspoon black pepper

16 Bibb lettuce leaves

Chopped fresh cilantro

IN a large skillet, cook the beef over medium-high heat, stirring with a wooden spoon to break it up, until no longer pink, 5 to 8 minutes. Use a slotted spoon to transfer the meat to a 4-quart slow cooker. Add 1 cup water, the potato, onion, carrot, bell pepper, salsa, garlic, jalapeño, chili powder, salt, cumin, oregano, and pepper.

COVER and cook on low for 7 to 8 hours or on high for 3½ to 4 hours.

SERVE in lettuce leaves, topped with cilantro and chopped onion.

TIP *Flavorful picadillo can also be served over 1 package (12 ounces) frozen riced cauliflower, prepared according to the package directions.*

ALEX SNODGRASS, THE DEFINED DISH

Alex Snodgrass is the Dallas-based blogger behind *The Defined Dish*. Alex is a stay-at-home mom and talented home cook with a love for sharing delicious, real food with lots of flavor.

In 2014, the Whole30 program totally transformed her life by not only changing her eating habits, but by helping her resolve her struggles with anxiety—and she's never looked back.

BEEF TACO SALAD

SERVES 6

PREP: 15 minutes

SLOW COOK: 2 hours (high)

TOTAL: 2 hours 15 minutes

For this beefy salad, cooking the ground beef in a skillet with onion and garlic is a crucial first step before it all goes into the cooker so that the meat breaks up into crumbles and all of the surface area gets browned and crisp.

1½ pounds lean ground beef

1 medium white onion, diced

2 cloves garlic, minced

2 Anaheim chile peppers, seeded and finely chopped

1 tablespoon ground cumin

1 teaspoon dried oregano

1 teaspoon chili powder

1 teaspoon coriander

1 teaspoon salt

1 teaspoon black pepper

1 bag (10 ounces) chopped romaine or 1 head romaine lettuce, chopped

3 green onions, sliced

2 tomatoes, diced

2 jalapeños, seeded if desired, and sliced

Whole30-compliant salsa (optional)

¼ cup chopped fresh cilantro (optional)

2 limes, cut into wedges

IN a large skillet, cook the beef, onion, and garlic over medium-high heat, stirring with a wooden spoon to break up the beef, until no longer pink, 5 to 8 minutes. Use a slotted spoon to transfer to a 4-quart slow cooker. Add the Anaheim chiles, cumin, oregano, chili powder, coriander, salt, and pepper. Stir to combine.

COVER and cook on high for 2 hours.

SERVE the taco meat on top of the chopped lettuce. Top servings with green onions, tomatoes, and jalapeños, along with salsa and cilantro, if desired. Serve with the lime wedges.

TERIYAKI BEEF WRAPS

SERVES 4

PREP: 20 minutes

SLOW COOK: 6 hours (low) or 3 hours (high)

TOTAL: 6 hours 20 minutes

There's no soy or sugar in this teriyaki, but it has the characteristic combo of sweet, salty, and umami flavors that makes it a perennial favorite.

2 red, yellow, orange, and/or green bell peppers, cut into strips

1 medium red onion, cut into wedges

¼ cup coconut aminos

¼ cup chopped pitted dates

1 piece (2 inches) fresh ginger, peeled and minced

1 teaspoon red pepper flakes

1 skirt steak (1½ to 2 pounds)

½ teaspoon salt

½ teaspoon black pepper

2 teaspoons arrowroot powder

1 head leaf lettuce, separated into leaves

2 green onions, green tops sliced

Sesame seeds, toasted (see Tip)

IN a 6-quart slow cooker, combine the bell peppers, onion, coconut aminos, dates, ginger, and red pepper flakes. Season the steak with salt and pepper, add to the cooker, and turn to coat.

COVER and cook on low for 6 hours or on high for 3 hours. Use a slotted spoon to transfer the steak, peppers, and onion to a cutting board or platter. Cover and let the steak rest 5 minutes.

MEANWHILE, skim the fat from the cooking liquid. Turn the slow cooker to high if using the low setting. Whisk the arrowroot into 2 tablespoons water, then stir into the cooking liquid. Cook, uncovered, until the sauce is thickened, about 5 minutes. Pour the sauce into individual small bowls.

SLICE the steak against grain. Spoon the steak, peppers, and onion into the lettuce leaves and sprinkle with the green onions and sesame seeds. Serve with the sauce for dipping.

TIP *To toast sesame seeds, heat in a dry skillet over medium heat, stirring, until fragrant and lightly browned, about 2 minutes.*

THAI LARB SALAD

SERVES 4

PREP: 20 minutes

SLOW COOK: 5 hours (low) or 2½ hours (high)

TOTAL: 5 hours 20 minutes

Traditionally, larb is a salad made with minced pork or chicken wrapped in lettuce leaves. This slow cooker version is made with small chunks of juicy chicken thighs, flavored the same way as the classic version—with shallot, lemongrass, lime juice, hot chile, fish sauce, cilantro, and mint—but served in bowls.

½ cup Whole30-compliant chicken broth or Chicken Bone Broth (page 294)

1½ pounds boneless, skinless chicken thighs, cut into ½-inch pieces

½ cup minced shallots

1 stalk lemongrass, bruised

1 Thai chile pepper, seeded (if desired) and finely chopped

4 tablespoons fresh lime juice

3 teaspoons Whole30-compliant fish sauce

½ teaspoon salt

2 green onions, thinly sliced

¼ cup chopped fresh mint, plus extra for serving

2 tablespoons chopped fresh cilantro, plus extra for serving

1 package (5 ounces) mixed salad greens

2 medium carrots, peeled and cut into matchsticks

½ English cucumber, sliced

Whole30 Sriracha (page 179)

IN a 4-quart slow cooker, combine the broth, chicken, shallots, lemongrass, Thai chile, 2 tablespoons of the lime juice, 2 teaspoons of the fish sauce, and the salt.

COVER and cook on low for 5 to 6 hours or on high for 2½ to 3 hours. Remove and discard the lemongrass.

USE a slotted spoon to transfer the chicken to a medium bowl. (Discard the cooking liquid.) Add the remaining 2 tablespoons lime juice, remaining 1 teaspoon fish sauce, the green onions, mint, and cilantro to the chicken.

TOP the greens with the chicken mixture, carrots, cucumber, and additional cilantro and mint. Serve with sriracha.

SOUPS, STEWS, AND NOODLE BOWLS

FRENCH CHICKEN STEW

SERVES 4

PREP: 30 minutes

SLOW COOK: 6 hours (low) or 3 hours (high)

TOTAL: 6 hours 30 minutes

Herbes de Provence is a blend of dried herbs frequently used in the cooking of southern France. Most versions include basil, fennel seeds, lavender, marjoram, rosemary, sage, savory, and thyme. Together with black olives and a generous dose of Dijon mustard, they give this elegant stew a decidedly French flavor.

1 medium onion, cut into wedges

2 cloves garlic, minced

4 slices Whole30-compliant bacon, chopped

4 medium carrots, peeled and cut into 1-inch pieces

1 large leek, white part only, sliced

12 small red potatoes (about 12 ounces)

Grated zest and juice of 1 lemon

½ cup Whole30-compliant chicken broth or Chicken Bone Broth (page 294)

1 tablespoon tapioca flour

1 teaspoon salt

½ teaspoon coarsely ground black pepper

8 meaty bone-in chicken pieces (breast halves, thighs, and drumsticks), skin removed

2 tablespoons extra-virgin olive oil

2 teaspoons herbes de Provence

2 tablespoons Whole30-compliant Dijon mustard

1 cup Whole30-compliant Kalamata olives or other black olives

Fresh tarragon leaves

IN a 6-quart slow cooker, combine the onion, garlic, bacon, carrots, leek, and potatoes. In a small bowl, stir together the lemon juice, broth, and tapioca flour; stir into the slow cooker. In another small bowl, combine the lemon zest, salt, and pepper. Coat the chicken with the olive oil and rub with the salt mixture. Add to the slow cooker. Sprinkle the herbes de Provence over the chicken.

COVER and cook on low for 6 to 7 hours or on high for 3 to 3½ hours.

TRANSFER the chicken to shallow serving bowls. Stir the mustard and olives into the cooking liquid. Ladle some of the cooking liquid over the chicken. Sprinkle with fresh tarragon leaves and serve.

INSTANT POT VARIATION *Follow the directions in the first step using a 6-quart Instant Pot, but leave out the carrots and potatoes. Lock the lid in place. Select Manual and cook at high pressure for 45 minutes. Use natural release for 10 minutes, then quick release. Remove the chicken. Stir in the carrots and potatoes. Lock the lid in place. Select Manual and cook at high pressure for 5 minutes. Use quick release. Return the chicken to the pot and continue with the remaining directions.*

HEARTY HERBED PORK STEW

SERVES 6

PREP: 25 minutes

SLOW COOK: 6 hours (low) or
3 hours (high)

TOTAL: 6 hours 25 minutes

Parsnips look like white carrots but have a sweeter, more intense flavor than their more common orange relatives. Look for slender or medium-size parsnips—larger ones can have woody cores.

1½ pounds Whole30-compliant boneless pork loin, cut into 1-inch pieces

½ small butternut squash, peeled and cut into 1-inch pieces (about 2 cups)

3 medium carrots, peeled and cut into ½-inch pieces

2 medium parsnips, peeled and cut into ½-inch pieces

1 medium yellow onion, chopped

2 teaspoons fresh thyme

½ teaspoon salt

½ teaspoon black pepper

4 cups Whole30-compliant chicken broth or Chicken Bone Broth (page 294)

Chopped fresh parsley

IN a 4-quart slow cooker, combine the pork, squash, carrots, parsnips, onion, thyme, salt, pepper, and broth. Cover and cook on low for 6 to 7 hours or on high 3 to 3½ hours.

SERVE, topped with parsley.

INSTANT POT VARIATION *Follow the directions in the first step using a 6-quart Instant Pot. Lock the lid in place. Select Manual and cook at high pressure for 4 minutes. Use natural release for 5 minutes, then quick release.*

NUTTY CHICKEN AND SWEET POTATO STEW

SERVES 6

PREP: 40 minutes

SLOW COOK: 6 hours (low) or 3 hours (high)

TOTAL: 6 hours 55 minutes

A bit of sunflower seed butter whisked into the cooking liquid right before serving gives this African-inspired stew (packed with nutrient-rich collard greens) a delicious nutty flavor.

1½ pounds boneless, skinless chicken thighs, cut into 1½-inch pieces

2 medium sweet potatoes (about 1¼ pounds total), peeled and cut into 1½ inch pieces

1 can (14.5 ounces) Whole30-compliant stewed tomatoes, undrained

1 medium yellow onion, chopped

3 cloves garlic, minced

1 piece (1 inch) fresh ginger, peeled and finely chopped

¼ teaspoon cayenne pepper

2½ cups Whole30-compliant chicken broth or Chicken Bone Broth (page 294)

1 bunch collard greens, trimmed and coarsely chopped

¼ cup Whole30-compliant sunflower seed butter

½ cup chopped almonds, toasted (see Tip)

½ cup chopped fresh cilantro or flat-leaf parsley

IN a 6-quart slow cooker, combine the chicken, sweet potatoes, tomatoes, onion, garlic, ginger, and cayenne. Add the broth. Cover and cook on low for 6 to 7 hours or on high for 3 to 3½ hours.

TURN the slow cooker to high if using the low setting. Use a ladle to remove ½ cup of the cooking liquid from the cooker; set aside. Stir the collard greens into the stew; cover and cook 15 minutes longer. Whisk the sunflower butter into the reserved ½ cup cooking liquid until smooth. Stir into the stew.

SERVE, sprinkled with almonds and cilantro.

TIP *To toast almonds, heat in a dry skillet over medium heat, stirring, until fragrant and lightly browned, about 2 minutes.*

INSTANT POT VARIATION *Follow the directions in the first step using a 6-quart Instant Pot. Lock the lid in place. Select Manual and cook at high pressure for 10 minutes. Use quick release. Remove ½ cup of the cooking liquid and set aside. Add the collard greens, select Sauté and adjust to Less/Low. Simmer, uncovered, for 15 minutes. Whisk the sunflower butter into the reserved cooking liquid and follow the remaining directions.*

SWEET POTATO AND JALAPEÑO PORK STEW

SERVES 6

PREP: 30 minutes

SLOW COOK: 6 hours (low) or 3 hours (high)

TOTAL: 6 hours 30 minutes

An apple adds a touch of sweetness to this autumnal pork stew and pairs really nicely with the fresh thyme. Braeburn apples are good for cooking—they hold their shape well without turning to mush.

2 pounds lean ground pork

1 quart Whole30-compliant vegetable broth

3 medium sweet potatoes, peeled and cut into 1-inch pieces

1 Braeburn apple, cored and cut into 1-inch pieces

2 jalapeños, seeded and diced

1 large shallot, minced

1 tablespoon fresh thyme, plus extra for serving

2 teaspoons ground ginger

½ teaspoon salt

½ teaspoon white pepper

Paprika

IN an extra-large skillet, cook the pork over medium-high heat, stirring, until no longer pink, about 10 minutes. Using a slotted spoon, transfer the pork to a 6-quart slow cooker. Add the broth, sweet potatoes, apple, jalapeños, shallot, thyme, ginger, salt, and white pepper.

COVER and cook on low for 6 hours or on high for 3 hours. Use a potato masher or fork to gently mash the sweet potatoes to thicken the stew.

SERVE, sprinkled with paprika and fresh thyme.

INSTANT POT VARIATION *Using a 6-quart Instant Pot, select Sauté and adjust to Normal/Medium to cook the pork until no longer pink, about 10 minutes. Add the broth, sweet potatoes, apple, jalapeños, shallot, thyme, ginger, salt, and white pepper. Lock the lid in place. Select Manual and cook at low pressure for 10 minutes. Use natural release for 5 minutes, then quick release. Follow the remaining directions.*

TUNISIAN LAMB STEW

SERVES 6
PREP: 35 minutes
SLOW COOK: 7 hours (low) or 3½ hours (high)
TOTAL: 7 hours 45 minutes

Warm, sweet spices—cumin, coriander, ginger, turmeric, cayenne, and cinnamon—are classics in North African cooking and complement the rich flavor of the lamb. If you can't find ground lamb—or aren't a fan—ground beef works equally well.

1½ pounds ground lamb or ground beef

1 to 2 tablespoons harissa

1 teaspoon ground cumin

1 teaspoon ground coriander

½ teaspoon ground ginger

½ teaspoon ground turmeric

¼ teaspoon cayenne pepper

¼ teaspoon ground cinnamon

1 medium butternut squash (about 1½ pounds), peeled, seeded, and cut into 1-inch cubes

1 medium green bell pepper, coarsely chopped

1 medium yellow onion, chopped

3 cloves garlic, minced

3 cups Whole30-compliant beef broth or Beef Bone Broth (page 294)

1 can (14.5 ounces) Whole30-compliant fire-roasted diced tomatoes, undrained

⅓ cup unsulfured golden raisins

⅓ cup chopped fresh parsley

⅓ cup pine nuts, toasted (see Tip)

Lemon wedges

IN a large skillet over medium heat, cook the lamb, breaking it up with a wooden spoon, until browned, about 5 minutes. Drain off the fat. Add the harissa, cumin, coriander, ginger, turmeric, cayenne, and cinnamon and stir until combined. Transfer the meat to a 3½- to 4-quart slow cooker. Stir in the squash, bell pepper, onion, and garlic. Pour the broth over all.

COVER and cook on low for 7 to 8 hours or on high for 3½ to 4 hours. Turn the slow cooker to high if using the low setting. Stir the tomatoes and raisins into the stew. Cover and cook for 10 minutes.

SERVE, topped with the parsley and pine nuts and accompanied by lemon wedges.

TIP *To toast pine nuts, heat in a dry skillet over medium heat, stirring, until fragrant and lightly browned, about 2 minutes.*

ASIAN PORK NOODLE BOWLS

SERVES 4
PREP: 10 minutes
SLOW COOK: 4½ hours (low) or 2¼ hours (high)
TOTAL: 4 hours 40 minutes

Five-spice powder is a spice blend that's commonly used in Chinese cooking. It's usually made of equal parts ground cinnamon, cloves, fennel seeds, star anise, and Szechuan peppercorns.

½ cup apple cider

½ cup coconut aminos

¼ teaspoon red pepper flakes

1½ pounds Whole30-compliant pork tenderloin, trimmed

2 teaspoons Whole30-compliant five-spice powder

½ teaspoon salt

2 tablespoons Clarified Butter (page 296) or ghee

1 package (12 ounces) frozen carrot noodles or 4 large carrots, peeled and spiralized (4 cups)

2 tablespoons sliced green onion

2 tablespoons chopped fresh cilantro

1 tablespoon sesame seeds, toasted (see Tip)

IN a 4-quart slow cooker, stir together the apple cider, coconut aminos, and red pepper flakes. Sprinkle the pork with the five-spice powder and salt. Add the pork to slow cooker and turn to coat.

COVER and cook on low for 4½ to 5 hours or on high for 2¼ to 2½ hours. Transfer the pork to a cutting board and cut into bite-size strips. Strain the cooking liquid.

IN a large skillet, heat the butter over medium heat. Add the carrot noodles and cook, stirring occasionally, until tender, 5 to 10 minutes.

SERVE the pork on the carrot noodles and drizzle with some of the strained cooking liquid. Top with the green onion, cilantro, and sesame seeds. If desired serve with additional coconut aminos.

TIP *To toast sesame seeds, heat in a skillet over medium heat, stirring, until fragrant and lightly browned, about 2 minutes.*

INSTANT POT VARIATION *Follow the directions for the first step, using a 6-quart Instant Pot. Lock the lid in place. Select Manual and cook at high pressure for 15 minutes. Use natural release for 5 minutes, then quick release. Follow the directions in the second step. Use the Instant Pot and follow the directions in the third step to cook the carrot noodles. Select Sauté and adjust to Normal/Medium. Cook, stirring occasionally, just until tender, 8 to 10 minutes. Continue with the remaining directions.*

CHICKEN, KALE, AND SAUSAGE STEW

SERVES 4

PREP: 20 minutes

SLOW COOK: 6 hours (low) or 3 hours (high)

TOTAL: 6 hours 20 minutes

Fennel and lemon are frequently paired up—they just seem to like each other a lot. Use a mortar and pestle to crush the fennel seeds, or place them in a plastic bag and roll over them with a rolling pin.

1 pound boneless, skinless chicken breast, cut into 1-inch pieces

4 cups Whole30-compliant chicken broth or Chicken Bone Broth (page 294)

1 can (14.5 ounces) Whole30-compliant fire-roasted diced tomatoes, undrained

1 large yellow onion, cut into thin wedges

2 cloves garlic, minced

2 teaspoons grated lemon zest, plus extra for serving

1½ teaspoons fennel seeds, crushed

8 ounces Whole30-compliant smoked kielbasa or chicken-apple sausage, sliced into ½-inch pieces

2 cups packed chopped fresh kale

IN a 6-quart slow cooker combine the chicken, broth, tomatoes, onion, garlic, lemon zest, and fennel seeds.

COVER and cook on low for 6 to 7 hours or on high for 3 to 3½ hours. Add the sausage and kale. Cover and let stand for 5 minutes or until the sausage is heated through and the kale is wilted. Serve, topped with additional lemon zest if desired.

BEEF FAJITA SOUP

SERVES 4

PREP: 10 minutes

SLOW COOK: 6 hours (low) or 3 hours (high)

TOTAL: 6 hours 10 minutes

If you are not actually doing a Whole30 but have adopted this way of eating as a lifestyle choice for the long haul, fajitas (minus the tortillas) are actually a decent choice when eating out. If you are doing a Whole30, this soup delivers all of the flavors of this Mexican favorite and is perfectly compliant.

1 pound ground beef

1 cup chopped onion

2 cloves garlic, minced

1 medium green bell pepper, coarsely chopped

1 medium red bell pepper, coarsely chopped

1 serrano chile pepper, seeded and chopped

4 cups Whole30-compliant beef broth or Beef Bone Broth (page 294)

1 can (14.5 ounces) Whole30-compliant fire-roasted diced tomatoes, undrained

2 teaspoons chili powder

½ teaspoon salt

Chopped fresh cilantro

Lime wedges

IN a large skillet, cook the beef, onion, and garlic over medium-high heat, breaking up the meat with a wooden spoon, until browned. Drain off any fat and transfer the beef mixture to a 3½- to 4-quart slow cooker. Add the bell peppers, serrano pepper, broth, tomatoes, chili powder, and salt. Cover and cook on low for 6 to 7 hours or on high for 3 to 3½ hours.

SERVE the soup with cilantro and lime wedges.

CINCINNATI CHILI BUTTERNUT-NOODLE BOWLS

SERVES 6

PREP: 15 minutes

SLOW COOK: 6 hours (low) or 3 hours (high)

TOTAL: 6 hours 25 minutes

Cincinnati chili—created in the 1920s by immigrant restaurateurs from Macedonia who added unsweetened dark chocolate and warm spices such as cinnamon to classic American chili—is traditionally served over spaghetti. In this Whole30 version, butternut squash noodles sub for the wheat pasta—and the dish doesn't miss a beat. Better yet, to save time, there's no need to brown the beef in a skillet first.

1 yellow onion, chopped

1 red bell pepper, chopped

1 jalapeño or serrano chile pepper, seeded (if desired) and finely chopped

3 cloves garlic, minced

1 can (28 ounces) Whole30-compliant fire-roasted diced tomatoes, undrained

1¾ cups Whole30-compliant beef broth or Beef Bone Broth (page 294)

2 tablespoons chili powder

1 tablespoon cocoa powder

1 teaspoon dried oregano, crushed

1 teaspoon ground cumin

½ teaspoon ground cinnamon

1½ pounds lean ground beef

½ teaspoon salt

½ teaspoon black pepper

1 package (12 ounces) frozen butternut squash noodles

Sliced green onions

IN a 4-quart slow cooker, combine the onion, bell pepper, chile pepper, and garlic. In a large bowl, stir together the tomatoes, broth, chili powder, cocoa powder, oregano, cumin, and cinnamon; pour into the cooker. Break the ground beef into small pieces and arrange it over the sauce mixture. Sprinkle with the salt and pepper.

COVER and cook on low for 6 to 7 hours or on high for 3 to 3½ hours.

IF on low, turn the slow cooker to the high setting. Stir in the butternut squash noodles. Cover and cook for 10 minutes longer, or until the squash is just tender (do not overcook). Serve, topped with sliced green onions.

CLASSIC SLOW COOKER BEEF STEW

SERVES 4

PREP: 25 minutes

SLOW COOK: 6 hours (low) or 3 hours (high)

TOTAL: 6 hours 25 minutes

All of the recipes in this book were created to be as dump-and-go as possible—just arrange or mix everything in the slow cooker, close the lid, push the button, and you're out the door. But this is one case where quickly browning the meat makes a big difference in the final result. Not only does browning caramelize the meat's natural sugars—infusing the stew with rich flavor—but it also avoids the protein bits that slough off raw meat during cooking and cloud the sauce.

2 tablespoons extra-virgin olive oil

1½ pounds beef stew meat, cut into ¾-inch pieces

4 medium carrots, peeled and diagonally sliced 1 inch thick

8 baby red potatoes, quartered

1 medium yellow onion, cut into thin wedges

2 cloves garlic, minced

½ teaspoon salt

½ teaspoon black pepper

1 bay leaf

2 cups Whole30-compliant beef broth or Beef Bone Broth (page 294)

2 cups Whole30-compliant vegetable juice

2 tablespoons coconut aminos

2 tablespoons tapioca flour (optional for a thicker stew)

IN a large skillet, heat the olive oil over medium-high heat. Add the beef and cook in batches if necessary, stirring occasionally, until browned on all sides.

TRANSFER the beef to a 4-quart slow cooker. Add the carrots, potatoes, onion, garlic, salt, pepper, bay leaf, broth, vegetable juice, and coconut aminos; stir to combine. Cover and cook on low for 6 to 8 hours or on high for 3 to 4 hours, or until the beef and vegetables are tender.

IF using the tapioca flour, turn the slow cooker to high if using the low setting. In a small bowl, stir together the tapioca flour and 2 tablespoons water. Stir into the stew. Cover and cook for 10 minutes. Remove and discard the bay leaf before serving.

INSTANT POT VARIATION *Follow the directions in the first step, using a 6-quart Instant Pot instead of a skillet, selecting Sauté and adjusting to High. In the second step, add the ingredients to the beef in the Instant Pot and lock the lid in place. Select Manual and cook at high pressure for 25 minutes. Use natural release for 10 minutes, then quick release. Continue with the last step, selecting Sauté and adjusting to High on the Instant Pot.*

SOUPS, STEWS, AND NOODLE BOWLS

59

ITALIAN SAUSAGE SOUP

SERVES 4

PREP: 10 minutes

SLOW COOK: 4 hours (low) or 2 hours (high)

TOTAL: 4 hours 25 minutes

Kids will love this soup—if yours can't tolerate any level of heat, simply leave out the crushed red pepper flakes. They can be sprinkled on the servings of those who do want a little spice in their soup.

1 pound Whole30-compliant sweet Italian chicken sausage, diagonally sliced ½ inch thick

4 cups Whole30-compliant chicken broth or Chicken Bone Broth (page 294)

1 can (14.5 ounces) Whole30-compliant diced tomatoes, undrained

½ cup chopped onion

2 cloves garlic, minced

1½ teaspoons Whole30-compliant Italian seasoning

¼ teaspoon salt

¼ teaspoon red pepper flakes

1½ cups cauliflower rice or cauliflower crumbles

4 cups baby spinach

IN a 3½- to 4-quart slow cooker, combine the sausage, broth, tomatoes, onion, garlic, Italian seasoning, salt, and red pepper flakes. Cover and cook on low for 4 to 5 hours or on high for 2 to 2½ hours.

TURN the slow cooker to high if using the low setting. Stir in the cauliflower. Cover and cook until the cauliflower is tender, 15 to 20 minutes. Stir in the baby spinach. Serve.

CAULIFLOWER RICE AND CRUMBLES

Nutritious cauliflower rice or "crumbles" can be used to replace couscous, grains, or rice and serves as a blank canvas for seasonings. You can buy bags of frozen riced cauliflower or refrigerated cauliflower crumbles in the produce section of your supermarket, but it takes just 5 minutes to make your own.

HOMEMADE CAULIFLOWER CRUMBLES: Cut 1 large head cauliflower into large florets. In batches, place the florets in a food processor (don't fill more than three-fourths full). Pulse the florets until processed into crumbles. Remove any unprocessed large pieces from the food processor. Transfer the crumbles or rice to bowl, then reprocess the large pieces. Makes about 7 cups.

HOMEMADE CAULIFLOWER RICE: Process as directed above, but pulse a bit longer, until the cauliflower is in rice-size pieces.

TO COOK CRUMBLES OR RICE: Place cauliflower crumbles or rice in a microwave-safe bowl. Drizzle with 1 tablespoon extra-virgin olive oil and stir to coat. Tightly cover the bowl with plastic wrap and cook until just tender, about 3 minutes. Or, heat 1 tablespoon extra-virgin olive oil in a large skillet over medium-high heat. Add the cauliflower and cook until just tender, 3 to 5 minutes.

Place any leftover cauliflower crumbles or rice in an airtight container and freeze for up to 3 months. Thaw at room temperature for 10 minutes before using.

KOREAN BEEF NOODLE BOWLS

SERVES 4

PREP: 30 minutes

SLOW COOK: 10 hours (low) or 5 hours (high)

TOTAL: 10 hours 30 minutes

The addition of kimchi as a topping—with its characteristic pungent, spicy-hot flavor—sparks up this rich, beefy bowl. The soft-boiled egg halves are an optional but traditional touch and add both color and protein.

1 cup Whole30-compliant beef broth or Beef Bone Broth (page 294)

1 Granny Smith apple, peeled, cored, and coarsely chopped

4 cloves garlic, minced

¼ cup coconut aminos

2 tablespoons toasted sesame oil

2 tablespoons cider vinegar

1 piece (2 inches) fresh ginger, grated

1 teaspoon Red Boat fish sauce

½ teaspoon paprika

½ teaspoon red pepper flakes

1 beef chuck roast (2 to 2½ pounds), fat trimmed, cut into 2-inch pieces

1 package (10.7 ounces) zucchini noodles or 2 small zucchini, spiralized

1 cup Whole30-compliant kimchi

½ cup thinly sliced red onion

2 large eggs, soft-boiled and halved (see recipe, right; optional)

Sesame seeds, toasted (see Tip)

IN a 4-quart slow cooker, combine the broth, apple, garlic, coconut aminos, sesame oil, vinegar, ginger, fish sauce, paprika, and red pepper flakes. Add the beef and stir to combine.

COVER and cook on low for 10 to 12 hours or on high for 5 to 6 hours. Remove the beef from the slow cooker. Turn the slow cooker to high if using the low setting. Add the zucchini noodles. Cover and cook until the noodles have softened, about 2 minutes. Using two forks, shred the beef.

SPOON the cooking liquid and noodles into serving bowls. Top each serving with the shredded beef, kimchi, onion, and an egg half, if desired. Sprinkle with toasted sesame seeds and serve.

TIP *To toast sesame seeds, heat in a skillet over medium heat, stirring, until fragrant and lightly browned, about 2 minutes.*

INSTANT POT VARIATION *Follow the directions in the first step using a 6-quart Instant Pot. Lock the lid in place. Select Manual and cook at high pressure for 55 minutes. Use natural release for 10 minutes, then quick release. Add the zucchini noodles, select Sauté and adjust to Less/Low. Follow the remaining directions.*

SOFT BOILED EGGS

Fill a medium saucepan with about 3 inches of water. Bring to a rolling boil over high heat. Reduce the heat to a rapid simmer (water bubbles are gently breaking the surface). Add the eggs, one at a time, and cook for 7 minutes for a barely set yolk. Remove the eggs with a slotted spoon and cool in a bowl of cold water. Carefully crack and peel the eggs.

MEXICAN PORK STEW

SERVES 6

PREP: 40 minutes

SLOW COOK: 6 hours (low) or
3 hours (high)

TOTAL: 6 hours 45 minutes

The generous yield of this veggie-packed stew makes it a good choice for a Sunday dinner when you have an extra-busy week coming up and would welcome leftovers.

1½ teaspoons chipotle powder

1 teaspoon ground cumin

1 teaspoon oregano

1 teaspoon garlic powder

½ teaspoon paprika

1 teaspoon sea salt

½ teaspoon black pepper

2½ to 3 pounds pork shoulder or butt roast

1 pound baby red potatoes

½ cup chopped onion

4 ounces button mushrooms, halved (about 2 cups)

1 can (14.5 ounces) Whole30-compliant whole tomatoes, drained

1 large zucchini (about 5 ounces), halved and cut into 2-inch chunks

2 cups packed chopped spinach

2 tablespoons tapioca flour

IN a small bowl, combine the chipotle powder, cumin, oregano, garlic powder, paprika, salt, and pepper. Sprinkle half of the seasoning on the pork. Place the pork in a 6-quart slow cooker. Add ¼ cup water, the potatoes, onion, and mushrooms.

IN a large bowl, crush the tomatoes with your hands. Add the remaining seasoning mix to the tomatoes; pour into the slow cooker. Cook for 6 hours on low or 3 hours on high, or until the pork and potatoes are tender. Transfer the pork to a platter and keep warm.

TURN the slow cooker to high if using the low setting. Stir the zucchini and spinach into the cooking liquid in the slow cooker.

IN a small bowl, stir the tapioca flour into 2 tablespoons water. Add to the stew and cook, stirring, for 3 minutes. Using two forks, shred the pork and stir it into the stew.

INSTANT POT VARIATION *Cut the pork into 3-inch pieces. Follow the directions in the first two steps using a 6-quart Instant Pot. Lock the lid in place. Select Manual and cook at high pressure for 20 minutes. Use natural release for 10 minutes, then quick release. In the third step, select Sauté and adjust to Normal. Continue with the remaining directions.*

BEEF AND BELL PEPPER SOUP

SERVES 4

PREP: 25 minutes

SLOW COOK: 5 hours (low) or 2½ hours (high)

TOTAL: 5 hours 25 minutes

For an additional flavor boost, use fire-roasted diced tomatoes in place of the plain ones.

1 pound lean ground beef

1 medium onion, chopped

1 can (14.5 ounces) Whole30-compliant diced tomatoes, undrained

1 can (15 ounces) Whole30-compliant tomato sauce

2 medium red or orange bell peppers, chopped

2 cloves garlic, minced

2 teaspoons Whole30-compliant Italian seasoning

½ teaspoon fennel seeds, crushed

½ teaspoon salt

2½ cups Whole30-compliant beef broth or Beef Bone Broth (page 294)

Fresh basil leaves (optional)

IN a large skillet, cook the beef and onion over medium heat, stirring occasionally and breaking up the beef with a wooden spoon, until browned, 8 to 10 minutes. Drain off the fat. Transfer to a 6-quart slow cooker.

STIR in the tomatoes, tomato sauce, bell peppers, garlic, Italian seasoning, fennel seeds, and salt, and then the broth.

COVER and cook on low for 5 to 6 hours or on high for 2½ to 3 hours. Top servings with fresh basil, if desired.

MOROCCAN SPICED MEATBALL AND GREENS STEW

SERVES 4

PREP: 40 minutes

SLOW COOK: 5 hours (low) or 2½ hours (high)

BAKE: 10 minutes

TOTAL: 6 hours

Take your pick of greens for this North African–inspired stew—kale, mustard, chard, or spinach. They're all great non-dairy sources of calcium as well as iron, potassium, magnesium, and vitamins A, C, K, and folate.

1 large shallot, finely chopped

1 large egg, lightly beaten

⅓ cup almond meal

1 teaspoon ground cumin

1 teaspoon ground coriander

1 teaspoon salt

½ teaspoon black pepper

½ teaspoon ground ginger

½ teaspoon ground cinnamon

1½ pounds ground beef

1 onion, chopped

2 carrots, peeled and chopped

4 cloves garlic, minced

1 teaspoon ground turmeric

2 cans (14.5 ounces each) Whole30-compliant beef broth or 3½ cups Beef Bone Broth (page 294)

1 can (14.5 ounces) Whole30-compliant diced tomatoes, undrained

8 cups chopped greens, such as kale, mustard greens, chard, and/or spinach

½ cup chopped fresh cilantro

PREHEAT the oven to 400°F.

IN a medium bowl, combine the shallot, egg, almond meal, cumin, coriander, salt, pepper, ginger, and cinnamon. Add the ground beef and mix just until combined. Form into 1½-inch meatballs. Place the meatballs on a foil-lined shallow baking pan. Bake for 10 minutes.

IN a 5- to 6-quart slow cooker, combine the onion, carrots, garlic, and turmeric. Add the broth and tomatoes. Arrange the meatballs in an even layer in the slow cooker. Cover and cook on low for 5 hours or on high for 2½ hours.

TURN the slow cooker to high if using the low setting. Gently stir in the greens. Cover and cook just until the greens are tender, 5 to 10 minutes. Stir in the cilantro just before serving.

SHRIMP HOT AND SOUR SOUP

SERVES 4

PREP: 15 minutes

SLOW COOK: 4 hours (low) or 2 hours (high)

TOTAL: 4 hours 15 minutes

Using frozen shrimp that are already peeled and deveined makes super-quick work of this Asian-style soup. To thaw the shrimp, place them in a bowl of cool water and let stand for 15 to 20 minutes while you chop the veggies, changing the water once, then drain.

6 cups Whole30-compliant chicken broth or Chicken Bone Broth (page 294)

1 pound peeled and deveined large shrimp

2 cups quartered cremini mushrooms

2 medium carrots, peeled and grated (½ cup)

2 cups thinly sliced green cabbage

½ cup canned sliced bamboo shoots, rinsed, drained, and cut into strips

½ to 1 serrano chile pepper, seeded, if desired, and minced

2 tablespoons minced fresh ginger

4 cloves garlic, minced

⅛ teaspoon ground white pepper

¼ cup rice wine vinegar

½ teaspoon sesame oil

1 large egg, lightly beaten

2 tablespoons sliced green onions

IN a 6-quart slow cooker, combine the broth, shrimp, mushrooms, carrots, cabbage, bamboo shoots, serrano chile, ginger, garlic, and white pepper. Cover and cook for 4 hours on low or 2 hours on high, or until the shrimp are pink and opaque and the cabbage is tender.

TURN the slow cooker to high if using the low setting. Add the vinegar and sesame oil, and then the beaten egg. Stir the soup until the egg is cooked and slightly thickens the soup.

SERVE, topped with the green onions and additional serrano pepper, if desired.

SPICY SESAME PORK MEATBALL AND NAPA CABBAGE SOUP

SERVES 4

PREP: 10 minutes

SLOW COOK: 6 hours (low) or 3 hours (high)

BAKE: 10 minutes

TOTAL: 6 hours 25 minutes

Partially baking the meatballs for 10 minutes at 400°F before they go in the slow cooker not only gives them a nice brown crust—which helps flavor the soup—but also helps them hold together better and keeps the garlicky, gingery broth nice and clear.

⅓ cup almond meal

1 large egg, lightly beaten

2 green onions, thinly sliced

1 tablespoon sesame seeds

2 cloves garlic, minced

1 teaspoon salt

½ teaspoon black pepper

1½ pounds lean ground pork

4 cups Whole30-compliant chicken broth or Chicken Bone Broth (page 294)

2 shallots, chopped

4 cloves garlic, thinly sliced

2 tablespoons coconut aminos

2 tablespoons minced fresh ginger

1 teaspoon toasted sesame oil

4 cups thinly sliced Napa cabbage

2 tablespoons sliced fresh basil

PREHEAT the oven to 400°F.

IN a medium bowl, combine the almond meal, egg, green onions, sesame seeds, garlic, salt, and pepper. Add the pork and mix just until combined. Form into 8 meatballs and place on a foil-lined rimmed baking sheet. Bake for 10 minutes.

IN a 4-quart slow cooker, combine the broth, shallots, garlic, coconut aminos, ginger, and sesame oil. Place the meatballs in the cooker in a single layer. Cover and cook on low for 6 to 7 hours or on high for 3 to 3½ hours.

TURN the slow cooker to high if using the low setting. Transfer the meatballs to serving bowls. Stir the cabbage into the liquid in the slow cooker. Cook on high for 5 minutes. Ladle the soup over the meatballs. Top servings with the basil.

THAI TURKEY AND CARROT NOODLE BOWL

SERVES 4

PREP: 10 minutes

SLOW COOK: 5 hours (low) or 2½ hours (high)

TOTAL: 5 hours 40 minutes

This flavorful noodle bowl is great with turkey, but lends itself to other ground meats as well—chicken, pork, or beef. Just be sure to cook the meat before adding it to the cooker with the other ingredients.

1 tablespoon coconut oil

1½ pounds lean ground turkey

1 tablespoon minced fresh ginger

2 cloves garlic, minced

2 teaspoons coconut aminos

¼ to ½ teaspoon red pepper flakes

3 cups Whole30-compliant chicken broth or Chicken Bone Broth (page 294)

1 package (12 ounces) carrot spirals or 4 large carrots, peeled and spiralized (4 cups)

1 can (13.5 ounces) Whole30-compliant coconut milk

¼ cup chopped fresh cilantro

1 lime, cut into quarters (optional)

IN a large skillet, heat the coconut oil over medium heat. Add the ground turkey and cook, stirring frequently and breaking it up with a wooden spoon, until no longer pink, 8 to 10 minutes. Drain off the fat.

IN a 4- to 5-quart slow cooker, combine the turkey, ginger, garlic, coconut aminos, and red pepper flakes. Add the chicken broth. Cover and cook on low for 5 to 6 hours or on high for 2½ to 3 hours.

STIR the carrot noodles and coconut milk into the slow cooker. Turn the slow cooker to high if using the low setting. Cover and cook until the carrot noodles are crisp-tender, about 30 minutes.

TOP servings with fresh cilantro and serve with lime wedges, if desired.

INSTANT POT VARIATION *Follow the directions in the first two steps using a 6-quart Instant Pot. Select Sauté and adjust to Normal/Medium to cook the turkey. Add the ginger, garlic, coconut aminos, and red pepper flakes. Add the broth. Lock the lid in place. Select Manual and cook at low pressure for 10 minutes. Use natural release for 5 minutes, then quick release. Stir in the carrot noodles and coconut milk. Select Sauté and adjust to Less/Low. Simmer, uncovered, until carrots are crisp-tender, about 10 minutes. Follow the remaining directions.*

EASY BEEF PHO

The base of any Vietnamese pho ("fuh") is the broth. This soup starts with good basic beef broth that's simmered with star anise, cinnamon, ginger, and fennel seeds to give it authentic flavor. The result is big, beautiful bowls of delicious and comforting beef soup that will cure anything that ails you—even if it's just hunger!

1½ pounds beef flank steak

3 tablespoons rice vinegar

3 tablespoons toasted sesame oil

3 cloves garlic, minced

¼ teaspoon salt

¼ teaspoon black pepper

3 star anise

1 cinnamon stick (3 inches), broken

1 piece (1 inch) fresh ginger, peeled and thinly sliced

2 teaspoons fennel seeds, crushed

2 quarts Whole30-compliant beef broth or Beef Bone Broth (page 294)

2 packages (3.2 ounces each) shiitake mushrooms, stemmed and thinly sliced

3 heads baby bok choy, trimmed and cut lengthwise into quarters

1 package (10.7 ounces) zucchini noodles or 2 small zucchini, spiralized

3 green onions, thinly sliced

1 fresh Thai or serrano chile pepper, seeded and thinly sliced

½ cup chopped fresh mint, cilantro, and/or basil

USE a sharp knife to score the steak on one side with shallow diagonal cuts 1 inch apart. Place the steak in a shallow dish. In a small bowl, whisk together the vinegar, sesame oil, garlic, salt, and pepper; pour over the steak and turn to coat. Cover and marinate in the refrigerator for 2 hours while making the broth. (For even more flavor, marinate the steak overnight.)

MEANWHILE, on a 6 x 6-inch piece of cheesecloth, combine the star anise, cinnamon stick, ginger, and fennel seeds; tie closed with kitchen string. In a 6-quart slow cooker combine the broth and spice bag. Cover and cook on high for 2 hours. Discard the spice bag.

REMOVE the steak from the marinade; discard the marinade. Cut the steak across the grain into thin slices. Add the sliced steak, mushrooms, bok choy, zucchini noodles, green onions, and chile to the hot broth. Cover and cook on high for 3 to 5 minutes or until the steak is cooked to desired doneness.

LADLE the pho into bowls and top with the fresh herbs.

INSTANT POT VARIATION *Marinate the steak as directed in the first step. Follow the directions for the broth in the second step using a 6-quart Instant Pot. Lock the lid in place. Select Soup/Broth and adjust to Less/Low; cook for 30 minutes. Use natural release for 5 minutes, then quick release. Discard the spice bag. Cook the steak and vegetables in the third step with the Instant Pot. Select Sauté, select Less/Low, and cook for 3 to 5 minutes or until the steak is cooked to desired doneness. Follow the remaining directions to serve.*

BORSCHT WITH BEEF AND DILL

SERVES 4

PREP: 20 minutes

SLOW COOK: 8 hours (low) or
4 hours (high)

TOTAL: 8 hours 40 minutes

This Russian beet soup gets an addition of beef and shredded cabbage, which it makes it super hearty and filling. If you love the earthy flavor of beets, you will love this beautiful soup!

1 can (8 ounces) Whole30-compliant tomato sauce

2 cups Whole30-compliant beef broth or Beef Bone Broth (page 294)

1 pound beef chuck roast, cut into ½-inch cubes

3 medium red beets (about 8 ounces total), peeled and cubed

2 medium carrots, peeled and sliced into ¼-inch pieces

1 medium red onion, diced

2 cloves garlic, minced

1 tablespoon cider vinegar

1 tablespoon fresh lemon juice

1 tablespoon chopped fresh dill, plus more for garnish

1 bay leaf

1 teaspoon salt

½ teaspoon coarse black pepper

2 cups shredded cabbage

1 lemon, cut into wedges

IN a 6-quart slow cooker, stir together the tomato sauce and broth. Add the beef, beets, carrots, onion, garlic, vinegar, lemon juice, dill, bay leaf, salt, and pepper. Cover and cook on low for 8 hours or on high for 4 hours. Remove the bay leaf.

STIR in the cabbage. Turn the slow cooker to high if using low setting. Cover and cook until the cabbage is tender-crisp, about 20 minutes.

SPRINKLE servings with additional fresh dill and serve with lemon wedges.

INSTANT POT VARIATION *Follow the directions in the first step using a 6-quart Instant Pot. Lock the lid in place. Select Manual and cook on high pressure for 10 minutes. Use natural release for 5 minutes, then quick release. In the second step, select Sauté and adjust to Less/Low. Simmer until the cabbage is tender-crisp, about 20 minutes.*

SOUPS, STEWS, AND NOODLE BOWLS

ITALIAN CHICKEN AND VEGETABLE SOUP

SERVES 4

PREP: 15 minutes

SLOW COOK: 6 hours (low) or 3 hours (high)

TOTAL: 6 hours 50 minutes

This light and fresh soup is super-simple to make and a good choice for a warm spring or summer day, when you want something comforting and satisfying but don't want to be weighed down. Just toss everything in the slow cooker, cover, and press start—and you are out the door or doing whatever else it is you need to do.

1¼ pounds bone-in chicken thighs, skin removed (see Tip, page 169)

1 medium onion, chopped

1 medium zucchini, cut into ½-inch pieces

4 medium carrots, cut into ½-inch pieces (2 cups)

4 cups Whole30-compliant chicken broth or Chicken Bone Broth (page 294)

½ teaspoon salt

¼ teaspoon black pepper

1½ cups sliced button mushrooms

1 can (28 ounces) Whole30-compliant fire-roasted diced tomatoes, undrained

¼ cup chopped fresh basil

IN a 4-quart slow cooker, combine the chicken, onion, zucchini, carrots, broth, salt, and pepper. Cover and cook on low for 6 to 7 hours or on high for 3 to 3½ hours.

REMOVE the chicken from the slow cooker. Use two forks to coarsely shred the chicken; discard the bones. Return the chicken to the cooker. Stir in the mushrooms and tomatoes. Cover and cook on high for 30 minutes. Serve topped with basil.

INSTANT POT VARIATION *Follow the directions of the first step using a 6-quart Instant Pot, but leave out the zucchini and carrots. Lock the lid in place. Select Manual and cook on high pressure for 20 minutes. Use natural release for 5 minutes, then quick release. In the second step, add the zucchini and carrots with the mushrooms and tomatoes. Select Sauté and adjust to Less/Low. Simmer, uncovered, until the vegetables are tender, 10 to 15 minutes. Follow the remaining directions to serve.*

CHICKEN AND ZOODLE SOUP

SERVES 6

PREP: 25 minutes

SLOW COOK: 6 hours (low) or
3 hours (high)

TOTAL: 6 hours 30 minutes

When the world has got you down—or you simply need a little mood boost—this chicken soup has all the comforting flavors of classic chicken noodle soup without getting weighed down by heavy wheat noodles.

2 pounds boneless, skinless chicken thighs, cut into 1-inch pieces

6 cups Whole30-compliant chicken broth or Chicken Bone Broth (page 294)

3 carrots, peeled and sliced

3 stalks celery with leaves, chopped ¼ inch thick

1 large white onion, coarsely chopped

1 tablespoon fresh lemon juice

1 teaspoon dried thyme

1 teaspoon dried marjoram

1 bay leaf

1 teaspoon salt

½ teaspoon black pepper

1 package (10.7 ounces) zucchini noodles or 2 small zucchini, spiralized

Coarse ground black pepper (optional)

Fresh thyme leaves (optional)

IN a 6-quart slow cooker, combine the chicken, broth, carrots, celery, onion, lemon juice, dried thyme, marjoram, bay leaf, salt, and pepper. Stir to combine.

COVER and cook on low for 6 hours or on high for 3 hours. Remove and discard the bay leaf. Turn the slow cooker to high if using the low setting. Add the zucchini noodles. Cover and cook for 5 minutes or until the noodles are tender.

IF desired, top servings with coarse ground black pepper and fresh thyme.

MONGOLIAN BEEF RAMEN NOODLE BOWLS

FROM GRACE BRINTON OF TRU PROVISIONS

SERVES 4

PREP: 45 minutes

SLOW COOK: 10 hours (low) or 5 hours (high)

TOTAL: 10 hours 45 minutes

For this dish, I took inspiration from the comfort of a noodle bowl and paired it with the flavors of Mongolian beef. The result is a rich, satisfying broth with fall-apart-tender beef ready to be slurped up with sesame zucchini noodles. To mix things up a bit, we're using beef stew meat instead of the traditional flank steak you usually see in Mongolian beef. If you want to prep ahead of time, spiralize your noodles and make the dressing, but don't mix them together until about 15 minutes before serving. You can also prep the sauce ahead of time. It thickens while cooking due to the arrowroot, which gives this dish a rich and flavorful finish.

FOR THE SAUCE

¾ cup coconut aminos

1 teaspoon extra-virgin olive oil

2 cloves garlic, finely minced

1 piece (1 inch) fresh ginger, peeled and grated

½ teaspoon red pepper flakes

FOR THE BEEF

2 pounds beef stew meat

3 tablespoons arrowroot powder

½ teaspoon salt

4 teaspoons avocado oil

2¼ cups Whole30-compliant beef broth or Beef Bone Broth (page 294)

(continued)

MAKE THE SAUCE: In a small bowl, whisk together the coconut aminos, olive oil, garlic, ginger, and red pepper flakes. Set aside.

MAKE THE BEEF: In a medium bowl, combine the beef, arrowroot, and salt; toss to coat. Heat a large skillet over medium-high heat; add 2 teaspoons of the avocado oil. Cook half the meat until browned, 4 to 5 minutes. Transfer the meat to a 4-quart slow cooker. Repeat with remaining 2 teaspoons oil and meat. Pour the sauce over the beef in the cooker and stir to coat. Pour 1¼ cups of the broth into the skillet. Stir, scraping the browned bits on the bottom of the skillet. Pour over the beef and stir to combine. Cover and cook on low for 10 hours or on high for 5 hours.

(continued)

FOR THE NOODLES AND DRESSING

2 packages (10.7 ounces each) zucchini noodles or 3 medium zucchini, spiralized

2 cups thinly sliced bok choy

½ cup thinly sliced green onions

4½ teaspoons toasted sesame oil

4 teaspoons rice vinegar

1 teaspoon extra-virgin olive oil

½ teaspoon salt

¼ teaspoon black pepper

MAKE THE NOODLES AND DRESSING: About 15 minutes before serving, place the noodles in a large bowl. Add the bok choy and half the green onions. In a small bowl, combine the sesame oil, vinegar, olive oil, salt, and pepper. Pour the dressing over the noodles and toss to coat. Set aside to let the noodles soften.

TRANSFER the beef to a bowl. Use two forks to coarsely shred the beef. Use a fine-mesh sieve to strain the cooking liquid into a small saucepan. Pour ½ cup of the strained cooking liquid over the beef; stir to coat. Add the remaining 1 cup broth to the saucepan with the cooking liquid and heat through, about 2 minutes.

DIVIDE the noodles among four bowls. Pour the hot broth over the noodles. Top the noodles with the beef. Serve with the remaining green onions.

PORK ADOBO STEW

FROM JOSH KATT OF KITCHFIX

SERVES 4

PREP: 35 minutes

SLOW COOK: 6 hours (low)

TOTAL: 6 hours 35 minutes

This is a fantastic recipe to make when having friends over. You can enjoy the stew simply on its own, or if you'd like, you can create a toppings bar for guests to fill their bowls with their favorite Mexican flavors. The stew itself is complex—chiles de arbol and annatto seeds contribute deep, rich flavors that are sure to impress.

FOR THE ANNATTO SEED OIL

2 tablespoons annatto seeds

¼ cup coconut oil

FOR THE STEW

2 pounds boneless pork shoulder, cut into 1-inch pieces

3 teaspoons salt

1 tablespoon ground cumin

1 teaspoon ground coriander

1 teaspoon dried oregano

8 garlic cloves, sliced

1 tablespoon Whole30-compliant tomato paste

(continued)

MAKE THE ANNATTO SEED OIL: In a small saucepan, combine the annatto seeds and coconut oil. Cook over medium heat for 2 minutes, just until you hear a sizzle (the oil should be dark red). Use a fine-mesh sieve to strain the seeds from the oil; discard the seeds.

MAKE THE STEW: In an extra-large skillet, heat the annatto seed oil over medium-high heat. Add the pork and sprinkle with 2 teaspoons of the salt. Cook until the pork is browned on all sides, 5 to 8 minutes. Add the cumin, coriander, oregano, garlic, and tomato paste and cook until the garlic is golden, about 1 minute. Add 1 cup of the broth. Stir, scraping up the browned bits from the bottom of the skillet.

(continued)

JOSH KATT, KITCHFIX

Josh Katt is the head chef and founder of Kitchfix, a Chicago meal delivery service and grocery company that focuses on locally sourced, high-quality ingredients and gluten-free, dairy-free options. While working as a personal chef for cancer survivors, Josh realized the incredible power of food as medicine. At Kitchfix, Josh aims to make this healthy, delicious food convenient and available to everyone by using whole, functional ingredients and leaving out unnecessary fillers.

2 quarts Whole30-compliant chicken broth or Chicken Bone Broth (page 294)

2 large Spanish or yellow onions, coarsely chopped

5 purple potatoes, coarsely chopped (about 2 cups)

2 medium carrots, peeled and coarsely chopped

2 medium stalks celery, coarsely chopped

¾ cup finely chopped poblano peppers

1 bay leaf

4 dried chiles de arbol

⅓ cup fresh lime juice

TOPPINGS

2 avocados, halved, pitted, peeled and diced

1 small cabbage, cored and sliced

1 small red onion, thinly sliced

Chopped fresh cilantro

1 lime, cut into wedges

TRANSFER the pork and sauce to a 6-quart slow cooker. Add the remaining broth, the onion, potatoes, carrots, celery, poblano peppers, bay leaf, chiles de arbol, and remaining 1 teaspoon salt. Cover and cook on low for 6 hours.

DISCARD the bay leaf and dried chiles. Stir in the lime juice and serve the stew with the toppings.

TOM YUM SOUP

SERVES 6

PREP: 25 minutes

SLOW COOK: 4 hours (low)

TOTAL: 4 hours 25 minutes

Makrut lime leaves (sometimes also called kaffir lime leaves) and spicy Thai basil are two ingredients you likely won't find at your local supermarket. If you have an Asian market close by it's worth seeking them out, as they lend this soup a touch of authentic flavor. If not, no worries. Fresh lime juice and regular sweet basil make a fine substitution.

1½ pounds boneless, skinless chicken breast, cut into ½-inch pieces

4 cups Whole30-compliant chicken broth or Chicken Bone Broth (page 294)

1 can (14.5 ounces) Whole30-compliant diced tomatoes, undrained

1 medium yellow onion, roughly chopped

8 ounces shiitake mushrooms, stemmed, caps sliced ¼ inch thick

1 large yellow bell pepper, chopped

2 stalks lemongrass, crushed

2 tablespoons fresh lime juice

3 tablespoons coconut aminos

2 teaspoons Whole30-compliant fish sauce

1 piece (1 inch) fresh ginger, peeled and minced

1 teaspoon salt

1 Thai chile pepper, seeded and chopped (optional)

4 fresh makrut lime leaves (optional)

Chopped fresh Thai basil or sweet basil

Chopped fresh cilantro

1 lime, cut into wedges

IN a 4-quart slow cooker, combine the chicken, broth, tomatoes, onion, mushrooms, bell pepper, lemongrass, lime juice, coconut aminos, fish sauce, ginger, and salt, along with the Thai pepper and lime leaves (if using). Stir to combine.

COVER and cook on low for 4 hours. Remove the lemongrass and lime leaves, if using. Top servings with basil and cilantro and serve with lime wedges.

SMOKY SWEET POTATO CHILI

SERVES 6

PREP: 30 minutes

SLOW COOK: 8 hours (low) or 4 hours (high)

TOTAL: 8 hours 30 minutes

While it's certainly not crucial that you use smoked salt in this chili, it is a fun ingredient to have on hand, and most larger supermarkets stock it. With just a sprinkle, it adds a new flavor dimension to simple roasted vegetables and meats.

1½ pounds lean ground beef

1 medium red onion, chopped

1 poblano pepper, seeded and diced

2 large sweet potatoes, peeled and cut into ½-inch cubes (4 cups)

1 can (10.75 ounces) Whole30-compliant tomato puree

1 can (15 ounces) Whole30-compliant crushed tomatoes

2 cups Whole30-compliant tomato juice

2 tablespoons cider vinegar

1 tablespoon chili powder

1½ teaspoons smoked paprika

1 teaspoon cumin

1 teaspoon garlic powder

½ teaspoon allspice

¼ teaspoon cayenne pepper

1 teaspoon smoked salt or regular salt

Finely chopped red onion (optional)

IN a large skillet, cook the beef over medium-high heat, stirring with a wooden spoon, until browned, about 10 minutes. Drain off the fat.

TRANSFER the beef to a 4- to 5-quart slow cooker. Add the onion, poblano pepper, sweet potatoes, tomato puree, crushed tomatoes, tomato juice, vinegar, chili powder, smoked paprika, cumin, garlic powder, allspice, cayenne, and salt to the cooker. Stir to combine.

COVER and cook on low for 8 hours or on high for 4 hours.

IF desired, top servings with chopped onions.

CHICKEN, LIME, AND AVOCADO SOUP

FROM ALEX SNODGRASS OF THE DEFINED DISH

SERVES 6

PREP: 25 minutes

SLOW COOK: 8 hours (low) or 4 hours (high)

TOTAL: 8 hours 25 minutes

This soup is a staple in our house. Not only is it easy to make, but it's filled with flavor and is oh-so satisfying. Why? Because avocado . . . and lots of it! I just love this soup, rain or shine, and I know you will, too.

2 quarts Whole30-compliant chicken broth or Chicken Bone Broth (page 294)

1 can (14.5 ounces) Whole30-compliant diced tomatoes

1 medium white onion, finely diced

1 jalapeño, seeded and finely diced

3 cloves garlic, minced

1 tablespoon chipotle powder or regular chili powder

1 teaspoon ground cumin

1 teaspoon dried oregano

½ teaspoon salt

½ teaspoon black pepper

4 boneless, skinless chicken breasts (2 pounds)

½ cup chopped fresh cilantro

½ cup fresh lime juice, plus lime wedges for serving

3 avocados, halved, pitted, peeled, and diced

IN a 6-quart slow cooker, stir together the broth, tomatoes, onion, jalapeño, garlic, chipotle powder, cumin, oregano, salt, and pepper. Add the chicken.

COVER and cook on low for 8 to 10 hours or on high for 4 to 5 hours.

USE tongs to transfer the chicken to a cutting board. Use two forks to shred the chicken. Return the chicken to the cooker and stir in the cilantro and lime juice.

TOP servings with avocado and serve with lime wedges.

WHITE CHICKEN CHILI WITH SWEET POTATOES

FROM MICHELE ROSEN OF PALEO RUNNING MOMMA

SERVES 4

PREP: 35 minutes

SLOW COOK: 5 hours (low) or 2½ hours (high)

TOTAL: 6 hours

A splash of coconut cream and ghee make this chili creamy and luxurious. It's also chunky, filling, and super yummy! The nutritional yeast is optional, but it does give the chili a rich, cheesy flavor without the use of dairy products. Look for it in the natural-foods section of your supermarket.

1½ pounds boneless, skinless chicken breasts

2 cups Whole30-compliant chicken broth or Chicken Bone Broth (page 294)

1 large white or Japanese sweet potato, peeled and cut into ¾-inch pieces (about 3 cups)

1 small yellow onion, diced

1 can (4 ounces) Whole30-compliant diced green chiles

1 tablespoon finely chopped seeded jalapeño

4 cloves garlic, minced

2 teaspoons ground cumin

1 teaspoon dried oregano

½ teaspoon chili powder

⅛ teaspoon cayenne pepper

1 teaspoon salt

¼ teaspoon black pepper

½ cup Whole30-compliant coconut cream (see Tip)

1 tablespoon Clarified Butter (page 296) or ghee

1 tablespoon fresh lime juice

2 tablespoons nutritional yeast (optional)

1 tablespoon minced fresh cilantro

1 avocado, halved, pitted, peeled, and diced

Chopped fresh cilantro or chives, for serving

PLACE the chicken in a 4-quart slow cooker. Add the broth, sweet potato, onion, green chiles, jalapeño, garlic, cumin, oregano, chili powder, cayenne, salt, and pepper. Stir to combine.

COOK on low for 5 to 6 hours or on high for 2½ to 3 hours.

TRANSFER the chicken to a plate; cover to keep warm. Turn the slow cooker to high if using the low setting. Add the coconut cream, butter, lime juice, and nutritional yeast (if using) to the slow cooker; stir to combine. Cover and cook for 20 minutes.

USE two forks to shred the chicken. Return the chicken to the slow cooker. Cover and cook for 10 minutes. Stir in the 1 tablespoon minced cilantro.

SERVE with the avocado and more cilantro.

TIP *Coconut cream is similar to coconut milk but contains less water, so it has a thicker consistency. Stir thoroughly before measuring.*

RIBS AND ROASTS

BALSAMIC AND ROSEMARY PORK TENDERLOIN

SERVES 4

PREP: 15 minutes

SLOW COOK: 2 hours (high)

TOTAL: 2 hours 25 minutes

Broccolini is actually a trademarked vegetable—a cross between broccoli and Chinese kale. It has slender, bright-green stalks that are sweet with just a touch of pepperiness, and bouquets of tiny green florets at the top. Either broccoli rabe or thin-stemmed broccoli can be substituted for the Broccolini.

2 teaspoons smoked salt or regular salt

1 teaspoon cracked black pepper

⅛ teaspoon garlic powder

½ teaspoon dried rosemary, crushed

½ teaspoon dried thyme

2 pounds Whole30-compliant pork tenderloin, trimmed

¼ cup balsamic vinegar

2 tablespoons coconut aminos

2 medium yellow onions, cut into 6 wedges, root partially attached

2 fresh rosemary sprigs

12 ounces Broccolini, trimmed

IN a small bowl, combine the salt, pepper, garlic powder, rosemary, and thyme. Rub the mixture on the pork.

IN a 6-quart slow cooker, combine the vinegar and coconut aminos. Place the pork and onions in the slow cooker and top with the fresh rosemary. Cover and cook on high for 2 hours. Remove and discard the fresh rosemary. Add the Broccolini to the slow cooker. Cover and cook until wilted, 8 to 10 minutes.

SLICE the pork and sprinkle with additional pepper. Serve with the onions and Broccolini.

COFFEE-RUBBED POT ROAST

SERVES 4

PREP: 25 minutes

SLOW COOK: 7 hours (low) or 3½ hours (high)

TOTAL: 7 hours 25 minutes

Poblano peppers—the glossy, dark green pepper used in chiles rellenos—are called ancho chiles when they are dried. Dark-red ancho chile powder has a rich, fruity flavor with just a touch of heat. It pairs beautifully with the earthy, bittersweet flavor of coffee in the rub for this beef roast.

1 tablespoon instant espresso coffee powder or ground instant coffee

2 teaspoons ancho chile powder

½ teaspoon salt

3 pounds boneless beef chuck, arm, or shoulder roast, trimmed

6 medium carrots, peeled and cut into 1-inch pieces

2 medium red onions, halved and cut into wedges

½ cup Whole30-compliant beef broth or Beef Bone Broth (page 294)

3 tablespoons Whole30-compliant tomato paste

Chopped fresh flat-leaf parsley

IN a small bowl, stir together the espresso powder, chile powder, and salt. Rub the roast on all sides with the espresso mixture.

IN a 6-quart slow cooker, add the carrots and onions. Add the broth and tomato paste; stir to combine. Place the seasoned roast on top of the vegetables.

COVER and cook on low for 7 to 8 hours or on high for 3½ to 4 hours. Transfer the meat and vegetables to a serving platter and top with the parsley. Serve with the strained cooking liquid, if desired.

INSTANT POT VARIATION *Follow the directions in the first step using a 6-quart Instant Pot, reserving the carrots. Lock the lid in place. Select Manual and cook at high pressure for 45 minutes. Use natural release for 10 minutes, then quick release. Transfer the roast to a plate; cover to keep warm. Add the carrots to the pot. Lock the lid in place. Select Manual and cook at high pressure for 3 minutes. Continue with the remaining directions.*

POMEGRANATE-ORANGE BBQ BRISKET WITH CELERY ROOT SLAW

SERVES 6

PREP: 15 minutes

SLOW COOK: 10 hours (low) or 5 hours (high)

REST: 10 minutes

TOTAL: 10 hours 25 minutes

Celery root—also called celeriac—is a homely, knobby, gnarly looking root covered with hairy tendrils. But inside, the creamy-white flesh is crisp and refreshing, with the flavors of celery and parsley. Look for firm roots with no soft spots and pick the roundest one you can find. The less gnarled it is, the less waste you'll have when peeling it.

FOR THE BRISKET

1 sweet onion, sliced

1 beef brisket or arm roast (3 to 4 pounds)

½ cup Whole30-compliant pomegranate juice

1 can (8 ounces) Whole30-compliant tomato sauce

1 tablespoon chili powder

1 teaspoon grated orange zest

½ teaspoon chipotle powder

½ teaspoon celery seeds

½ teaspoon salt

FOR THE SLAW

⅓ cup Whole30-compliant mayonnaise

2 tablespoons fresh orange juice

½ teaspoon celery seeds

½ teaspoon salt

½ teaspoon black pepper

1 large celery root, peeled and coarsely shredded (about 4 cups)

2 carrots, peeled and shredded

Sliced green onions (optional)

MAKE THE BRISKET: Place the onions and brisket in a 6-quart slow cooker. In a medium bowl, combine the pomegranate juice, tomato sauce, chili powder, orange zest, chipotle powder, celery seeds, and salt. Pour the pomegranate mixture over the brisket and onions. Cover and cook on low for 10 to 12 hours or on high for 5 to 6 hours, or until the brisket is tender.

MAKE THE SLAW: In a medium bowl, combine the mayonnaise, orange juice, celery seeds, salt, and pepper. Add the celery root and carrots; toss to combine. Cover and chill for 1 to 4 hours.

REMOVE the roast from the cooker; reserve the cooking liquid. Cover the brisket with foil and let it rest for 10 minutes. Thinly slice the brisket and serve with the cooking liquid and the slaw. If desired, top the slaw with green onions.

INSTANT POT VARIATION *Follow the directions in the first step using a 6-quart Instant Pot. Lock the lid in place. Select Meat/Stew and cook at high pressure for 2 hours. Use quick release. Follow the remaining directions.*

PORK AND VEGETABLE YELLOW CURRY

SERVES 4

PREP: 20 minutes

SLOW COOK: 5 hours (low) or 2½ hours (high)

TOTAL: 5 hours 20 minutes

Pork loin is a lean cut. Cooking it in coconut milk spiked with warm Indian spices infuses it with flavor and keeps it from drying out over the long simmering time.

1 can (14.5 ounces) Whole30-compliant coconut milk

1½ teaspoons grated fresh ginger

1 teaspoon salt

1 teaspoon ground turmeric

1 teaspoon Whole30-compliant yellow curry powder

½ to 1 teaspoon Whole30-compliant garam masala

½ teaspoon ground cinnamon

½ teaspoon red pepper flakes

½ teaspoon garlic powder

1½ pounds Whole30-compliant boneless pork loin, cut into 1-inch cubes

1 package (10 ounces) shredded carrots

1 medium yellow onion, roughly chopped

1 medium head (2 pounds) cauliflower, cut into florets, or 4 cups purchased cauliflower florets

2 Roma (plum) tomatoes, cored and chopped

1 serrano chile pepper, seeded and minced (optional)

1 package (12 ounces) frozen riced cauliflower and broccoli, prepared according to package directions, or 3 cups raw cauliflower and broccoli rice (see Tip)

Chopped fresh cilantro

IN a small bowl, whisk together the coconut milk, ginger, salt, turmeric, curry powder, garam masala, cinnamon, red pepper flakes, and garlic powder until thoroughly combined.

IN a 4-quart slow cooker, combine the pork, carrots, onion, cauliflower florets, tomatoes, and serrano pepper (if using). Add the coconut milk mixture and stir gently to combine.

COVER and cook on low for 5 hours or on high for 2½ hours. Serve the stew over the riced cauliflower and broccoli and top with chopped cilantro.

TIP *To make homemade cauliflower and broccoli rice, place 1 cup cauliflower florets and 1 cup broccoli florets in a food processor. Pulse the florets until processed into rice-size pieces.*

INSTANT POT VARIATION *Follow the directions in the first two steps using a 6-quart Instant Pot. Lock the lid in place. Select Manual and cook at low pressure for 5 minutes. Use natural release for 5 minutes, then quick release. Follow the remaining directions.*

POT ROAST WITH BUTTERNUT SQUASH AND DATES

SERVES 4

PREP: 25 minutes

SLOW COOK: 7 hours (low) or 3½ hours (high)

TOTAL: 7 hours 25 minutes

Dates add a touch of caramel-y sweetness—but not too much—to this simple but rich-tasting dish. A peppery arugula salad dressed with olive oil, lemon juice, salt, and pepper makes a nice accompaniment.

½ cup Whole30-compliant tomato paste

½ teaspoon salt

½ teaspoon black pepper

2 pounds boneless beef chuck roast, trimmed

1 medium butternut squash (about 1½ pounds), peeled, seeded, and cut into 1½-inch pieces

2 medium onions, each cut into 6 wedges

1 cup Whole30-compliant beef broth or Beef Bone Broth (page 294)

½ cup fresh orange juice

8 pitted dates, cut in half

2 bay leaves

Chopped fresh parsley (optional)

IN a small bowl, stir together the tomato paste, salt, and pepper. Spread the mixture over all sides of the roast. Place the roast in a 5- to 6-quart slow cooker. Add the squash, onions, broth, orange juice, dates, and bay leaves.

COVER and cook on low for 7 to 8 hours or on high for 3½ to 4 hours. Remove and discard the bay leaves.

SERVE the beef and vegetables with the cooking juices and top with parsley, if desired.

INSTANT POT VARIATION *Follow the directions in the first step using a 6-quart Instant Pot, reserving the squash. Lock the lid in place. Select Manual and cook at high pressure for 40 minutes. Use natural release for 10 minutes, then quick release. Transfer the roast to a plate; cover to keep warm. Add the squash to the pot. Lock the lid in place. Select Manual and cook at high pressure for 3 minutes. Follow the remaining directions.*

GARLIC PEPPER PORK WITH COLLARDS

SERVES 6

PREP: 20 minutes

SLOW COOK: 5 hours (low) or 2½ hours (high)

TOTAL: 5 hours 20 minutes

Collard greens are a Southern side-dish specialty—served mostly with various types of pork. If you like, sprinkle hot pepper vinegar over the cooked collards for an extra shot of tanginess.

3 pounds pork butt roast

1 tablespoon Whole30-compliant garlic pepper seasoning

8 cups chopped collard greens, tightly packed

3 slices Whole30-compliant bacon, chopped

½ large red onion, sliced

¼ cup chopped garlic

¼ teaspoon black pepper

1 tablespoon cider vinegar

RUB the pork roast on all sides with the garlic pepper seasoning. Place the seasoned roast in a 6-quart slow cooker with ¼ cup water. Add the collards, bacon, onion, and garlic. Sprinkle with the pepper.

COOK for 5 to 6 hours on low or 2½ to 3 hours on high, or until the pork falls apart easily with a fork. Transfer the pork to a platter or cutting board; tent with foil to rest 10 minutes.

STIR the vinegar into the collard greens. If the pork is wrapped in a string mesh, cut it apart carefully with kitchen shears. Slice the pork and serve with the collard greens.

INSTANT POT VARIATION *Follow the directions in the first two steps using a 6-quart Instant Pot. Lock the lid in place. Select Manual and cook at high pressure for 45 minutes. Use natural release for 10 minutes, then quick release. Continue with the remaining directions.*

TERIYAKI PORK

SERVES 4

PREP: 20 minutes

SLOW COOK: 4 hours (low) or 2 hours (high)

TOTAL: 4 hours 20 minutes

Bottled teriyaki sauce contains high-fructose corn syrup, wheat, soy (in the soy sauce), and synthetic preservatives. Our version of the popular Japanese sauce has the same sweet-savory-salty appeal but is made entirely of compliant foods.

¼ cup pineapple juice

¼ cup coconut aminos

2 cloves garlic, minced

½ teaspoon ground ginger

Dash cayenne pepper

1½ pounds Whole30-compliant pork tenderloin, trimmed

¼ teaspoon black pepper

1 cup chopped fresh pineapple

¼ cup sliced green onions

1 package (12 ounces) frozen cauliflower rice, prepared according to package directions or 3 cups raw cauliflower rice (page 60)

IN a 3½- to 4-quart slow cooker, stir together the pineapple juice, coconut aminos, garlic, ginger, and cayenne. Sprinkle the pork with the pepper; add to the slow cooker and turn to coat.

COVER and cook on low for 4 to 5 hours or on high for 2 to 2½ hours.

TRANSFER the pork to a cutting board; strain the cooking liquid. Cut the pork into ½-inch slices. Drizzle the pork with some of the cooking liquid and top with the pineapple and green onions. Serve with the cauliflower rice.

INSTANT POT VARIATION *Follow the directions in the first two steps using a 6-quart Instant Pot. Lock the lid in place. Select Manual and cook at high pressure for 15 minutes. Use natural release for 5 minutes, then quick release. Continue with the remaining directions.*

ASIAN POT ROAST WITH SHIITAKES AND SNOW PEAS

Several hours of cook time makes the meat butter-knife tender—and just 10 to 15 minutes for the vegetables keeps them bright in color and perfectly fresh so that everything is at its best taste and texture.

1 large sweet onion, halved and cut lengthwise into thin wedges

1 green bell pepper, thinly sliced lengthwise

1 boneless beef arm roast (2½ to 3 pounds), trimmed

Salt and black pepper

3 tablespoons coconut aminos

4 cloves garlic, minced

2 tablespoons grated fresh ginger

1 teaspoon sesame oil

2 cups snow peas, trimmed

8 ounces shiitake mushrooms, stemmed and sliced

1 bunch green onions, white and green parts, cut into 1-inch pieces

IN a 5- to 6-quart slow cooker, combine the onion and bell pepper. Season the beef with salt and pepper and add to the slow cooker. In a small bowl, combine the coconut aminos, garlic, ginger, and sesame oil. Drizzle over the beef.

COVER and cook on low for 7 to 8 hours or on high for 3½ to 4 hours, or until tender. Remove the roast from the cooker. Cover with foil to keep warm.

TURN the slow cooker to high if using the low setting. Stir the snow peas, mushrooms, and green onions into the slow cooker. Cover and cook until the snow peas are crisp-tender and mushrooms are softened, 10 to 20 minutes. Slice or shred the beef and serve with the vegetables and mushrooms.

INSTANT POT VARIATION *Follow the directions in the first step using a 6-quart Instant Pot. Lock the lid in place. Select Manual and cook at high pressure for 45 minutes. Use natural release for 10 minutes, then quick release. Add the vegetables, select Sauté, and adjust to Less/Low. Simmer, uncovered, until the snow peas are crisp-tender and the mushrooms have softened, 10 to 20 minutes. Continue with the remaining directions.*

BEEF BARBACOA

SERVES 8

PREP: 15 minutes

SLOW COOK: 8 hours (low) or 4 hours (high)

TOTAL: 8 hours 15 minutes

It's probably no surprise that *barbacoa* is the root word of *barbecue*. And while it can apply to different meats depending on where you are in the world (beef, lamb, pork, goat) and can involve a variety of cooking methods (over an open fire, in a hole in the ground, even steamed), it always means meat that is cooked long and low until it is falling-apart-tender: perfect for the slow cooker!

3 pounds boneless beef chuck roast, trimmed and cut into large pieces

1 tablespoon chili powder

2 teaspoons chipotle powder

1½ teaspoons salt

1 teaspoon ground cumin

1 cup chopped yellow onion

¾ cup Whole30-compliant beef broth or Beef Bone Broth (page 294)

4 cloves garlic, minced

1 jalapeño, seeded and finely chopped

Butterhead lettuce or jicama tortillas (see Tip)

Lime wedges

Chopped fresh cilantro

ADD the beef to a 4-quart slow cooker. Sprinkle the beef with the chili powder, chipotle powder, salt, and cumin; stir to coat. Add the onion, broth, garlic, and jalapeño.

COVER and cook on low for 8 to 10 hours or on high for 4 to 5 hours. Transfer the beef to a bowl and shred using two forks. Add enough of the cooking liquid to moisten. Serve in lettuce leaves or jicama tortillas with lime wedges and cilantro.

TIP *To make jicama tortillas, peel one medium jicama and trim so it will fit into a mandoline, about 4 inches wide. Place the mandolin on the thinnest setting and carefully slice the jicama. One jicama makes approximately 18 tortillas.*

INSTANT POT VARIATION *Follow the directions in the first step using a 6-quart Instant Pot. Lock the lid in place. Select Manual and cook at high pressure for 50 minutes. Use natural release for 10 minutes, then quick release. Follow the remaining directions.*

MUSTARD-BRAISED BRISKET WITH POTATOES AND CABBAGE

SERVE 6

PREP: 20 minutes

SLOW COOK: 10 hours (low) or 5 hours (high)

TOTAL: 10 hours 50 minutes

With potatoes, cabbage, caraway, mustard, and dill, this dish has echoes of hearty Eastern European fare—perfect for a cold fall or winter night.

1 tablespoon Whole30-compliant coarse-grain mustard

3 cloves garlic, minced

1 teaspoon caraway seeds, crushed

½ teaspoon coarse salt

¼ teaspoon black pepper

2 to 2½ pounds beef brisket, trimmed

1 to 1¼ pounds 2- to 3-inch Yukon gold potatoes, scrubbed and halved

1 medium onion, cut into thin wedges

1 small head cabbage, cored and cut into 8 wedges

2 tablespoons cider vinegar

1 tablespoon Clarified Butter (page 296) or ghee

1½ teaspoons snipped fresh dill

IN a small bowl, combine the mustard, garlic, caraway seeds, salt, and pepper. Spread all over brisket. Place the potatoes, onion, and ½ cup water in a 3½- to 4-quart slow cooker. Lay the brisket on top of the vegetables. Cover and cook on low for 10 to 11 hours or on high for 5 to 5½ hours.

TURN the slow cooker to high if using the low setting. Add the cabbage to the slow cooker. Cover and cook until tender, about 30 minutes.

TRANSFER the brisket and vegetables to a serving platter. Skim the fat from the cooking juices; add the vinegar, butter, and dill. Whisk until well combined. Drizzle the liquid over the beef and vegetables and serve.

INSTANT POT VARIATION *Follow the directions in the first step using a 6-quart Instant Pot, but leave out the potatoes. Lock the lid in place. Select Meat/Stew and cook at high pressure for 90 minutes. Use natural release for 10 minutes, then quick release. In the second step, transfer the brisket to a serving platter. Add the potatoes and cabbage to the pot. Lock the lid in place. Select Meat/Stew and cook at high pressure for 5 minutes. Use quick release. Continue with the third step.*

HOT BEEF

SERVES 6

PREP: 35 minutes

SLOW COOK: 8 hours (low) or
4 hours (high)

TOTAL: 8 hours 40 minutes

When you're craving something hearty and comforting, this take on the old-fashioned open-faced hot beef sandwich slathered with gravy will make you smile. The Whole30 version substitutes garlic mashed potatoes for the toasted bread. Serve it with some steamed broccoli tossed with a little melted ghee. All will feel right with the world, we promise.

1 beef arm roast (2½ to 3 pounds)

6 cloves garlic, peeled

½ teaspoon dried rosemary

1 teaspoon salt

¼ teaspoon black pepper

2 pounds russet potatoes, peeled and cut into 2-inch chunks

1 package (8 ounces) button mushrooms, halved

1 medium yellow onion, sliced

2 tablespoons tapioca flour

¼ teaspoon garlic powder

2 tablespoons Clarified Butter (page 296) or ghee

CUT three slits each into the top and bottom of the roast. Insert a garlic clove into each slit. In a small bowl, combine the rosemary, salt, and pepper. Sprinkle on both sides of roast. Place the roast in a 6-quart slow cooker with ¼ cup water. Add the potatoes, mushrooms, and onion.

COVER and cook on low for 8 to 10 hours or on high for 4 to 5 hours. Transfer the beef to a cutting board or platter. Cover and keep warm. Transfer the potatoes to a large bowl.

TURN the slow cooker to high if using the low setting. In a small bowl, stir together the tapioca flour and 2 tablespoons water. Pour into the slow cooker. Cook, stirring occasionally, until the gravy has thickened, about 5 minutes.

MEANWHILE, sprinkle the potatoes with the garlic powder; add the butter. Use a potato masher or fork to mash the potatoes to your desired consistency.

SERVE the roast over the mashed potatoes, with gravy ladled over the top.

PORK TENDERLOIN WITH BUTTERNUT SQUASH

SERVES 4

PREP: 20 minutes

SLOW COOK: 5 hours (low) or 2½ hours (high)

TOTAL: 5 hours 25 minutes

If you use 24 ounces pre-cubed butternut squash, available in the produce sections of most supermarkets, the prep for this recipe is 10 minutes or less.

1 medium butternut squash (about 1½ pounds), peeled, seeded, and cut into 1-inch cubes

2 medium shallots, coarsely chopped

½ cup apple cider

¾ teaspoon salt

½ teaspoon black pepper

1 teaspoon smoked paprika

1 teaspoon dried thyme

1½ pounds Whole30-compliant pork tenderloin, trimmed

Fresh thyme (optional)

IN a 4-quart slow cooker, combine the squash, shallots, cider, ¼ teaspoon of the salt, and ¼ teaspoon of the pepper. In a small bowl, stir together the paprika, dried thyme, and the remaining ½ teaspoon salt and ¼ teaspoon pepper; sprinkle over the pork. Add the pork to the slow cooker. Cover and cook on low for 5 to 6 hours or on high for 2½ to 3 hours.

TRANSFER the pork to a cutting board. Let rest for 5 minutes, then cut into ½-inch slices. Strain the cooking liquid. Drizzle servings of the pork and vegetables with some of the cooking liquid. If desired, sprinkle with additional pepper and fresh thyme and serve.

SHORT RIBS PIZZAIOLA WITH CAULIFLOWER RICE

SERVES 4 TO 6

PREP: 35 minutes

SLOW COOK: 7 hours (low) or 3½ hours (high)

TOTAL: 7 hours 35 minutes

Pizzaiola is an Italian word for a pizza maker. And while the tomato, basil, olives, and pickled pepperoncini in this yummy dish make it taste like pizza, it doesn't have the globs of cheese and bready crust that make you wish hadn't just eaten a slice (or a few) of that pie.

FOR THE SHORT RIBS

2 teaspoons dried oregano, crushed

2 teaspoons fennel seeds, crushed

½ to 1 teaspoon red pepper flakes

1 teaspoon salt

12 bone-in beef short ribs

2 tablespoons extra-virgin olive oil (optional)

1 onion, chopped

1 bulb fennel, trimmed and chopped

1 green bell pepper, chopped

½ cup sliced pickled pepperoncini peppers

4 cloves garlic, minced

1 can (14.5 ounces) Whole30-compliant diced tomatoes

FOR THE CAULIFLOWER RICE

2 packages (12 ounces each) frozen riced cauliflower or 6 cups raw cauliflower rice (page 60)

1 tablespoon extra-virgin olive oil

½ teaspoon dried oregano, crushed

½ teaspoon garlic powder

Salt and black pepper

½ cup fresh basil leaves, torn

¼ cup sliced Whole30-compliant black or green olives

MAKE THE SHORT RIBS: In a small bowl, combine the oregano, fennel seeds, red pepper flakes, and salt; rub onto the short ribs. If desired, in a large skillet, heat the olive oil and cook the short ribs on all sides until browned, about 10 minutes. In a 6-quart slow cooker, combine the onion, chopped fennel, bell pepper, pepperoncini peppers, and garlic. Add the short ribs; top with the tomatoes.

COVER and cook on low for 7 to 8 hours or on high for 3½ to 4 hours, or until the short ribs are tender. Remove the ribs from the cooker. Skim the fat from the cooking liquid.

MAKE THE CAULIFLOWER RICE: Cook the cauliflower rice according to the package directions; drain well. Stir in the olive oil, oregano, and garlic powder. Season to taste with salt and pepper.

SERVE the short ribs and cooking liquid (not strained) over the cauliflower rice. Top with fresh basil and olives.

INSTANT POT VARIATION *Follow the directions in the first step using a 6-quart Instant Pot. If desired, brown the short ribs in the Instant Pot by selecting Sauté, then More/High. In the second step, lock the lid in place. Select Meat/Stew, select More/High, and cook for 1 hour 15 minutes. Use natural release for 10 minutes, then quick release. Continue with the remaining directions.*

SPICY CITRUS SHORT RIBS

SERVES 4

PREP: 20 minutes

SLOW COOK: 8 hours (low) or
4 hours (high)

TOTAL: 8 hours 20 minutes

Short ribs are marbled with a fair amount of fat—that's part of what makes them so good! Searing the ribs renders some of the fat, but this recipe skips that step in the interest of saving time, so you'll want to thoroughly skim the cooking liquid before drizzling it over the meat and vegetables.

1 medium onion, chopped

1 tablespoon grated orange zest, plus extra for sprinkling

½ cup fresh orange juice

2 tablespoons Whole30-compliant tomato paste

1 teaspoon chipotle powder

2 cloves garlic, minced

1 teaspoon salt

12 bone-in beef short ribs (about 4½ pounds)

1 package (12 ounces) riced cauliflower and sweet potato, prepared according to package directions

IN a 6-quart slow cooker, stir together the onion, orange zest, orange juice, tomato paste, chipotle powder, garlic, and salt. Place the ribs in the slow cooker; add the orange juice mixture and toss to coat.

COVER and cook on low for 8 to 9 hours or on high for 4 to 4½ hours.

TRANSFER the ribs to a serving platter. Skim the fat from the cooking liquid. Serve the ribs on the riced cauliflower and sweet potato, drizzled with the cooking liquid and topped with additional orange zest.

INSTANT POT VARIATION *Follow the directions in the first two steps using a 6-quart Instant Pot. Lock the lid in place. Select Meat/Stew, select More/High, and cook 1 hour 15 minutes. Use natural release for 10 minutes, then quick release. Continue with the remaining directions.*

SWEET AND SPICY SHREDDED PORK

SERVES 6 TO 8

PREP: 20 minutes

SLOW COOK: 9 hours (low) or 4½ hours (high)

Ground chipotle pepper (chipotle powder) provides the heat and smoke—and just a few dates provide the sweetness—to this slow-simmered pork shoulder. Paper-thin slices of jicama serve as fresh and crunchy "tortillas" to serve with the richly flavored meat. You could also serve it over greens for a hearty salad.

1 cup coarsely chopped seeded tomatoes

1 small onion, cut into thin wedges

4 pitted unsweetened dates

1 teaspoon coarse salt

1 teaspoon garlic powder

½ teaspoon dry mustard

½ teaspoon black pepper

¼ teaspoon ground cloves

¼ teaspoon chipotle powder

2 pounds boneless pork shoulder, trimmed and cut into 3 portions

⅓ cup Whole30-compliant tomato paste

2 teaspoons Whole30-compliant coarse-grain mustard

Jicama tortillas (see Tip, page 113)

Chopped fresh chives or parsley

PLACE the tomatoes, onion, and dates in a 4-quart slow cooker. In a small bowl, combine the salt, garlic powder, dry mustard, pepper, cloves, and chipotle powder. Sprinkle the seasoning over the pork pieces; rub in with your fingers. Arrange the pork in the cooker over the vegetables. Pour ½ cup water over all.

COVER and cook on low for 9 to 10 hours or on high for 4½ to 5 hours. Using a slotted spoon, transfer the pork to a cutting board. Using two forks, pull the meat into shreds. Set aside.

CAREFULLY transfer the cooking liquid to a blender. Add the tomato paste and coarse-grain mustard. Cover and blend until smooth; pour back into the cooker. Add the shredded meat. Toss to combine.

SERVE the pork in jicama tortillas and top with chives or parsley.

INSTANT POT VARIATION *Follow the directions in the first two steps using a 6-quart Instant Pot. Lock the lid in place. Select Manual and cook at high pressure for 40 minutes. Use natural release for 10 minutes, then quick release. Continue with the remaining directions.*

ASIAN-STYLE RIBS WITH BOK CHOY–CARROT SALAD

SERVES 4

PREP: 15 minutes

SLOW COOK: 8 hours (low) or 4 hours (high)

TOTAL: 8 hours 25 minutes

If you have the time and don't mind an extra step, brown the ribs before putting them into the cooker. You will have less fat in the end and a nice crust on the meat. The crunchy slaw-like salad of baby bok choy ribbons and shredded carrot tossed with a compliant bottled lemon-garlic dressing provides a refreshing contrast to the rich, meaty ribs.

FOR THE RIBS

4 green onions

½ cup coconut aminos

4 cloves garlic, minced

1 piece (1 inch) fresh ginger, peeled and minced

1 tablespoon cider vinegar

2 teaspoons Whole30-compliant fish sauce

1 teaspoon salt

8 bone-in beef short ribs (about 4½ pounds)

FOR THE SALAD

3 baby bok choy, trimmed and thinly sliced into ribbons

½ cup shredded carrots

Whole30-compliant lemon-garlic dressing (Tessamae's)

1 tablespoon sesame seeds, toasted (see Tip)

MAKE THE RIBS: Thinly slice the green onions; separate the white and green parts and set the green parts aside. In a small bowl, stir together the white parts, the coconut aminos, garlic, ginger, vinegar, fish sauce, and salt.

PLACE the ribs in a single layer in a 4- to 5-quart slow cooker. Pour the coconut amino mixture over the ribs.

COVER and cook on low for 8 to 9 hours or on high for 4 to 4½ hours. Transfer the ribs to a platter; cover to keep warm.

STRAIN the cooking liquid through a fine-mesh sieve into a medium saucepan. Discard the solids. Skim the fat. Bring the cooking liquid to a boil over medium heat and reduce to a simmer. Cook the sauce until reduced by half, about 10 minutes.

MAKE THE SALAD: In a large bowl, combine the bok choy and carrots. Drizzle with the lemon-garlic dressing and toss to coat. Sprinkle with the sesame seeds and toss again.

SERVE the ribs drizzled with the sauce and sprinkled with remaining green onions. Serve the salad alongside.

TIP *To toast sesame seeds, heat in a dry skillet over medium heat, stirring, until fragrant and lightly browned, about 2 minutes.*

BARBECUE PORK RIBS WITH WATERMELON-TOMATO SALAD

SERVES 4

PREP: 20 minutes

SLOW COOK: 5 hours (low) or 2½ hours (high)

TOTAL: 5 hours 20 minutes

The sweetness and acidity of watermelon salad is a welcome accompaniment to the richness of ribs. Don't make it too far ahead of serving time; the salad can chill for only up to 1 hour before the watermelon starts breaking down.

FOR THE RIBS

3 pounds pork loin back ribs, membrane removed (see Tip), cut into individual ribs

1 tablespoon Whole30-compliant barbecue rub

¾ cup Whole30-compliant chicken broth or Chicken Bone Broth (page 294)

1 cup Whole30-compliant barbecue sauce

Grated orange zest

FOR THE SALAD

3 cups 1-inch chunks seedless watermelon

2 cups halved cherry tomatoes

½ cup thinly sliced red onion

3 tablespoons extra-virgin olive oil

2 tablespoons white balsamic vinegar or white wine vinegar

⅛ teaspoon salt

¼ cup lightly packed chopped fresh mint or basil

MAKE THE RIBS: Sprinkle the ribs with the barbecue rub; rub in with your fingers. Add the ribs and broth to a 4-quart slow cooker.

COVER and cook on low for 5 to 6 hours or on high for 2½ to 3 hours.

MAKE THE SALAD: Meanwhile, in a medium bowl, combine the watermelon, tomatoes, and onion. In a small bowl, whisk together the olive oil, vinegar, and salt. Drizzle the dressing over the watermelon salad; toss to coat. Cover and chill for up to 1 hour. Sprinkle with the mint just before serving.

TRANSFER the ribs to a serving platter; discard the cooking liquid. Brush the ribs with the barbecue sauce and top with orange zest. Serve with the watermelon-tomato salad.

TIP *To remove the membrane (silver skin) from the back of the ribs, start at one end of the rack and slide a table knife under the membrane. Lift and loosen the membrane. Use a paper towel to grab the edge of the membrane and pull it off. Or you can ask the butcher to do this for you.*

BRAISED SHORT RIBS WITH CAULIFLOWER–SWEET POTATO PILAF

SERVES 4

PREP: 20 minutes

SLOW COOK: 8 hours (low) or 4 hours (high)

TOTAL: 8 hours 30 minutes

The term "convenience product" used to mean something that was highly processed and likely contained preservatives and fake flavor enhancers. But with the move toward clean eating, there are now great convenience products for Whole30-ers, such as the frozen riced cauliflower and sweet potato that serves as the base of the pilaf that accompanies these ribs. Just a few stir-ins—chopped parsley, capers, olive oil, and lemon—give this pure product great flavor.

2 tablespoons dried sage

2 tablespoons dried oregano

2 teaspoons garlic powder

1 teaspoon salt

1 teaspoon coarse black pepper

8 to 12 bone-in beef short ribs (3 to 4 pounds)

3 medium carrots, peeled and sliced diagonally ½ inch thick

2 medium yellow onions, coarsely chopped

4 cloves garlic, crushed

1 cup Whole30-compliant tomato juice

1 package (12 ounces) frozen riced cauliflower and sweet potato

Grated zest and juice of 1 lemon

¼ cup chopped fresh parsley

2 teaspoons Whole30-compliant capers, drained

2 teaspoons extra-virgin olive oil

Fresh thyme sprigs

IN a small bowl, combine the sage, oregano, garlic powder, salt, and pepper. Rub the ribs with the spice mixture. Place the carrots, onions, garlic, and tomato juice in a 6-quart slow cooker. Add the ribs.

COVER and cook on low for 8 hours or on high for 4 hours. Use a slotted spoon to transfer the beef and vegetables to a platter; cover to keep warm.

TRANSFER the cooking liquid to a medium saucepan. Skim the fat. Bring the sauce to a boil over medium heat. Reduce the heat and simmer until reduced by half, about 10 minutes.

MEANWHILE, for the pilaf, prepare the riced cauliflower and sweet potatoes according to the package directions. Stir in the lemon zest and juice, parsley, capers, and olive oil.

DRIZZLE the sauce over the ribs and vegetables and top with fresh thyme. Serve on top of the pilaf.

INSTANT POT VARIATION *Follow the directions of the first two steps using a 6-quart Instant Pot, but leave out the carrots. Lock the lid in place. Select Manual and cook on high pressure for 50 minutes. Use natural release for 5 minutes, then quick release. Remove the ribs from the pot. Add the carrots to the pot. Select Sauté and adjust to Medium. Simmer until the liquid is reduced by half and the carrots are tender, about 10 minutes. Continue with the last three steps.*

ISLAND BRAISED SHORT RIBS
FROM CRISTINA CURP OF THE CASTAWAY KITCHEN

SERVES 4

PREP: 45 minutes

SLOW COOK: 3 hours (high)

TOTAL: 3 hours 45 minutes

This recipe is warm and spiced with sweet notes—the perfect dish to serve to dinner guests. It will have the house smelling inviting and delicious! The pineapple and papaya not only add sweetness to the dish, they help break down the short rib meat for fall-off-the-bone tenderness and a deliciously sweet and spiced sauce.

4 slices Whole30-compliant bacon, cut into 1-inch pieces

3 pounds English-cut beef short ribs, cut into 2- to 3-inch pieces

1 tablespoon fine Himalayan salt or regular salt

1 large onion, diced

¼ medium head cabbage, chopped (4 cups)

4 cloves garlic, minced

1 tablespoon dry mustard

2 teaspoons ground cinnamon

1 teaspoon black pepper

⅓ cup tapioca flour

3 cups Whole30-compliant beef bone broth or Beef Bone Broth (page 294)

¼ cup white wine vinegar

1 cup diced pineapple

½ cup diced papaya or additional pineapple

½ cup unsweetened apple sauce

2 tablespoons coconut aminos

3 fresh rosemary sprigs

Chopped fresh parsley

HEAT an extra-large heavy-bottom skillet over medium-high heat. Add the bacon and cook, stirring occasionally, until crisp, 5 to 8 minutes. Transfer the bacon to paper towels.

SPRINKLE the ribs with the salt. Add to the skillet and cook in the bacon fat until browned, turning once, 2 minutes. Transfer the ribs to a plate.

ADD the onion and cabbage to the skillet and cook until tender, 6 to 8 minutes. Add the garlic, dry mustard, cinnamon, and pepper. Stir in the tapioca flour. Immediately add the broth and vinegar. Cook, stirring, until the sauce thickens. Add the pineapple, papaya, and coconut aminos. Add the short ribs and the bacon. Bring to a boil, stirring. Reduce the heat and simmer, stirring frequently, for 5 minutes. Transfer to a 6-quart slow cooker. Add the rosemary.

COVER and cook on high for 3 hours. Remove and discard the bones and rosemary. Serve the sauce over the ribs, topped with parsley.

CLASSIC BBQ RIBS WITH BRUSSELS SPROUTS

SERVES 4

PREP: 25 minutes

SLOW COOK: 6 hours (low) or 3 hours (high)

TOTAL: 6 hours 25 minutes

It's not absolutely necessary to broil the ribs after they come out of the slow cooker, but it does give them a nice caramelized brown crust.

1 teaspoon salt

¼ teaspoon black pepper

1 teaspoon onion powder

3½ pounds baby back ribs, membrane removed (see Tip), cut into 4 portions

1 bottle (10 ounces) Whole30-compliant barbecue sauce

1 medium red onion, minced

4 cloves garlic, minced

¼ cup pitted dates, finely chopped

1 package (10 ounces) frozen roasted Brussels sprouts or 12 ounces fresh Brussels sprouts

IN a small bowl, combine the salt, pepper, and onion powder. Rub the ribs with the seasoning. Lay the ribs, bone sides down, in a 6-quart slow cooker. Pour the barbecue sauce over the ribs. Add the onion, garlic, and dates.

COVER and cook on low for 6 to 7 hours or on high for 3 to 3½ hours. Transfer the ribs to a platter, or to a large foil-lined baking sheet if broiling. Skim the fat from the cooking liquid. Spoon some of the cooking liquid over the ribs.

MEANWHILE, prepare the frozen Brussels sprouts according to the package directions, or roast fresh sprouts (see Tip).

BROIL the ribs, if desired: Place an oven rack 4 inches from the broiler and preheat the broiler. Broil the ribs for 3 to 5 minutes, or until the sauce begins to bubble.

SERVE the ribs with the Brussels sprouts alongside.

TIP *To remove the membrane (silver skin) from the back of the ribs, start at one end of the rack and slide a table knife under the membrane. Lift and loosen the membrane. Use a paper towel to grab the edge of the membrane and pull it off. Or you can ask the butcher to do this for you.*

TIP *To roast fresh Brussels sprouts, place trimmed and halved Brussels sprouts on a rimmed baking sheet. Drizzle with olive oil and sprinkle with salt and pepper. Roast in a 400°F oven until tender, about 20 minutes.*

DECONSTRUCTED PORK GYROS

SERVES 6

PREP: 45 minutes

SLOW COOK: 9 hours (low) or 4½ hours (high)

TOTAL: 9 hours 45 minutes

These bowls of tender chunks of pork flavored with Greek seasonings and a crunchy salad of cucumber, radishes, and red onion topped with a mayo-based tzatziki sauce is so absolutely delicious, the pita bread of a traditional gyro won't even cross your mind.

FOR THE TZATZIKI

⅔ cup Whole30-compliant avocado mayonnaise or Basic Mayonnaise (page 295)

2 teaspoons fresh lemon juice

1 small cucumber, shredded (¼ cup)

½ cup shredded radishes

2 tablespoons snipped fresh dill

1 clove garlic, minced

⅛ teaspoon salt

FOR THE PORK

1½ teaspoons dried oregano

1 teaspoon garlic powder

1 teaspoon grated lemon zest

¾ teaspoon dried marjoram

½ teaspoon salt

½ teaspoon black pepper

2½ to 3 pounds Whole30-compliant boneless pork shoulder, trimmed and cut into large chunks

1 cup Whole30-compliant chicken broth or Chicken Bone Broth (page 294)

1 tablespoon fresh lemon juice

1 medium cucumber, thinly sliced

6 radishes, thinly sliced

1 small red onion, thinly sliced

Lemon wedges

Fresh dill

MAKE THE TZATZIKI: In a medium bowl, stir together the mayonnaise, lemon juice, cucumber, radishes, dill, garlic, and salt. Cover and refrigerate until serving.

MAKE THE PORK: In a small bowl, combine the oregano, garlic powder, lemon zest, marjoram, salt, and pepper. Rub the pork with the seasoning. Place the pork in a 4-quart slow cooker and add the broth.

COVER and cook on low for 9 to 10 hours or on high 4 ½ to 5 hours. Use tongs or a slotted spoon to transfer the pork to a platter. Use two forks to coarsely shred the pork. Add the lemon juice to the cooking liquid. Drizzle the pork with some of the cooking liquid.

SERVE the shredded pork in bowls with piles of cucumber, radishes, and onion and drizzle with the tzatziki. Serve with lemon wedges and top with fresh dill.

HERB-STUFFED PORK LOIN AND SPICED CAULIFLOWER

SERVES 8

PREP: 20 minutes

SLOW COOK: 4½ hours (low) or 2 hours (high)

TOTAL: 5 hours 10 minutes

A savory combination of fresh parsley, oregano, thyme, garlic, and lemon zest is tucked into the center of a pork roast to infuse the meat with incredible flavor over the long cooking time. Be sure to tie the roast with clean, 100-percent cotton kitchen string to keep everything intact as it cooks.

1 Whole30-compliant boneless pork loin or sirloin roast (3 pounds)

¼ cup chopped fresh parsley

1 tablespoon chopped fresh oregano

1 tablespoon fresh thyme leaves

2 cloves garlic, minced

2 teaspoons grated lemon zest

½ teaspoon salt

½ teaspoon black pepper

1 can (28 ounces) Whole30-compliant whole tomatoes, undrained, cut up

1 tablespoon fresh lemon juice

1 tablespoon dried oregano, crushed

2 teaspoons ground ancho chile powder

1 teaspoon ground allspice

6 cups small cauliflower florets

2 tablespoons chopped fresh parsley

MAKE a lengthwise cut down the center of the pork, cutting to within 1 inch of the other side. Butterfly it open. In a small bowl, combine the parsley, oregano, thyme, garlic, lemon zest, salt, and pepper. Spread the herb mixture over the pork. Fold the pork back together and tie in three or four places with kitchen string. Place in a 6-quart slow cooker.

IN a medium bowl, combine the tomatoes, lemon juice, oregano, ancho chile, and allspice. Pour over the pork.

COVER and cook on low for 4½ to 5½ hours or on high for 2 to 2½ hours. Turn the slow cooker to high if using the low setting. Stir in the cauliflower. Cover and cook for 15 to 20 minutes, or until the cauliflower is tender. Stir in the parsley.

TRANSFER the roast to a cutting board; cut the strings. Let the roast rest for 5 minutes before slicing. Serve the pork with the cauliflower and sauce.

INSTANT POT VARIATION *Follow the directions in the first step using a 6-quart Instant Pot. Lock the lid in place. Select Manual and cook on high pressure for 40 minutes. Use natural release for 10 minutes, then quick release. For the cauliflower in the third step, select Sauté and adjust to Normal/Medium. Simmer until the cauliflower is tender, 15 to 20 minutes.*

SESAME-GINGER SHORT RIBS WITH COLESLAW

SERVES 4

PREP: 15 minutes

SLOW COOK: 7 hours (low) or 3½ hours (high)

TOTAL: 7 hours 15 minutes

Crunchy angel-hair slaw is a refreshing accompaniment to rich, meaty ribs. Make it at the same time you put the ribs in the slow cooker and chill in the refrigerator while the ribs cook. Not only will everything be ready to eat when you get home, but the slaw will be nice and cold.

FOR THE RIBS

2 teaspoons Whole30-compliant five-spice powder

1 teaspoon salt

8 bone-in beef short ribs (about 4 pounds)

2 green onions

⅓ cup fresh orange juice

2 tablespoons rice vinegar

2 tablespoons coconut aminos

1 tablespoon toasted sesame oil

1 piece (1 inch) fresh ginger, peeled and finely chopped

2 cloves garlic, minced

¼ teaspoon red pepper flakes

FOR THE COLESLAW

1 package (10 ounces) angel-hair coleslaw

¼ cup lightly packed chopped fresh parsley

½ cup Whole30-compliant mayonnaise or Basic Mayonnaise (page 295)

2 tablespoons rice vinegar

⅛ teaspoon cayenne pepper

¼ teaspoon Whole30-compliant five-spice powder

¼ teaspoon salt

2 teaspoons sesame seeds, toasted (see Tip)

MAKE THE RIBS: In a small bowl, combine the five-spice powder and salt. Rub the ribs with the spice mixture. Place the ribs in a 4-quart slow cooker. Thinly slice the green onions; reserve the green tops until ready to serve. Add the white parts to the slow cooker. In a small bowl, whisk together the orange juice, vinegar, coconut aminos, oil, ginger, garlic, and red pepper flakes; pour over the ribs.

COVER and cook on low for 7 to 8 hours or on high for 3½ to 4 hours.

ADJUST an oven rack to 4 inches below the broiler. Preheat the broiler. Remove the ribs from the cooker and place them, meaty sides up, in a large baking pan. Broil until browned, about 4 minutes. Cover to keep warm.

SKIM the fat from the cooking liquid. Transfer the cooking liquid to a saucepan and bring to a boil. Reduce the heat and simmer, stirring occasionally, until the sauce is slightly thickened, about 5 minutes. Brush the ribs with the sauce.

MAKE THE COLESLAW: Meanwhile, in a large bowl combine the coleslaw and parsley. In a small bowl, whisk together the mayonnaise, vinegar, cayenne, five-spice powder, and salt. Stir the dressing into the coleslaw mixture.

SPRINKLE the ribs with the reserved sliced green onion tops and the sesame seeds. Serve the coleslaw alongside.

TIP *Toast sesame seeds in dry skillet over medium heat until fragrant and lightly toasted, about 2 minutes.*

KOREAN POT ROAST WITH JICAMA SALAD

SERVES 4

PREP: 30 minutes

SLOW COOK: 8 hours (low) or 4 hours (high)

TOTAL: 8 hours 30 minutes

Gochugaru—Korean red chile flakes—is increasingly available and would be a fun, authentic substitute for the red pepper flakes here if you can find them. Most gochugaru is made from dried chiles that have been seeded. It is often milder than red pepper flakes, so you could actually use more of it, if you like.

FOR THE POT ROAST

1 teaspoon onion powder

2 teaspoons coarse ground black pepper

1 chuck roast (2 pounds), trimmed

Grated zest and juice of 1 orange

¼ cup coconut aminos

2 tablespoons Whole30-compliant fish sauce

2 tablespoons rice wine vinegar

4 cloves garlic, crushed

1 piece (½ inch) fresh ginger, peeled and thinly sliced

1 jalapeño, seeded and halved

2 teaspoons red pepper flakes

FOR THE JICAMA SALAD

¾ pound jicama, peeled and cut into matchsticks (3 cups)

½ orange bell pepper, finely diced

¼ cup slivered red onion

1 small orange, segmented

¼ cup fresh lime juice

1 tablespoon extra-virgin olive oil

1 small jalapeño, seeded and minced

MAKE THE POT ROAST: In a small bowl, combine the onion powder and pepper. Rub the roast on all sides with the spice mixture. In a 6-quart slow cooker, combine the orange juice and zest, coconut aminos, fish sauce, vinegar, garlic, ginger, jalapeño, and red pepper flakes. Add the roast and turn to coat.

COVER and cook on low for 8 to 10 hours or on high for 4 to 5 hours.

MAKE THE JICAMA SALAD: Meanwhile, in a medium bowl, combine the jicama, bell pepper, onion, and orange segments. Drizzle with the lime juice and olive oil; toss to combine. Sprinkle with the jalapeño.

REMOVE the roast from the slow cooker. Use two forks to shred the meat. Drizzle with some of the cooking juices and serve with the jicama salad.

PORK BELLY BREAKFAST BOWLS
FROM CHRISTI LAZAR OF BAZAARLAZARR

SERVES 6

PREP: 1 hour

MARINATE: 8 hours

SLOW COOK: 3½ hours (high)

TOTAL: 12½ hours

Hi, everyone! Christi here from @BazaarLazarr, openly admitting my love for pork belly! I wanted to do a new take on a breakfast bowl, but instead of bacon, use slow cooked pork belly. Slow cooking makes the pork belly exceptionally tender, and hints of citrus and Asian flavors make this pork belly a completely delicious experience. Feel free to use the pork belly beyond a breakfast bowl. It would be fantastic in a soup or simply served over sautéed vegetables. I hope you enjoy this recipe as much as I do!

FOR THE MARINADE AND PORK BELLY

1 cup fresh blood orange juice (about 7 medium blood oranges)

1 cup pomegranate juice

Juice of 1 large lime

⅛ teaspoon red pepper flakes

¼ teaspoon white pepper

2 green onions, green parts only, chopped

6 large cloves garlic, 3 crushed and 3 sliced

1 piece (2 inches) fresh ginger, peeled and roughly chopped

2½ teaspoons kosher salt or 1¼ teaspoons regular salt

2 pounds pork belly, skin scored (see Tip, page 142)

¼ cup coconut aminos

1 tablespoon Whole30-compliant fish sauce

1 tablespoon toasted sesame oil

(continued)

MARINATE THE PORK BELLY: In a container large enough to fit the pork, whisk together the blood orange juice, pomegranate juice, lime juice, red pepper flakes, white pepper, green onions, crushed garlic, half of the ginger, and 2 teaspoons of the salt. Submerge the pork. Cover and refrigerate for 8 hours or up to overnight.

IN a 4-quart slow cooker, combine the remaining ginger, the coconut aminos, fish sauce, and sliced garlic.

COOK THE PORK BELLY: Remove the pork from the container; brush any garlic or ginger pieces into the marinade. Season both sides of the pork with the remaining ½ teaspoon salt. Heat a large cast-iron skillet over medium heat and add the sesame oil. Add the pork to the skillet, skin side down, and cook until browned, 3 minutes.

POUR the marinade into the slow cooker; stir to combine. Place the pork in the slow cooker, skin side up.

COVER and cook on high for 3½ to 4 hours, or until tender. Transfer the pork to a platter and cover to keep warm.

MAKE THE SALAD: Meanwhile, preheat the oven to 450°F.

PLACE the sweet potatoes on a large rimmed baking sheet. Drizzle with the olive oil, sprinkle with ½ teaspoon salt and the pepper, and toss to coat. Arrange the potatoes in a single layer and roast in the oven, stirring once halfway through, until fork-tender and starting to brown, 30 to 35 minutes.

(continued)

FOR THE BREAKFAST SALAD

3 large sweet potatoes, peeled and cut into ½-inch cubes (about 6 cups)

2 tablespoons extra-virgin olive oil

1½ teaspoons salt

¼ teaspoon black pepper

1 tablespoon white vinegar

6 large eggs, at room temperature

1 large container (10 ounces) mixed salad greens

3 avocados, halved, pitted, peeled, and cubed

Chopped green onions

Red pepper flakes

POACH THE EGGS: Combine 6 cups water and the vinegar in an extra-large skillet, bring to a boil, and add 1 teaspoon salt. Reduce the heat to a simmer. Break an egg into a custard cup or ramekin. Gently slip the egg into the water; repeat with remaining eggs, allowing each egg an equal amount of space in the water. Simmer until the whites are completely set and the yolks begin to thicken, about 4 minutes. Use a slotted spoon to remove the eggs.

SLICE the pork. Divide the greens among six bowls. Add the sweet potatoes, pork, poached eggs, and avocado. Top with green onions and additional red pepper flakes. Slice the poached eggs open and serve.

TIP *To score the pork belly skin, use a sharp knife to make shallow diagonal cuts in a diamond pattern at 1-inch intervals. Do not cut into the meat.*

PORK RIBS WITH MOLE VERDE

SERVES 4

PREP: 25 minutes

SLOW COOK: 4½ hours (low) or 2¼ hours (high)

TOTAL: 4 hours 35 minutes

One of the elements of an authentic mole is the incorporation of ground nuts or seeds. While this green and tangy tomatillo-based sauce isn't the traditional brick-red sauce based on dried chiles with a touch of dark chocolate, it does have a subtly nutty flavor from roasted and ground pepitas (pumpkin seeds).

½ cup roasted pepitas, plus more for serving

1 can (28 ounces) tomatillos, undrained

1 medium white onion, coarsely chopped

½ cup packed coarsely chopped fresh cilantro, plus more for serving

1 jalapeño, seeded (if desired) and roughly chopped

3 cloves garlic, minced

¾ teaspoon salt

2½ pounds pork loin back ribs, membrane removed (see Tip), cut into 4 portions

¼ teaspoon black pepper

1 tablespoon fresh lime juice

1 package (12 ounces) frozen riced butternut squash

MAKE THE MOLE VERDE: In a spice grinder, process the pepitas in batches until finely ground. Transfer to a food processor or blender. Add the tomatillos, onion, cilantro, jalapeño, garlic, and ¼ teaspoon of the salt. Cover and process until smooth.

LIGHTLY season the ribs with the remaining ½ teaspoon salt and the pepper. Place in a 4-quart slow cooker. Pour the mole verde over the ribs.

COVER and cook on low for 4½ to 5 hours or on high for 2¼ to 2½ hours. Remove the ribs from the cooker.

ADJUST an oven rack to 4 inches below the broiler. Preheat the broiler. Place the ribs, meaty sides up, in a large baking pan. Broil until browned, about 4 minutes. Cover to keep warm.

SKIM the fat from the mole verde sauce and transfer to a medium saucepan. Bring to a boil. Reduce the heat and simmer, stirring occasionally, until slightly thickened, about 10 minutes. Stir in the lime juice.

MEANWHILE, prepare the butternut squash according to the package directions.

SERVE the mole verde sauce with the ribs and butternut squash. Top with additional roasted pepitas and cilantro.

TIP *To remove the membrane (silver skin) from the back of the ribs, start at one end of the rack and slide a table knife under the membrane. Lift and loosen the membrane. Use a paper towel to grab the edge of the membrane and pull it off. Or you can ask the butcher to do this for you.*

PORK LOIN WITH SWEET POTATO, APPLE, AND PEAR SMASH

SERVES: 6

PREP: 25 minutes

SLOW COOK: 6 hours (low) or 3 hours (high)

TOTAL: 6 hours 25 minutes

Although this dish is delicious any time of year, it's definitely one to make in the fall. It's packed with fall veggies and fruits—even cranberries. The cinnamon gives the smash a warm, slightly sweet flavor that's perfect with the savory pork.

2½ pounds Whole30-compliant pork loin

1 teaspoon dried thyme

½ teaspoon Whole30-compliant garlic and herb seasoning

¼ teaspoon black pepper

1½ pounds sweet potatoes, peeled and cut into 2-inch chunks

2 cooking apples, such as Fuji, peeled, cored, and quartered

2 cooking pears, such as Bartlett, peeled, cored, and quartered

1 teaspoon ground cinnamon

½ teaspoon salt

½ cup fresh or frozen cranberries

1 tablespoon cider vinegar

PLACE the pork in a 6-quart slow cooker and add ¼ cup water. In a small bowl, stir together the thyme, seasoning blend, and pepper. Rub the spice mixture over the pork.

IN a large bowl, combine the sweet potatoes, apples, and pears. Sprinkle with the cinnamon and salt and toss to combine. Add to the cooker and top with the cranberries.

COVER and cook for 6 hours on low or for 3 hours on high.

USE a slotted spoon to transfer the sweet potatoes, apples, pears, and cranberries to a large bowl. Use a potato masher or fork to mash to desired consistency. Stir in the vinegar.

SLICE the pork and serve with the smash.

SPICY ITALIAN POT ROAST WITH FINGERLING POTATOES, CARROTS, ONIONS, AND PEPPERONCINI

FROM SIMON HALL OF SIMON HALL PRIVATE CHEF

SERVES 6

PREP: 30 minutes

SLOW COOK: 8 hours (low) or 4½ hours (high)

TOTAL: 8 hours 30 minutes

Whether it's a mid-week slump or a Friday evening dinner, I want something that is elegant, healthy, and—most important—filling. This spicy pot roast is always my go-to when I need a satisfying dinner for one (with leftovers!) or an impressive meal for a tableful of dinner guests. No one will ever know that you just tossed everything in the slow cooker!

1 chuck roast (2½ pounds)

1 teaspoon salt

½ teaspoon black pepper

2 tablespoons extra-virgin olive oil

1 pound fingerling potatoes

1 pound carrots, peeled and cut into 1-inch pieces

2 medium yellow onions, cut into large pieces

4 cups Whole30-compliant beef broth or Bone Beef Broth (page 294)

1 can (28 ounces) Whole30-compliant diced tomatoes, undrained

1 jar (16 ounces) Whole30-compliant sliced pepperoncini, drained, half the liquid reserved

¼ cup Whole30-compliant Italian seasoning

1 tablespoon paprika

¼ teaspoon cayenne pepper (optional)

6 cloves garlic, peeled

1 bay leaf

Chopped fresh parsley

SPRINKLE the roast with the salt and pepper. Heat the olive oil in a large heavy skillet over medium heat. Add the roast and cook until browned on both sides, about 6 minutes.

TRANSFER the roast to a 6-quart slow cooker. Add the potatoes, carrots, onions, broth, tomatoes, pepperoncini and reserved liquid, Italian seasoning, paprika, cayenne (if using), garlic, and bay leaf.

COVER and cook on low for 8 to 10 hours or on high for 4½ to 5 hours. Discard the bay leaf.

USE a slotted spoon to transfer the meat and vegetables to a platter; drizzle with the cooking liquid and sprinkle with the parsley. Serve.

TIP *This roast can also be served as a stew. Simply break up the cooked roast into smaller chunks. Divide the roast, vegetables, and cooking liquid among bowls and sprinkle servings with parsley.*

POULTRY

BACON-MUSHROOM CHICKEN WITH SWEET POTATOES

SERVE 6

PREP: 30 minutes

SLOW COOK: 6 hours (low) or 3 hours (high)

TOTAL: 6 hours 30 minutes

Crisp-cooked and crumbled bacon provides a smoky, salty counterpoint to the sweetness of the mashed potatoes in this dish. Look for Whole30-compliant bacon at natural-foods grocery stores—it won't contain added sweeteners, nitrates, nitrites, gluten, lactose, or MSG.

1 cup Whole30-compliant chicken broth or Chicken Bone Broth (page 294)

3 cloves garlic, minced

4 small sweet potatoes, scrubbed and halved lengthwise (about 1 pound total)

1 teaspoon dried thyme

¾ teaspoon salt

¾ teaspoon black pepper

12 small bone-in chicken thighs, skin removed (see Tip, page 169)

3 cups thinly sliced cremini mushrooms

½ cup chopped red onion

1 tablespoon coconut oil, melted

3 strips Whole30-compliant bacon, crisp-cooked and crumbled

Fresh thyme leaves (optional)

IN a 6-quart slow cooker, combine the chicken broth and garlic. Place the potatoes, cut sides down, in the cooker. In a small bowl, combine the dried thyme, ½ teaspoon of the salt, and ½ teaspoon of the pepper. Place half the chicken thighs, meaty sides up, on the potatoes. Sprinkle with half the thyme mixture. Repeat with remaining chicken and thyme mixture. Add the mushrooms and red onion to the cooker in an even layer.

COVER and cook on low for 6 to 7 hours or on high for 3 to 3½ hours. Remove the chicken and potatoes from the cooker. When cool enough to handle, remove the potato skins. Place the potato flesh in a medium bowl; add the coconut oil and the remaining ¼ teaspoon salt and ¼ teaspoon pepper. Using a potato masher, mash potatoes until smooth.

SERVE the chicken and vegetables with the mashed potatoes and drizzle with the cooking liquid. Top the servings with bacon and, if desired, fresh thyme.

CHICKEN THIGHS AND BABY POTATOES WITH GREEN CHILE SAUCE

SERVES 4

PREP: 25 minutes

SLOW COOK: 6 hours (low) or 3 hours (high)

TOTAL: 6 hours 25 minutes

The sauce for this chicken dish is essentially salsa verde—savory and tart with the lemon–green apple flavor of tomatillos and lime and just a touch of heat from green chiles. Serve it with a simple slaw of grated jicama dressed with lime.

1½ pounds baby red or gold potatoes

8 bone-in chicken thighs (about 2 pounds total), skin removed (see Tip, page 169)

1 can (4 ounces) Whole30-compliant diced green chiles

½ cup Whole30-compliant chicken broth or Chicken Bone Broth (page 294)

2 medium tomatillos, husks removed and diced

3 cloves garlic, minced

2 teaspoons ground cumin

1 teaspoon ground coriander

1 teaspoon salt

½ teaspoon black pepper

Grated zest and juice of 1 lime

½ cup chopped fresh cilantro

PLACE the potatoes in a 5- to 6-quart slow cooker. Arrange the chicken over the potatoes. In a medium bowl, combine the green chiles, broth, tomatillos, garlic, cumin, coriander, salt, and pepper. Pour over the chicken and potatoes in the cooker. Cover and cook on low for 6 hours or on high for 3 hours.

DRIZZLE the chicken and potatoes with the lime juice and sprinkle with the lime zest and cilantro.

INSTANT POT VARIATION *Follow the directions in the first step using a 6-quart Instant Pot. Lock the lid in place. Select Manual and cook at high pressure for 35 minutes. Use natural release for 10 minutes, then quick release. Follow the remaining directions.*

CHICKEN THIGHS WITH PARSNIPS AND POTATOES

SERVES 4

PREP: 25 minutes

SLOW COOK: 6 hours (low) or 3 hours (high)

TOTAL: 6 hours 30 minutes

A generous amount of ghee gives the simple sauce for this chicken rich, buttery flavor that is brightened with lemon and briny green olives.

2 teaspoons garlic powder

2 teaspoons dried oregano

1 teaspoon salt

½ teaspoon paprika

½ teaspoon black pepper

8 boneless, skinless chicken thighs (about 2 pounds total)

1 lemon, thinly sliced

½ cup chopped Whole30-compliant pitted green olives

2 medium parsnips, peeled and sliced ½-inch thick

2 medium russet potatoes, peeled and sliced ½-inch thick

¼ cup melted Clarified Butter (page 296) or ghee

2 tablespoons tapioca flour

IN a small bowl, combine the garlic powder, oregano, salt, paprika, and pepper. Sprinkle 2 teaspoons of the garlic seasoning over the chicken. Place the chicken in a 6-quart slow cooker. Add ½ cup water, the lemon slices, and olives.

IN a medium bowl, combine the parsnips and potatoes; sprinkle with the remaining garlic seasoning. Add to the slow cooker and pour the melted butter over all.

COVER and cook on low for 6 hours or on high for 3 hours. Transfer the chicken, potatoes, and parsnips to a platter; cover and keep warm.

TURN the slow cooker to high if using the low setting. In a small bowl, stir together the tapioca powder and ¼ cup water; add to the cooking liquid. Stir until the sauce is thickened, about 3 minutes. Serve the sauce over the chicken, potatoes, and parsnips.

INSTANT POT VARIATION *Follow the directions the first two steps using a 6-quart Instant Pot. Lock the lid in place. Select Manual and cook at high pressure for 15 minutes. Use natural release for 5 minutes, then quick release. After stirring in the tapioca slurry, select Sauté and adjust to Less/Low. Follow the remaining directions.*

CHIPOTLE CHICKEN THIGHS

SERVES 4

PREP: 15 minutes

SLOW COOK: 5 hours (low) or
2½ hours (high)

TOTAL: 5 hours 15 minutes

A generous dose of chipotle powder contributes a fair amount of heat to this simple tomato-based chicken dish. Serve over cauliflower rice to soak up all of the yummy sauce.

1 can (14.5 ounces) Whole30-compliant fire-roasted crushed tomatoes

1 medium yellow bell pepper, coarsely chopped

2 cloves garlic, minced

2 teaspoons chili powder

1 teaspoon chipotle powder

½ teaspoon salt

8 boneless, skinless chicken thighs (1½ to 2 pounds total)

1 package (12 ounces) frozen cauliflower rice, prepared according to package directions or 3 cups raw cauliflower rice (page 60)

Sliced green onions

Lime wedges

IN a 5- to 6-quart slow cooker, stir together the tomatoes, bell pepper, garlic, chili powder, chipotle powder, and salt. Add the chicken and turn to coat. Cover and cook on low for 5 to 6 hours or on high for 2½ to 3 hours.

SERVE the chicken on cauliflower rice and top with green onions. Serve with lime wedges.

INSTANT POT VARIATION *Follow the directions in the first step using a 6-quart Instant Pot. Lock the lid in place. Select Manual and cook at high pressure for 15 minutes. Use natural release for 5 minutes, then quick release. Follow the remaining directions.*

HERB-ROASTED CHICKEN WITH VEGETABLES

SERVES 4

PREP: 30 minutes

SLOW COOK: 6 hours (low) or 3 hours (high)

BROIL: 5 minutes

TOTAL: 6 hours 35 minutes

This whole bird benefits from two methods of cooking. Slow cooking with moist heat makes it impossibly succulent and juicy, and a quick broil right before serving crisps up the skin. Perfection!

1 lemon, quartered

4 sprigs fresh herbs (rosemary, thyme, and/or oregano); plus more for serving (optional)

1 whole chicken (3 to 3½ pounds)

1 tablespoon extra-virgin olive oil

1 tablespoon grated lemon zest

1½ teaspoons fresh lemon juice

½ teaspoon salt

¼ teaspoon black pepper

2 large onions, cut into wedges

1 pound baby Yukon Gold potatoes

6 medium carrots, peeled and cut into 1-inch slices

Lemon wedges (optional)

PLACE the lemon quarters and the herb sprigs in the cavity of the chicken. In a small bowl, combine the olive oil, lemon zest, lemon juice, salt, and pepper. Rub the mixture all over the chicken. Tie the legs together with cotton kitchen string.

IN a 6-quart slow cooker, combine the onions, potatoes, and carrots. Place the chicken, breast side up, on the vegetables. Cover and cook on low for 6 to 7 hours or on high for 3 to 3½ hours, or until the chicken is no longer pink and a thermometer registers 170°F when inserted into a thigh.

PREHEAT the oven to broil.

CAREFULLY transfer the chicken to a broiler-safe 13 x 6-inch baking pan. Remove and discard the lemon and herbs from the cavity. Use a slotted spoon to transfer the vegetables to the baking pan; discard the cooking liquid. Broil the chicken and vegetables until the chicken skin is golden brown and crispy, about 5 minutes. Serve the chicken with the vegetables. If desired, top with additional fresh herb leaves and/or serve with lemon wedges.

> **TIP** *The chicken can be shredded or chopped and used in recipes calling for cooked chicken. This recipe makes 3 to 3½ cups shredded or chopped chicken.*

> **TIP** *The joints of a slow-cooked chicken are a little loose, and tying with cotton kitchen string makes removal from the cooker easier. It's not crucial to making the recipe, so just skip this step if you don't have kitchen string handy.*

LEMON CHICKEN THIGHS WITH GREEN BEANS

SERVES 4

PREP: 15 minutes

SLOW COOK: 8 hours (low) or 4 hours (high)

TOTAL: 8 hours 15 minutes

Chicken thighs are made for the slow cooker—they stay juicy and delicious even with a long cooking time. Cooking meat on the bone, as is done here, makes it extra-flavorful as well. Be sure to remove the skin, though. A dry-heat method of cooking—such as roasting—makes chicken skin crisp and delectable, but the moist heat of the slow cooker does not give it that same appeal.

1 cup Whole30-compliant chicken broth or Chicken Bone Broth (page 294)

¾ pound green beans, trimmed and halved crosswise

1 small white onion, diced

3 Roma (plum) tomatoes, cored and quartered

8 bone-in chicken thighs (2 to 2½ pounds total), skin removed (see Tip, page 169)

¾ teaspoon salt

½ teaspoon black pepper

½ teaspoon dried thyme

2 lemons, cut into ¼-inch-thick slices, seeds removed

IN a 6-quart slow cooker, combine the broth, green beans, onion, and tomatoes. Place the chicken on the vegetables and sprinkle with the salt, pepper, and thyme. Top the chicken with the lemon slices.

COVER and cook on low for 8 hours or on high for 4 hours. Serve the chicken with the vegetables.

LEMON THAI CURRY CHICKEN WITH SESAME ZUCCHINI NOODLES

SERVES 6

PREP: 30 minutes

SLOW COOK: 4½ hours (low) or 2¼ hours (high)

TOTAL: 5 hours

If you have the time, let the chicken marinate for 2 hours in the refrigerator before cooking to allow the flavors to more fully permeate the meat.

3 tablespoons Whole30-compliant red curry paste

4 tablespoons light sesame oil

1 tablespoon grated fresh ginger

1 teaspoon grated lemon zest

12 small bone-in chicken thighs, skin removed (see Tip, page 169)

6 medium carrots, peeled and cut into 1½-inch pieces

1 small red onion, cut into thin wedges

⅔ cup Whole30-compliant chicken broth or Chicken Bone Broth (page 294)

2 packages (10.7 ounces each) zucchini noodles or 3 medium zucchini, spiralized, long noodles snipped if desired

1 tablespoon sesame seeds, toasted (see Tip)

⅓ cup chopped fresh cilantro

¼ cup slivered almonds, toasted (see Tip)

Lemon wedges

IN a small bowl, combine the curry paste, 2 tablespoons of the sesame oil, the ginger, and lemon zest. Place half the chicken in a large bowl. Spoon half the curry mixture on the chicken and rub all over. Repeat with remaining chicken and curry mixture. (If desired, cover and marinate the chicken in the refrigerator for up to 2 hours.)

TRANSFER the chicken to a 6-quart slow cooker. Top with the carrots and onion. Pour the broth over all. Cover and cook on low for 4½ to 5 hours or on high for 2¼ to 2½ hours.

MEANWHILE, in a large skillet, cook the zucchini noodles in the remaining 2 tablespoons sesame oil over medium heat, stirring frequently, until the noodles are crisp, 3 to 4 minutes. Remove from the heat. Stir in 2 teaspoons of the sesame seeds.

IN a small bowl, combine the cilantro, almonds, and remaining 1 teaspoon sesame seeds. Serve the chicken and vegetables over the zucchini noodles; spoon some of the cooking juices on top. Sprinkle with the cilantro-almond-sesame mixture and serve with lemon wedges.

TIP *To toast seeds or nuts, heat in a skillet over medium heat, stirring, until fragrant and lightly browned, about 2 minutes.*

INSTANT POT VARIATION *Follow the directions in the first two steps using a 6-quart Instant Pot. Lock the lid in place. Select Manual and cook at high pressure for 25 minutes. Use natural release for 5 minutes, then quick release. Follow the remaining directions.*

SPAGHETTI SQUASH AND TURKEY MEATBALLS WITH MEDITERRANEAN SAUCE

SERVE 4

PREP: 45 minutes

SLOW COOK: 5 hours (low) or 2½ hours (high)

BAKE: 10 minutes

TOTAL: 6 hours

Even if you're the only one doing a Whole30, no one in the family will complain about this tasty spaghetti(ish) and meatball dish for dinner. Crushing the fennel seeds before mixing them with the ground turkey releases their distinctive flavor.

1 large egg

½ cup finely chopped onion

¼ cup almond flour

½ teaspoon fennel seeds, finely crushed (see Tip)

½ teaspoon ground coriander

1 teaspoon salt

¼ teaspoon black pepper

1 pound ground turkey

2 cups Whole30-compliant canned crushed tomatoes, undrained

⅓ cup finely chopped drained Whole30-compliant roasted red peppers

¼ cup Whole30-compliant tomato paste

3 cloves garlic, minced

1 bay leaf

1 spaghetti squash (about 2 pounds), halved lengthwise and seeds removed

1 tablespoon extra-virgin olive oil

⅓ cup coarsely chopped Whole30-compliant pitted green olives

2 tablespoons fresh lemon juice

½ cup chopped flat-leaf parsley

PREHEAT the oven to 400°F.

IN a large bowl, whisk the egg together with 2 tablespoons water. Stir in the onion, almond flour, fennel seeds, coriander, ¾ teaspoon of the salt, and the pepper. Add the turkey and mix well. Shape into 12 meatballs and place in a foil-lined rimmed baking pan. Bake for 10 minutes.

MEANWHILE, in a medium bowl, stir together the crushed tomatoes, roasted peppers, tomato paste, garlic, and bay leaf. Pour about half of the sauce into a 6-quart slow cooker. Place the squash halves, cut sides down, on the sauce. (If necessary to fit in the slow cooker, cut squash halves in half.) Place the meatballs around and on top of the squash. Spoon the remaining sauce over the meatballs.

COVER and cook on low for 5 hours or on high for 2½ hours. Use a large spoon to transfer the squash halves to a cutting board; cool for about 10 minutes. Use a fork to scrape the strands into a large bowl. Drizzle the squash strands with the olive oil and sprinkle with the remaining ¼ teaspoon salt. Toss to coat.

REMOVE and discard the bay leaf. Gently stir the olives and lemon juice into the sauce and meatballs. Serve the meatballs and sauce over the squash. Sprinkle with parsley.

TIP *To crush fennel seeds, use a mortar and pestle, spice grinder, or place in a plastic bag and lay the bag on a cutting board. Crush the seeds with a rolling pin, heavy pot, or meat tenderizer.*

SPANISH CHICKEN MEATBALLS IN SMOKY TOMATO SAUCE

SERVES 6

PREP: 40 minutes

SLOW COOK: 6 hours (low) or 3 hours (high)

TOTAL: 6 hours 40 minutes

Smoked paprika is an almost magical ingredient. Just a little bit adds rich, smoky flavor to this tomato sauce for meatballs that are spiked with green olives, serrano chile, orange zest, and garlic. When shaping the meatballs, keep a bowl of cool water nearby; dipping your hands will help prevent the meat from sticking.

1 can (15 ounces) Whole30-compliant tomato sauce

1 can (14.5 ounces) Whole30-compliant diced fire-roasted tomatoes

¼ cup fresh orange juice

1 teaspoon Spanish (sweet) paprika

½ teaspoon smoked paprika

⅓ cup almond meal

1 large egg, lightly beaten

2 tablespoons chopped Whole30-compliant green olives

1 serrano chile pepper, seeded and finely chopped

½ teaspoon grated orange zest

2 cloves garlic, minced

½ teaspoon salt

1½ pounds ground chicken

1 tablespoon extra-virgin olive oil

2 packages (10 ounces each) frozen riced butternut squash, prepared according to package directions

Chopped fresh parsley

IN a 5- to 6-quart slow cooker, combine the tomato sauce, tomatoes, orange juice, Spanish paprika, and smoked paprika. In a medium bowl, combine the almond meal, egg, olives, serrano, orange zest, garlic, and salt. Add the chicken and, using wet hands, mix well. Shape into 1½-inch meatballs. Arrange the meatballs over the sauce in the cooker. Drizzle with the olive oil. Cover and cook on low for 6 hours or on high for 3 hours.

SERVE the meatballs and sauce over the riced squash. Sprinkle with parsley.

FIVE-SPICE CHICKEN WINGS

SERVES 4

PREP: 20 minutes

SLOW COOK: 3 hours (high)

TOTAL: 3 hours 20 minutes

Broiling the wings after they're cooked isn't a necessary step, but it takes only 3 to 4 minutes and gives them a nice glossy, crisp skin.

3 pounds chicken wings

2 tablespoons Whole30-compliant five-spice powder

1 teaspoon cayenne pepper

1 teaspoon salt

3 green onions, trimmed

½ cup unsweetened pineapple juice

2 tablespoons coconut aminos

1 tablespoon grated fresh ginger

1 tablespoon sesame seeds, toasted (see Tip)

½ to 1 teaspoon red pepper flakes

Whole30-compliant creamy ranch dressing

Mixed salad greens (optional)

USE kitchen shears or a very sharp chef's knife to remove the tips of the chicken wings (discard the tips or save them for making stock). Cut along the edge of the drumette through the joint to separate the wingette and the drumette (you should have 8 of each). Place the chicken pieces in a large bowl.

IN a small bowl, combine the five-spice powder, cayenne, and salt. Sprinkle over the chicken and toss to coat.

SLICE and set aside the green tops of the green onions. Trim the root of the white ends. Add the white green onion ends, pineapple juice, coconut aminos, and ginger to a 6-quart slow cooker. Add the wings and toss to coat.

COVER and cook on high for 3 hours. Using a slotted spoon, transfer the chicken to a large bowl and carefully toss with the sliced green onion tops, sesame seeds, and red pepper flakes. Discard the cooking liquid. Serve the wings with the ranch salad dressing for dipping and, if desired, drizzled over mixed greens.

> **TIP** *To toast sesame seeds, heat them in a skillet over medium heat, stirring until fragrant and lightly browned, about 2 minutes.*

> **TIP** *For crispier wings, position the oven rack 4 to 5 inches from the broiler. Preheat the oven to broil. Line a large shallow baking pan with foil. Transfer the wings from the slow cooker to the prepared pan with a slotted spoon. Broil for 4 to 5 minutes, or until browned. Carefully toss the wings with the green onion tops, red pepper flakes, and sesame seeds and serve the wings with mixed greens and dressing.*

ARTICHOKE AND OLIVE CHICKEN LEGS

SERVES 4

PREP: 20 minutes

SLOW COOK: 6 hours (low) or 3 hours (high)

TOTAL: 6 hours 20 minutes

This Mediterranean-inspired dish is for the dedicated Kalamata olive–lovers out there. You can enjoy a generous amount of these briny, buttery-textured fruits, guilt-free, in every serving. As you might guess, they are rich in the same monounsaturated healthy fat found in olive oil. Eat up!

2 teaspoons garlic powder

1 teaspoon salt

½ teaspoon black pepper

8 chicken legs, skin removed (see Tip)

2 medium white onions, roughly chopped

2 cans (14 ounces each) Whole30-compliant whole artichoke hearts, drained and halved

1½ cups pitted Whole30-compliant Kalamata olives

1 lemon, cut into wedges

3 sprigs fresh thyme, plus additional leaves for garnish

IN a small bowl, combine the garlic powder, salt, and pepper. Rub the chicken with the seasoning. Place the onions, artichoke hearts, and olives in a 6-quart slow cooker. Add the chicken. Top with lemon wedges and thyme sprigs.

COVER and cook on low for 6 to 7 hours or on high for 3 to 3½ hours. Remove and discard the lemon wedges and thyme. Serve the chicken with the artichokes, onions, and olives. Sprinkle with additional thyme.

TIP *To remove the skin from chicken pieces, use a paper towel to grip the skin and pull it away from the flesh. For drumsticks, start at the meaty end and pull toward the bony end. Then use kitchen shears to cut the skin at the joint.*

CHICKEN BREASTS WITH ROASTED PEPPERS AND OLIVES

SERVES 4

PREP: 10 minutes

SLOW COOK: 4 hours (low) or 2 hours (high)

TOTAL: 4 hours 10 minutes

Mediterranean flavors infuse this super-quick-to-prep chicken entree. A sprinkle of fresh parsley and lemon zest brightens the chicken and peppers.

1 jar (12 ounces) Whole30-compliant roasted red peppers, drained and sliced

1 cup thinly sliced onion

½ cup Whole30-compliant chicken broth or Chicken Bone Broth (page 294)

2 cloves garlic, minced

½ teaspoon salt

1½ pounds boneless, skinless chicken breasts

2 teaspoons Whole30-compliant garlic and herb seasoning

¼ cup pitted Whole30-compliant Kalamata olives, quartered

1 tablespoon chopped flat-leaf parsley

1 teaspoon grated lemon zest

1 tablespoon extra-virgin olive oil

IN a 3½- to 4-quart slow cooker, combine the red peppers, onion, broth, garlic, and salt. Top with the chicken; sprinkle with the garlic and herb seasoning. Cover and cook on low for 4 hours or on high for 2 hours.

TRANSFER the chicken and vegetables to a serving platter. Discard the cooking liquid. Top the chicken with the olives, parsley, and lemon zest. Drizzle with the olive oil.

HERBED CHICKEN AND VEGETABLES

SERVES 4

PREP: 15 minutes

SLOW COOK: 6 hours (low) or 3 hours (high)

TOTAL: 6 hours 15 minutes

Boneless, skinless chicken thighs are a cook's best friend. They are inexpensive, tasty, and juicy—and you almost can't over-cook them. In a very simple dish such as this one, the fact that they are more flavorful than boneless, skinless breasts is especially important.

1 pound new red potatoes, halved

4 medium carrots, peeled, halved lengthwise, and cut into 1-inch pieces

1 medium onion, cut into thin wedges

½ cup Whole30-compliant chicken broth or Chicken Bone Broth (page 294)

1 teaspoon salt

½ teaspoon black pepper

8 bone-in chicken thighs, skin removed (see Tip, page 169)

1½ teaspoons Whole30-compliant Italian seasoning

½ teaspoon garlic powder

Chopped fresh flat-leaf parsley

IN a 5- to 6-quart slow cooker, combine the potatoes, carrots, onion, broth, ½ teaspoon of the salt, and ¼ teaspoon of the pepper. Top with the chicken. Sprinkle with the Italian seasoning, garlic powder, and remaining salt and pepper.

COVER and cook on low for 6 to 8 hours or on high for 3 to 4 hours.

STRAIN the cooking liquid. Serve the chicken and vegetables drizzled with some of the cooking liquid. Top with parsley.

INDIAN CHICKEN NOODLE BOWLS

SERVES 4

PREP: 15 minutes

SLOW COOK: 5 hours (low) or 2½ hours (high)

TOTAL: 5 hours 30 minutes

You can use any kind (or combination) of curry powder you like in this dish, depending on your taste. If you like mild curry, use regular curry powder. If you like a little heat, use 1 teaspoon each mild and hot curry powder. Or if you like a lot of heat, use all hot curry powder.

1½ pounds boneless, skinless chicken thighs

3 tablespoons Clarified Butter (page 296) or ghee, melted

2 teaspoons Whole30-compliant garam masala

2 teaspoons Whole30-compliant curry powder

½ teaspoon salt

½ cup Whole30-compliant chicken broth or Chicken Bone Broth (page 294)

1 cup Whole30-compliant coconut milk

3 packages (10.7 ounces each) spiralized butternut squash (about 8 cups)

½ cup roasted cashews, chopped

2 tablespoons chopped fresh cilantro

IN a 4-quart slow cooker, combine the chicken, 1 tablespoon of the clarified butter, the garam masala, curry powder, and salt; stir to coat. Pour the broth over the chicken. Cover and cook on low for 5 to 6 hours or on high for 2½ to 3 hours.

TRANSFER the chicken to a cutting board and cut into bite-size pieces. Return the chicken to the slow cooker with ½ cup of the cooking liquid and the coconut milk. If on low, turn the slow cooker to the high setting. Cover and cook until heated through, 15 to 20 minutes longer.

HEAT the remaining 2 tablespoons clarified butter in a large skillet over medium heat. Add the spiralized squash and cook, stirring occasionally, until just tender, 3 to 4 minutes.

SERVE the chicken and sauce on top of the squash noodles. Top with cashews and cilantro.

INSTANT POT VARIATION *Follow the directions in the first two steps using a 6-quart Instant Pot. Lock the lid in place. Select Manual and cook at high pressure for 10 minutes. Use quick release. After adding the coconut milk, select Sauté and adjust to Less/Low. Simmer, uncovered, until heated through, 5 to 10 minutes. Follow the remaining directions.*

ITALIAN CHICKEN WITH FENNEL

SERVES 4

PREP: 10 minutes

SLOW COOK: 4 hours (low) or
2 hours (high)

TOTAL: 4 hours 10 minutes

If your fennel bulb still has the lacy green fronds attached—
and they look fresh—you can snip and use them to garnish the
finished dish instead of the parsley.

¼ cup Whole30-compliant
tomato paste

5 cloves garlic, minced

1 teaspoon dried oregano

¾ teaspoon salt

¼ teaspoon black pepper

8 bone-in chicken thighs, skin
removed (see Tip, page 169)

1 bulb fennel, cored and cut into
thin wedges

1 medium red, orange, or yellow
bell pepper, cut into 1-inch pieces

1 can (14.5 ounces) Whole30-
compliant fire-roasted diced
tomatoes

¼ cup Whole30-compliant
capers, drained

Chopped fresh flat-leaf parsley

IN a 6-quart slow cooker, stir together the tomato paste, garlic,
oregano, salt, and pepper. Add the chicken and turn to coat. Place the
fennel under the chicken. Top the chicken with the bell pepper and
tomatoes.

COVER and cook on low for 4 to 5 hours or on high for 2 to 2½ hours.
Serve the chicken and vegetables topped with the capers and fresh
parsley.

SPICY TURKEY-STUFFED PEPPERS

SERVES 4
PREP: 40 minutes
SLOW COOK: 2½ hours (low)
TOTAL: 3 hours 10 minutes

A simple guacamole spooned on after cooking cools the fire of these spicy stuffed peppers. For the best flavor, use 93% lean turkey (a blend of white and dark meat) rather than ground turkey breast, which can be dry.

FOR THE PEPPERS
4 medium red, green, or yellow bell peppers

1 pound ground turkey

2 cups chopped button mushrooms

1 stalk celery, thinly sliced

½ cup chopped onion

3 cloves garlic, minced

1 teaspoon paprika

½ teaspoon ground coriander

½ teaspoon coarse salt

¼ to ½ teaspoon cayenne pepper

1 large Roma (plum) tomato, finely chopped

FOR THE GUACAMOLE
1 medium avocado, halved, pitted, and peeled

1 tablespoon fresh lemon juice

1 clove garlic, minced

½ teaspoon coarse salt

⅛ teaspoon black pepper

2 tablespoons chopped flat-leaf parsley

Whole30 Sriracha (page 179) (optional)

MAKE THE PEPPERS: Place a small rack in a 5- to 6-quart slow cooker. Add ¼ cup water to the slow cooker. Cut a thin slice across the top of each pepper to remove the stem. Use a small sharp knife to cut out the seeds and membranes, keeping the pepper intact. Set the peppers, cut sides up, on the rack in the cooker.

IN a large skillet over medium heat, cook the turkey, mushrooms, celery, and onion, stirring occasionally and breaking up the meat with a wooden spoon, until the turkey is browned. Drain off the fat. Add the 3 cloves minced garlic, the paprika, coriander, ½ teaspoon salt, and the cayenne pepper. Cook, stirring, over medium heat for 30 seconds. Remove from the heat. Stir in the tomato. Spoon the turkey mixture into the peppers.

COVER and cook on low for 2½ to 3 hours. Carefully transfer the stuffed peppers to serving plates.

MAKE THE GUACAMOLE: In a medium bowl combine the avocado, lemon juice, 1 clove minced garlic, ½ teaspoon salt, and the black pepper. Mash with a fork or potato masher until almost smooth. Stir in the parsley. Top the peppers with the guacamole and serve with sriracha, if desired.

WHOLE30 SRIRACHA

This spicy condiment has been all the rage for years now, but the bottled stuff contains sugar. This totally compliant version gets a touch of sweetness from a single dried date—so go crazy with it!

MAKES 1½ CUPS **PREP:** 15 minutes **COOK:** 10 minutes **TOTAL:** 25 minutes

1 pound Fresno chile peppers, seeded and roughly chopped
5 cloves garlic, smashed and peeled
2 tablespoons apple cider vinegar
2 tablespoons tomato paste
1 medium dried Medjool date, pitted
2 tablespoons Red Boat fish sauce
½ teaspoon salt

In a high-power blender (see Tip), combine all the ingredients and process until smooth.

Transfer to a small saucepan and bring to a boil. Reduce the heat and simmer, stirring occasionally, for 10 minutes. Taste the sauce and adjust for salt. If the sauce is too thick, add water, 1 tablespoon at a time, until it reaches the desired consistency. Let cool.

Use immediately, or store in an airtight container in the refrigerator for up to 1 week.

TIP *If using a regular blender, chop the peppers into smaller pieces and mince the garlic for a smoother consistency.*

SWEET AND SPICY APRICOT DRUMSTICKS

SERVES 4

PREP: 15 minutes

SLOW COOK: 5 hours (low) or 2½ hours (high)

TOTAL: 5 hours 15 minutes

Be sure to buy unsulfured apricots to make the sauce for this dish. They will be dark brown and not as plump as those treated with sulfites—a preservative—but you don't want to consume those on a Whole30. Or ever, really.

½ cup water

2 tablespoons coconut aminos

2 tablespoons Whole30-compliant Dijon mustard

1 clove garlic, minced

½ teaspoon salt

¼ teaspoon red pepper flakes

8 chicken drumsticks (1½ to 2 pounds total), skin removed (see Tip, page 169)

6 ounces dried apricots, chopped

1 shallot, thinly sliced (about ⅓ cup)

2 packages (12 ounces each) frozen riced cauliflower, prepared according to package directions, or 3 cups raw cauliflower rice (page 60)

Chopped fresh parsley (optional)

IN a 3½- to 4-quart slow cooker, combine the water, coconut aminos, mustard, garlic, salt, and red pepper flakes. Add the chicken, apricots, and shallot and toss to coat.

COVER and cook on low for 5 to 6 hours or on high for 2½ to 3 hours. Transfer the chicken to a plate and cover to keep warm. Use an immersion blender to blend the mixture in the cooker until smooth. Add water, 1 tablespoon at a time, if needed for desired consistency. Return the chicken to the slow cooker and toss gently with tongs to coat.

SERVE the drumsticks over the cauliflower rice. Top with the sauce and chopped parsley, if desired.

INSTANT POT VARIATION *Follow the directions in the first step using a 6-quart Instant Pot. Lock the lid in place. Select Manual and cook at high pressure for 25 minutes. Use quick release. Follow the remaining directions.*

VERDE CHICKEN

SERVES 4

PREP: 20 minutes

SLOW COOK: 4 hours (low) or
2 hours (high)

TOTAL: 4 hours 20 minutes

Fresh cilantro and lime juice added right before blending brighten the flavor of this beautiful green sauce. If you'd like to turn up the heat a bit, add a seeded jalapeño to the blender or food processor along with the cooked vegetables.

1 to 1½ pounds boneless, skinless chicken breast

¼ teaspoon ground cumin

¼ teaspoon sea salt

¼ teaspoon black pepper

2 cups quartered husked tomatillos (4 to 5)

2 poblano peppers, stems removed and quartered

½ cup diced onion

2 tablespoons sliced garlic

2 cups chopped fresh cilantro

Juice of ½ lime

½ teaspoon salt

PLACE the chicken breasts and ¼ cup water in a 6-quart slow cooker. Sprinkle with the cumin, salt, and pepper. Add the tomatillos, poblano peppers, onion, and garlic.

COVER and cook on low for 4 hours or on high for 2 hours.

TRANSFER the chicken to a platter with a slotted spoon; cover and keep warm. Transfer the tomatillos, peppers, onion, and garlic to a blender or food processor. Add the cilantro, lime juice, and salt. Cover and blend or process until almost smooth. Chop or shred the chicken, stir into the sauce, and serve over cooked riced vegetables or veggie noodles.

TURKEY BREAST TENDERLOIN PICCATA WITH CHERRY TOMATOES AND GREEN BEANS

SERVES 4

PREP: 20 minutes

SLOW COOK: 6 hours (low) or 3 hours (high)

TOTAL: 6 hours 40 minutes

Dishes prepared in the classic "piccata" style are usually thin scallops of meat or chicken that are floured and pan-fried, then served with a pan sauce made from butter, lemon, garlic, capers, and parsley. This dish features all of those great flavors without the cook having to stand over a stove.

1½ pounds Whole30-compliant turkey breast tenderloins

½ cup Whole30-compliant chicken broth or Chicken Bone Broth (page 294)

3 tablespoons fresh lemon juice

2 tablespoons chopped garlic

2 tablespoons melted Clarified Butter (page 296) or ghee

1 bay leaf

1 teaspoon salt

½ teaspoon black pepper

1 pint cherry tomatoes

2 tablespoons chopped fresh flat-leaf parsley

1 tablespoon Whole30-compliant capers, drained

2 teaspoons grated lemon zest

1 package (16 ounces) frozen whole green beans

PLACE the turkey in a 5- to 6-quart slow cooker. In a medium bowl, combine the broth, lemon juice, garlic, 1 tablespoon of the butter, the bay leaf, salt, and pepper. Pour over the turkey in the cooker.

COVER and cook on low for 6 to 7 hours or on high for 3 to 3½ hours. Remove the turkey from cooker; cover with foil and let rest for about 10 minutes. If on low, turn the slow cooker to the high setting. Stir in the tomatoes. Cover and cook until the tomatoes are softened and beginning to burst, about 20 minutes. Stir in the parsley, capers, and 1 teaspoon of the lemon zest.

MEANWHILE, cook the green beans according to the package directions. Drain well and stir in the remaining 1 tablespoon butter and 1 teaspoon lemon zest. Season to taste with salt and pepper.

SLICE the turkey and serve with the tomato sauce and green beans.

TACO TURKEY-STUFFED PEPPERS

SERVES 4

PREP: 15 minutes

SLOW COOK: 2½ hours (low)

TOTAL: 2 hours 45 minutes

Mix up the colors of the bell peppers you use for the prettiest finished dish.

1 tablespoon extra-virgin olive oil

1½ pounds ground turkey

½ cup chopped onion

3 cloves garlic, minced

1 tablespoon Whole30-compliant taco seasoning (see Tip)

¾ cup Whole30-compliant salsa

4 medium red or yellow bell peppers

Chopped fresh cilantro

IN a large skillet, heat the oil over medium-high heat. Add the turkey, onion, garlic, and taco seasoning and cook, stirring with a wooden spoon to break up the meat, until browned. Stir in the salsa.

PLACE a small rack in a 5- to 6-quart slow cooker. Add ¼ cup water to the slow cooker. Cut a thin slice from the top of each pepper to remove the stem. Use a small, sharp knife to cut out the seeds and membranes, keeping the peppers intact. Set the peppers, cut sides up, on the rack in the cooker. Spoon the turkey mixture into the peppers. Cover and cook on low for 2½ to 3 hours, until the peppers are tender.

CAREFULLY transfer the peppers to a serving platter. Discard the cooking liquid. Serve, topped with cilantro.

TIP *If you can't find a Whole30-compliant taco seasoning, it's easy to make your own: In a container with an airtight lid, combine 2 tablespoons chili powder, 2½ teaspoons ground cumin, 1½ teaspoons sea salt, 1½ teaspoons ground black pepper, 1 teaspoon each garlic and onion powder, 1 teaspoon paprika, ½ teaspoon crushed red pepper flakes, and ½ teaspoon dried oregano. Store in a cool, dark place for up to 6 months. Stir or shake well before using.*

INSTANT POT VARIATION *Follow the directions in the first two steps using a 6-quart Instant Pot. Select Sauté and adjust to Normal/Medium to cook the turkey. After stuffing the peppers, add ¼ cup water and a trivet to the pot. Place the peppers on the trivet. Lock the lid in place. Select Manual and cook at high pressure for 5 minutes. Use quick release. Follow the remaining directions.*

CAJUN FAJITAS

FROM CHARLOTTE SMYTHE OF CONFESSIONS OF A CLEAN FOODIE

SERVES 4

PREP: 25 minutes

SLOW COOK: 4 hours (high)

TOTAL: 4 hours 25 minutes

Two great cuisines—Mexican and Cajun—come together in this easy dinner. The peppers and onions are added to the cooker with only 1 hour left of cooking so they stay crisp-tender, fresh-tasting, and brightly colored.

1 pound boneless, skinless chicken thighs, cut into ½-inch pieces

1 teaspoon Korean pepper flakes or Aleppo pepper

1 teaspoon smoked paprika

1 teaspoon salt

½ teaspoon chili powder

½ teaspoon garlic powder

¼ teaspoon turmeric

1 medium green bell pepper, sliced

1 medium red bell pepper, sliced

1 large onion, sliced

2 tablespoons Whole30-compliant tomato sauce

1 teaspoon Whole30-compliant Cajun seasoning

1 teaspoon melted Clarified Butter (page 296) or ghee

1 tablespoon fresh lemon juice

1 package (12 ounces) frozen riced cauliflower or 3 cups raw cauliflower rice (see page 60)

1 avocado, halved, pitted, peeled, and sliced

IN a 4-quart slow cooker, combine the chicken, pepper flakes, paprika, salt, chili powder, garlic powder, and turmeric.

COVER and cook on high for 3 hours. Add the peppers, onion, tomato sauce, Cajun seasoning, and butter; stir to combine. Cover and cook for 1 hour.

ADD the lemon juice and stir to combine. Serve the chicken and vegetables over the cauliflower rice and top with the avocado.

CHARLOTTE SMYTHE, CONFESSIONS OF A CLEAN FOODIE

Charlotte is the blogger behind *Confessions of a Clean Foodie*, where she encourages her readers to think beyond the surface meaning of the word health. From creating delicious recipes to sharing budget-saving strategies and kitchen organization tips, Charlotte is always happy, honored, and excited to help another person change their life through real food.

CHICKEN SHAWARMA

SERVES 4

PREP: 45 minutes

SLOW COOK: 2 hours (high)

TOTAL: 2 hours 45 minutes

In the Middle East—its place of origin—shawarma is made of highly seasoned minced meat that is wrapped around a spit and slowly roasted. This slow-cooker version is still highly seasoned, but with *ras el hanout*—a North African spice blend that can include ginger, anise, cinnamon, nutmeg, peppercorns, cloves, cardamom, nigella, mace, galangal, turmeric, and dried flowers such as lavender and rose. *Ras el hanout* means "head of the shop," because each spice shop owner would create their own unique blend.

FOR THE LEMON-DILL SAUCE

1 cup unsalted cashews, rinsed

1 clove garlic

1 tablespoon fresh lemon juice

⅛ teaspoon salt

1 tablespoon fresh dill or
1 teaspoon dried dill

FOR THE PICKLED VEGGIES

1 cup shredded carrots

½ cup thinly sliced red onion

¼ cup apple cider vinegar

1 tablespoon 100% apple juice

⅛ teaspoon salt

FOR THE CHICKEN

1 tablespoon ras el hanout

½ teaspoon salt

1½ pounds boneless, skinless chicken thighs

1 cup Whole30-compliant chicken broth or Chicken Bone Broth (page 294)

Bibb lettuce leaves

MAKE THE SAUCE: Place the cashews in a medium bowl and add enough water to cover by 1 inch. Cover the bowl and let stand for 4 hours or up to overnight. Drain the cashews and rinse under cold water. Place the cashews, ¾ cup fresh water, the garlic, lemon juice, and salt in a high-speed blender. Cover and blend until smooth. Add cold water, 2 tablespoons at a time, to reach drizzling consistency. Transfer to a bowl; stir in the dill.

MAKE THE PICKLED VEGGIES: Meanwhile, in a small bowl, combine the carrots, onion, vinegar, apple juice, and salt. Cover and marinate in the refrigerator until serving.

MAKE THE CHICKEN: In a small bowl, combine the ras el hanout and salt. Rub the chicken with the seasoning. Place the chicken in a 4-quart slow cooker and add the broth.

COVER and cook on high for 2 hours. Transfer the chicken to a cutting board. Discard the cooking liquid.

SLICE the chicken and divide among lettuce leaves. Use a slotted spoon to top the chicken with the pickled veggies. Drizzle with the sauce and serve.

INSTANT POT VARIATION *Make the sauce and pickled vegetables. Follow the directions in the third and fourth steps using a 6-quart Instant Pot. Lock the lid in place. Select Manual and cook on high pressure for 10 minutes. Use natural release for 5 minutes, then quick release. Follow the remaining directions to serve.*

CHICKEN TIKKA MASALA
FROM CHRISTI LAZAR OF BAZAARLAZARR

SERVES 6

PREP: 45 minutes

MARINATE: 8 hours or overnight

SLOW COOK: 4 hours (high)

TOTAL: 12 hours 45 minutes

This tikka masala is a curry that doesn't feel overwhelming to make, and is a breeze in the slow cooker! As you know, take-out magically tastes even better the next day, and this dish is no different. If you're not a fan of heat, feel free to omit the cayenne pepper; the chicken will taste just as good! The chicken and sauce are fantastic served by themselves, over cauliflower rice, or even for breakfast, topping potatoes and eggs!

2½ pounds boneless, skinless chicken thighs

2 teaspoons kosher salt

2 cans (13.6 ounces) Whole30-compliant coconut milk, refrigerated overnight

1 tablespoon turmeric

2 teaspoons ground coriander

2 teaspoons Whole30-compliant curry powder

2 teaspoons ground cumin

2 teaspoons Whole30-compliant garam masala

5 large garlic cloves, crushed

1 piece (1 inch) fresh ginger, peeled and minced

¼ teaspoon cayenne pepper (optional)

1 medium onion, chopped

1 can (28 ounces) Whole30-compliant crushed tomatoes

2 tablespoons Whole30-compliant tomato paste

1 tablespoon fresh lemon juice

2 packages (12 ounces each) frozen riced cauliflower or 6 cups raw cauliflower rice (see page 60)

¼ teaspoon salt

Chopped fresh parsley

SPRINKLE both sides of the chicken with the salt. Cut each piece of chicken in half, then into 1-inch strips. Set aside.

OPEN one of the cans of coconut milk carefully; the top part should be solid. Spoon the solid portion into a large bowl and add ½ cup of the liquid. Stir in the turmeric, coriander, curry powder, cumin, garam masala, garlic, ginger, and cayenne pepper (if using). Add the chicken to the marinade. If needed, add more of the liquid portion of the coconut milk to cover. Cover and refrigerate overnight.

COMBINE the onion, crushed tomatoes, tomato paste, and lemon juice in a 6-quart slow cooker. Add the chicken and marinade and stir.

COVER and cook on high for 4 hours.

FOR the coconut cream, open the second can of coconut milk and spoon the solid portion into a medium bowl. Add ½ cup of the liquid and stir until no lumps remain.

PREPARE the riced cauliflower according to the package directions.

USE a slotted spoon to transfer the chicken to a bowl; cover to keep warm. Use an immersion blender to blend the cooking liquid in the slow cooker until smooth. Add ¾ cup of the coconut cream; blend well. (Or transfer the cooking liquid to a blender, add the coconut cream, and blend.) Add the salt.

SERVE the chicken over the cauliflower rice. Top with the sauce and sprinkle with parsley.

CHRISTI LAZAR, BAZAARLAZARR

Christi Lazar is the food writer, photographer, and creator of the popular blog *BazaarLazarr*, where the guiding principle is that healthy food should be fun! In 2016, Christi found food freedom through Whole30, which has been life-altering. Christi is a New York–based digital marketer who loves helping people navigate clean eating with her colorful and fun recipes. Having spent many years using her career as an excuse to deprioritize healthy eating, Christi is passionate about sharing her tips and tricks for balancing both.

INDIAN-SPICED DRUMSTICKS AND THIGHS

SERVES 4

PREP: 25 minutes

SLOW COOK: 5 hours (low) or 2½ hours (high)

TOTAL: 5 hours 30 minutes

Indian cooks are known for their way with spices, and this dish has no shortage of them. Cloves, fennel seeds, cinnamon, nutmeg, cumin, turmeric, coriander, cayenne, and cardamom are combined with ghee to make a paste that's rubbed over the chicken before cooking.

---

2 cups Whole30-compliant chicken broth or Chicken Bone Broth (page 294)

½ cup chopped onion

4 cloves garlic, minced

1 piece (2 inches) fresh ginger, peeled and grated

3 tablespoons Clarified Butter (page 296) or ghee

2 teaspoons ground cumin

1 teaspoon ground turmeric

1 teaspoon salt

¾ teaspoon cayenne pepper

¾ teaspoon ground cardamom

½ teaspoon ground cinnamon

½ teaspoon ground coriander

¼ teaspoon fennel seeds, crushed

¼ teaspoon ground nutmeg

⅛ teaspoon ground cloves

4 chicken drumsticks and 4 thighs, skin removed (see Tip, page 169)

2 tablespoons Whole30-compliant tomato paste

½ cup Whole30-compliant coconut milk (see Tip)

2 tablespoons tapioca flour

2 packages (10 ounces each) riced butternut squash, beets, or kohlrabi

Fresh mint leaves

IN a 6-quart slow cooker, combine the broth, onion, garlic, and ginger. In a small bowl, combine the clarified butter, cumin, turmeric, salt, cayenne, cardamom, cinnamon, coriander, fennel, nutmeg, and cloves. Rub the spice paste over the chicken. Add the chicken to the slow cooker.

COVER and cook on low for 5 to 6 hours or on high for 2½ to 3 hours. Transfer the chicken to a plate; cover to keep warm.

SKIM the fat from the cooking liquid. Stir in the tomato paste and coconut milk. In a small, bowl, stir together the tapioca flour and 2 tablespoons water. Stir the mixture into the cooking liquid. If on low, turn the slow cooker to the high setting. Cover and cook until the sauce is slightly thickened, about 5 minutes.

MEANWHILE, prepare the riced squash according to the package directions.

SERVE the chicken and sauce with the squash. Sprinkle with fresh mint.

> **TIP** *Canned coconut milk separates in the can with the cream rising to the top. Be sure to whisk the coconut milk well before measuring.*

> **INSTANT POT VARIATION** *Follow the directions of the first two steps using a 6-quart Instant Pot. Lock the lid in place. Select Manual and cook on high pressure for 20 minutes. Use natural release for 5 minutes, then quick release. Follow the remaining directions.*

ITALIAN TURKEY MEATBALLS WITH MARINARA

SERVES 4

PREP: 30 minutes

BAKE: 10 minutes

SLOW COOK: 6 hours (low) or 3 hours (high)

TOTAL: 6 hours 40 minutes

This family-friendly dish of meatballs and sauce served over zoodles is one that even picky eaters will love. Partially baking the meatballs before placing them in the slow cooker helps them hold their shape and renders off some of the not-so-pretty protein bits that slough off raw meat during moist cooking.

FOR THE MEATBALLS
1 package (19 ounces) ground turkey breast

¼ cup minced onion

¼ cup minced mushrooms

1 tablespoon minced garlic

4 teaspoons tapioca flour

1 tablespoon Whole30-compliant Italian seasoning

½ teaspoon fennel seeds, crushed

¼ teaspoon red pepper flakes

¼ teaspoon sea salt

¼ teaspoon black pepper

1 large egg, lightly beaten

FOR THE SAUCE
1 can (28 ounces) Whole30-compliant crushed tomatoes

½ cup grated carrots

¼ cup grated onion

1 tablespoon minced garlic

1 tablespoon Whole30-compliant Italian seasoning

1 bay leaf

TO SERVE
2 packages (10.7 ounces each) zucchini noodles or 3 medium zucchini, spiralized

2 tablespoons chopped fresh parsley

MAKE THE MEATBALLS: Preheat the oven to 400°F. In a large bowl, combine the turkey, minced onion, mushrooms, and garlic. In a small bowl, stir together the tapioca flour, Italian seasoning, fennel seeds, red pepper flakes, salt, and black pepper. Add the tapioca mixture and the egg to the turkey mixture and mix until thoroughly combined. Let sit 5 minutes. Shape into 16 meatballs. Place on a foil-lined baking pan and bake for 10 minutes.

MAKE THE SAUCE: In a 6-quart slow cooker, combine 1 cup water with the tomatoes, carrots, grated onion, garlic, Italian seasoning, and bay leaf. Add the meatballs.

COVER and cook on low for 6 hours or on high for 3 hours. Discard the bay leaf.

MEANWHILE, prepare the zucchini noodles according to the package directions. Divide the noodles among four serving bowls. Top each with four meatballs and sauce. Sprinkle with parsley and serve.

CHICKEN, SHRIMP, AND SAUSAGE JAMBALAYA

FROM GRACE BRINTON OF TRU PROVISIONS

SERVES 4

PREP: 35 minutes

SLOW COOK: 5 hours (low)

TOTAL: 5 hours 35 minutes

When I think of jambalaya, I picture layers of flavor that make a particular recipe unique to whomever created it. For this version, I wanted to keep things flavorful and a little spicy but, most important, simple. The most time you'll spend on this dish will be searing the meat and sautéing the veggies, which adds texture and depth to the dish.

4½ teaspoons Clarified Butter (page 296) or ghee

2 Whole30-compliant andouille sausages (6 ounces total), sliced into 1-inch pieces

1 pound boneless, skinless chicken thighs, cut into 1-inch pieces

1 teaspoon salt

2 red, green, or orange bell peppers, diced

½ medium yellow onion, diced

3 large cloves garlic, minced

1 cup Whole30-compliant chicken broth or Chicken Bone Broth (page 294)

¼ cup Whole30-compliant tomato paste

1 pound parsnips, peeled and riced (see Tip)

2 tablespoons minced fresh parsley, plus more for serving

1½ teaspoons dried thyme

1 teaspoon paprika

1 teaspoon turmeric

½ teaspoon black pepper

8 peeled and deveined shrimp

MELT 1 teaspoon of the clarified butter in a large skillet over medium heat. Add the sausage and cook, turning once, until browned, about 5 minutes. Transfer the sausage to a 4-quart slow cooker.

ADD 1 teaspoon of the butter to the skillet. Add the chicken and sprinkle with ¼ teaspoon of the salt. Cook the chicken until browned, about 5 minutes. Transfer the chicken to the slow cooker.

ADD the remaining 2½ teaspoons butter to the skillet. Add the bell peppers, onion, and garlic. Cook, stirring, until softened, about 5 minutes. Transfer the vegetables to the slow cooker. Add the broth and tomato paste to the skillet and stir to scrape up any brown bits on the bottom. Pour into the slow cooker. Stir in the parsnip rice, parsley, thyme, paprika, turmeric, remaining ¾ teaspoon salt, and the pepper.

COVER and cook on low for 5 to 6 hours. If using the shrimp, add them for the last 20 minutes of cooking (submerge the shrimp in the sauce).

SERVE the jambalaya in bowls, topped with parsley.

TIP *For riced parsnips, place 2-inch pieces of parsnip in a food processor. Cover and pulse until the parsnip is in rice-size pieces.*

SOUTHWEST TURKEY LEGS

SERVES 4

PREP: 25 minutes

SLOW COOK: 7 hours (low) or 3½ hours (high)

TOTAL: 7 hours 25 minutes

A cooling fruit salad of melon, pineapple, orange, and fresh mint makes a refreshing accompaniment to meaty, spicy turkey legs.

FOR THE TURKEY LEGS

2 teaspoons salt

1 teaspoon black pepper

1 teaspoon cumin

1 teaspoon coriander

1 teaspoon cayenne

1 teaspoon onion powder

4 turkey legs (3 pounds)

FOR THE FRUIT SALAD

2 cups assorted melon chunks, such as cantaloupe and honeydew

1 cup fresh pineapple chunks

2 oranges, peeled and sectioned (see Tip)

¼ cup fresh orange juice

2 tablespoons fresh lime juice

2 tablespoons extra-virgin olive oil

¼ teaspoon coriander

¼ cup chopped fresh mint

COOK THE TURKEY LEGS: Pour 1 cup water into a 6-quart slow cooker and add a steamer basket. In a small bowl, combine the salt, pepper, cumin, coriander, cayenne, and onion powder. Rub the seasoning over the turkey legs. Tightly wrap each leg in a piece of aluminum foil about 12 x 12 inches. Place the legs on the steamer basket.

COVER and cook on low for 7 hours or on high for 3½ hours. Remove the turkey from the slow cooker; let cool for 10 minutes before removing the foil.

MAKE THE FRUIT SALAD: Meanwhile, in a medium bowl, combine the melon, pineapple, and oranges. In a small bowl, combine the orange juice, lime juice, olive oil, and coriander. Add to the fruit and toss. Sprinkle with the mint.

SERVE the turkey legs with the fruit salad.

TIP *If you have a few extra minutes, you can supreme the oranges (remove the membrane so they can easily be served in slices): With a sharp knife, trim the fruit's ends. Set one end on a cutting board and slice off the peel and pith in sections. Set the fruit on its side. Cut toward the center, along the membrane. Then slice along the adjacent membrane until the cuts meet, releasing the segment. Repeat with the remaining segments.*

INSTANT POT VARIATION *Follow the directions in the first two steps using a 6-quart Instant Pot. Lock the lid in place. Select Manual and cook on high pressure for 40 minutes. Use natural release for 5 minutes, then quick release. Continue with the remaining directions.*

TURKEY-PORK MEATLOAF WITH SMOKY TOMATO SAUCE

SERVES 6

PREP: 20 minutes

SLOW COOK: 4 hours (low) or 2 hours (high)

TOTAL: 4 hours 25 minutes

Making a foil sling for the meatloaf allows you to easily get it into and out of the slow cooker. Poking holes in it ensures that the fats and cooking juices will drain off during cooking and allow the meatloaf to develop a nice browned crust.

FOR THE MEATLOAF

2 large eggs, lightly beaten

¼ cup almond flour

1 teaspoon salt

½ teaspoon black pepper

½ teaspoon dry mustard

½ teaspoon dried thyme

½ cup coarsely chopped yellow onion

½ small red bell pepper, coarsely chopped

1 medium carrot, coarsely chopped

2 cloves garlic, peeled

1 package (19 ounces) ground turkey breast

8 ounces lean ground pork

FOR THE SAUCE

½ cup hot water

4 medjool dates, pitted

1 can (6 ounces) Whole30-compliant tomato paste

2 tablespoons cider vinegar

½ teaspoon onion powder

½ teaspoon garlic powder

½ teaspoon salt

¼ teaspoon smoked paprika

4 small sweet potatoes, scrubbed and pricked with a fork

Chopped fresh parsley

Clarified Butter (page 296) or ghee

MAKE THE MEATLOAF: In a medium bowl, stir together the eggs, almond flour, salt, pepper, dry mustard, and thyme.

IN a food processor, combine the onion, bell pepper, carrot, and garlic. Cover and pulse until finely chopped. Stir into the egg mixture. Add the turkey and pork; mix gently to combine (do not overmix). Poke a few holes in a 12 x 18-inch piece of foil for drainage. Shape the meat mixture into two 6 x 3-inch loaves and place on the foil.

PLACE a steamer rack in a 4-quart slow cooker. Add 1 cup water to the cooker. Use the foil to lower the loaves onto the rack. Tuck the foil into the pot.

COVER and cook on low for 4 to 4½ hours or on high for 2 to 2¼ hours, or until a thermometer inserted into the loaves registers 160°F.

MEANWHILE, MAKE THE SAUCE: In a small bowl, pour the hot water over the dates and let sit until softened, about 5 minutes. In a food processor or blender, combine the dates and soaking water, tomato paste, vinegar, onion powder, garlic powder, salt, and paprika. Cover and process until smooth.

MICROWAVE the sweet potatoes until tender, turning once, 8 to 10 minutes.

ADJUST an oven rack to 8 inches below the broiler. Preheat the broiler and line a baking sheet with foil. Use the foil to transfer the loaves to the baking sheet. Spoon about ½ cup of the sauce over each loaf. Broil just until the sauce starts to bubble, 4 to 5 minutes.

TOP the loaves with parsley and serve with the sweet potatoes topped with clarified butter.

TIP *Store leftover sauce in an airtight container in the refrigerator for up to 2 weeks.*

FISH AND SHELLFISH

SHRIMP GUMBO

SERVES 4

PREP: 25 minutes

SLOW COOK: 4 hours (low) or 2 hours (high)

TOTAL: 4 hours 25 minutes

Filé powder is made from the dried, ground leaves of the sassafras tree. It acts as a thickener in this gumbo, and also gives the gumbo its characteristic woodsy flavor and a pleasantly "sandy" texture. Look for it in the spice aisle of your supermarket.

1 pound fresh or frozen peeled and deveined medium shrimp

2 Whole30-compliant chicken and apple sausage links or 6 ounces Whole30-compliant andouille sausage, coarsely chopped

1 cup fresh or frozen sliced okra

½ cup diced green bell pepper

½ cup diced onion

½ cup diced celery

1 can (14.5 ounces) Whole30-compliant whole tomatoes, drained and cut-up

1 bay leaf

¾ teaspoon Whole30-compliant Cajun seasoning

¼ teaspoon salt

¼ teaspoon black pepper

½ teaspoon filé powder

1 package (16 ounces) cauliflower crumbles, prepared according to package directions or 3 cups raw cauliflower rice (page 60)

Chopped fresh flat-leaf parsley

Whole30-compliant hot sauce (optional)

THAW the shrimp, if frozen. In a 6-quart slow cooker, combine the shrimp, sausage, okra, bell pepper, onion, celery, tomatoes, bay leaf, Cajun seasoning, salt, and pepper.

COVER and cook on low for 4 hours or on high for 2 hours, or just until the shrimp is opaque and the vegetables are cooked through. Turn the slow cooker to high if using the low setting. Stir in the filé powder. Cook, stirring, until slightly thickened, about 3 minutes.

DISCARD the bay leaf. Serve the gumbo over the cauliflower, and sprinkle with parsley. If desired, pass hot sauce at the table.

TIP *If desired, substitute 2 tablespoons tapioca flour stirred into 1 tablespoon cold water for the filé.*

INSTANT POT VARIATION *Follow the directions in the first two steps using a 6-quart Instant Pot. Lock the lid in place. Select Manual, adjust to Less/Low, and cook for 5 minutes. Use natural release for 2 minutes, then quick release. Leave the keep warm function active while stirring in the filé powder. Continue with the remaining directions.*

FISH AND SHELLFISH

SHRIMP WITH NAPA CABBAGE AND PEACH-HARISSA VINAIGRETTE

SERVES 4

PREP: 50 minutes

SLOW COOK: 2 hours (low) or 1 hour (high)

TOTAL: 2 hours 50 minutes

The vinaigrette for this fresh, crunchy salad is a yummy balance of sweet (from the peaches) and heat (from the harissa). Harissa is a North African condiment made with chiles, garlic, cumin, coriander, caraway, and olive oil. It comes in a variety of heat levels, from mild to fiery. Choose one that suits your taste.

FOR THE SHRIMP
¼ cup pickling spice

1 pound peeled and deveined jumbo shrimp

1 bottle (8 ounces) clam juice

½ teaspoon salt

¼ teaspoon black pepper

FOR THE VINAIGRETTE
¾ cup sliced peaches, fresh or thawed frozen

¼ cup avocado oil

3 tablespoons white wine vinegar

1 teaspoon harissa paste

¼ teaspoon salt

FOR THE SALAD
6 cups shredded Napa cabbage

1 cup chopped tomatoes

½ cup thinly sliced cucumber

¼ cup sliced green onions

¼ cup almond slices, toasted (see Tip)

MAKE THE SHRIMP: Place the pickling spice on a 6 x 6-inch piece of cheesecloth. Fold up the edges, tie with cotton kitchen string, and place in a 4-quart slow cooker. Add the shrimp, clam juice, salt, and pepper. Cover and cook for 2 hours on low or 1 hour on high, or until the shrimp are pink and opaque. Transfer to a large plate with a slotted spoon; cover and chill for 30 minutes. Discard the cooking liquid and spice bag.

MAKE THE VINAIGRETTE: In a food processor or blender, combine the peaches, avocado oil, vinegar, harissa, and salt. Cover and process or blend until smooth. If the vinaigrette is thick, add water, 1 teaspoon at a time. Cover and refrigerate until serving.

MAKE THE SALAD: Divide the cabbage among four serving plates. Top with the tomatoes, cucumber, and chilled shrimp. Drizzle with the vinaigrette and sprinkle with green onion and almond slices.

TIP *To toast almonds, heat in a skillet over medium heat, stirring, until fragrant and lightly browned, about 2 minutes.*

SHRIMP SCAMPI NOODLE BOWLS

SERVES 4

PREP: 15 minutes

SLOW COOK: 2 hours (high)

TOTAL: 2 hours 15 minutes

Both the yellow-squash noodles and shrimp are sufficiently delicate that you don't want to overcook either one of them (the noodles would get mushy and the shrimp would get tough). Just about 2 hours on high yields perfectly cooked crisp-tender noodles and tender shrimp in a buttery, garlicky sauce.

1 pound fresh or frozen peeled and deveined medium shrimp

4 cups Whole30-compliant chicken broth or Chicken Bone Broth (page 294)

2 unpeeled medium yellow summer squash (about 1 pound total), spiralized, long noodles snipped, if desired

2 tablespoons Clarified Butter (page 296) or ghee

4 cloves garlic, minced

¼ teaspoon red pepper flakes, plus extra for serving

½ teaspoon salt

2 tablespoons fresh lemon juice

¼ cup chopped flat-leaf parsley

THAW the shrimp, if frozen. In a 4-quart slow cooker, combine the shrimp, broth, yellow squash noodles, butter, garlic, red pepper flakes, and salt. Cover and cook on high for 2 to 2½ hours, or until the shrimp are opaque and the noodles are tender. Stir in the lemon juice.

SERVE in bowls, topped with parsley and additional red pepper flakes if desired.

BALSAMIC-GLAZED SWEET POTATOES AND SALMON

SERVES 6

PREP: 15 minutes

SLOW COOK: 4 hours (low) or 2 hours (high)

TOTAL: 4 hours 45 minutes

Even though fish doesn't take long to cook, the slow cooker provides an ideal environment for cooking it. Just 25 minutes sitting on top of sweet potatoes in the gentle, moist heat of the slow cooker renders salmon tender, buttery, and perfectly done.

2 pounds sweet potatoes, peeled and cut into 1-inch pieces

1 medium red onion, cut into thin wedges

3 tablespoons balsamic vinegar

2 teaspoons Whole30-compliant coarse-grain mustard

1 teaspoon salt

1½ pounds fresh or frozen salmon fillet, thawed if frozen, skin removed

½ teaspoon dried thyme

½ teaspoon ground coriander

¼ teaspoon ground ginger

¼ teaspoon black pepper

IN a 6-quart slow cooker, combine the sweet potatoes, onion, ⅓ cup water, the vinegar, mustard, and ½ teaspoon of the salt. Toss to coat and spread in an even layer. Cover and cook on low for 4 to 5 hours or on high for 2 to 2½ hours, or just until the potatoes are tender.

RINSE the salmon with cold water; pat dry with paper towels. Cut the salmon crosswise in half. In a small bowl, combine the remaining ½ teaspoon salt, the thyme, coriander, ginger, and pepper. Sprinkle evenly over the salmon.

TURN the slow cooker to high if using the low setting. Gently stir the potato mixture. Lay the salmon pieces on the potatoes. Cover and cook on high until the salmon flakes easily when tested with a fork, about 25 minutes.

TRANSFER the salmon to a cutting board; cut into 6 portions. Serve the salmon and potatoes drizzled with some of the cooking liquid.

INSTANT POT VARIATION *Follow the directions to the cook the potatoes in the first step using a 6-quart Instant Pot. Lock the lid in place. Select Manual, adjust to More/High, and cook for 3 minutes. Use quick release. Follow the directions in the third step to cook the salmon. Lock the lid in place. Select Manual, adjust to More/High, and cook for 5 minutes. Use quick release. Continue with the remaining directions.*

FISH AND SHELLFISH

CARIBBEAN FISH AND SHRIMP

SERVES 4

PREP: 1 hour

SLOW COOK: 3 hours (low) or 1½ hours (high)

TOTAL: 4 hours

Although the fried plantains—technically called *tostones*—are optional, definitely make them if you have the time. They're crisp and a little bit salty and a perfect way to round out this beautiful, fresh-tasting dish. Look for plantains that are still green for the best results.

FOR THE FISH AND SHRIMP

1 bottle (8 ounces) clam juice

1 bay leaf

½ teaspoon grated fresh ginger

1 pound mahi-mahi or cod fillets

½ pound peeled and deveined jumbo shrimp

1 teaspoon dehydrated minced onion

¾ teaspoon ground allspice

½ teaspoon ground cinnamon

¼ teaspoon ground ginger

¼ teaspoon dried thyme

¼ teaspoon cayenne pepper

½ teaspoon sea salt

3 slices lemon, quartered

1 mango, diced

½ cup sliced fennel

FOR THE CITRUS SALSA

⅓ cup minced Vidalia onion

1 orange, peeled, segmented, and chopped

½ grapefruit, peeled, segmented, and chopped

¼ cup minced jicama

½ to 1 serrano chile pepper, seeded if desired, and minced

1 teaspoon minced garlic

¼ teaspoon salt

1 tablespoon chopped fresh cilantro

FOR THE PLANTAINS (OPTIONAL)

2 tablespoons Clarified Butter (page 296) or ghee

2 plantains, peeled and sliced ¼ inch thick

½ teaspoon garlic salt

MAKE THE FISH AND SHRIMP: In a 6-quart slow cooker, combine the clam juice, bay leaf, and fresh ginger. Rinse and pat dry the fish and shrimp. In a small bowl, combine the dehydrated onion, allspice, cinnamon, ground ginger, thyme, cayenne pepper, and salt and sprinkle over the fish and shrimp. Add to the slow cooker and top with the lemon slices, half the diced mango, and the fennel. Cook for 3 hours on low or 1½ hours on high, or until the fish flakes easily when tested with a fork and the shrimp are pink and opaque. Discard the bay leaf.

MEANWHILE, MAKE THE CITRUS SALSA: In a medium bowl, combine the remaining mango, the onion, orange, grapefruit, jicama, serrano pepper, garlic, and salt. Taste, and add more salt, if desired. Keep the salsa covered in the refrigerator until serving.

MAKE THE PLANTAINS: Heat the butter in large nonstick skillet over medium-high heat. Add the plantain slices in a single layer and cook until caramelized on both sides, 7 to 10 minutes. Transfer the plantains to a paper towel–lined bowl. Sprinkle with the garlic salt and toss to coat.

STIR the cilantro into the citrus salsa. Use a slotted spoon to serve the salsa with the fish, shrimp, and plantains.

INSTANT POT VARIATION *Follow the instructions in the first step using a 6-quart Instant Pot. Lock the lid in place. Select Manual, adjust to Less/Low, and cook for 3 minutes. Use natural release for 2 minutes, then quick release. For the plantains, select Sauté and adjust to More/High. Continue with the remaining directions.*

COD WITH PEPPERS AND TOMATOES

SERVES 4

PREP: 10 minutes

SLOW COOK: 4 hours (low) or
2 hours (high)

TOTAL: 4 hours 40 minutes

The quickest way to prep a bell pepper? Stand it upright on a cutting board, then slice down each of the four "sides." You'll be left with pieces that are ready for slicing—and the stem and seedy core that can be tossed.

2 medium yellow bell peppers, sliced

3 medium shallots, sliced

3 cloves garlic, minced

1 can (14.5 ounces) Whole30-compliant diced tomatoes

4 cod fillets (5 to 6 ounces each)

¼ teaspoon salt

¼ teaspoon black pepper

1 tablespoon chopped fresh flat-leaf parsley

1 tablespoon Whole30-compliant capers, drained

1 teaspoon grated lemon zest

1 tablespoon extra-virgin olive oil

IN a 3½- to 4-quart slow cooker, combine the bell peppers, shallots, garlic, and tomatoes. Cover and cook on low for 4 to 5 hours or on high for 2 to 2½ hours.

IF on low, turn the slow cooker to the high setting. Place the fish fillets on the sauce. Sprinkle with the salt and pepper. Cover and cook just until the fish starts to flake with a fork, 30 to 40 minutes.

TOP the cod with the parsley, capers, lemon zest, and olive oil, and serve.

INSTANT POT VARIATION *In a 6-quart Instant Pot, combine the bell peppers, shallots, garlic, and tomatoes. Place the fish on the vegetables. Sprinkle with the salt and pepper. Lock the lid in place. Select Manual, adjust to Less/Low, and cook for 3 minutes. Use natural release for 2 minutes, then quick release. Continue with the remaining serving directions.*

GREEN-CHILE SQUASH WITH SEED-CRUSTED FISH

SERVES 4

PREP: 25 minutes

SLOW COOK: 4 hours (low) or 2 hours (high)

TOTAL: 5 hours

A blend of sesame seeds, cumin seeds, and mustard seeds adds flavor and crunch to this interesting dish that can be made with any of several types of fish, including cod, salmon, and halibut.

FOR THE GREEN-CHILE SQUASH

4 cups diced butternut squash

2 poblano peppers, seeded and chopped

1 jalapeño, seeded and finely chopped

2 cloves garlic, minced

1 teaspoon ground cumin

½ teaspoon garlic powder

¾ teaspoon salt

½ teaspoon black pepper

2 tablespoons extra-virgin olive oil

FOR THE FISH

2 tablespoons extra-virgin olive oil

2 teaspoons sesame seeds

1½ teaspoons cumin seeds

1 teaspoon brown or yellow mustard seeds

¾ teaspoon salt

½ teaspoon black pepper

4 cod, salmon, or halibut fillets (5 to 6 ounces each)

MAKE THE GREEN-CHILE SQUASH: In a 5- to 6-quart slow cooker, combine the squash, poblanos, jalapeño, garlic, cumin, garlic powder, salt, and pepper. Drizzle with the olive oil and toss to coat. Cover and cook on low for 4 to 6 hours or on high for 2 to 3 hours, or until the squash is just tender.

MAKE THE FISH: In a small bowl, combine the olive oil, sesame seeds, cumin seeds, mustard seeds, salt, and pepper. Rub the seed paste on the fish. Place the fish in the cooker on top of the squash mixture. Turn the slow cooker to high if using the low setting. Cover and cook for 30 to 35 minutes, or until the fish flakes easily with a fork.

USE a slotted spoon to serve the fish with the chiles and squash.

SMOKY COD AND GREEN BEANS EN PAPILLOTE

SERVES 4

PREP: 20 minutes

SLOW COOK: 2 hours (high)

TOTAL: 2 hours 20 minutes

Cooking *en papillote* is a French technique in which food (usually delicate foods such as fish and vegetables) is wrapped up and cooked in parchment paper. The steam that builds up in the packet during cooking helps retain moisture and nutrients. Place a packet on each dinner plate and cut them open at the table. The aroma that comes wafting out is heavenly!

1 pound haricot verts or slender green beans, trimmed

2 red or yellow bell peppers, thinly sliced (3 cups)

1 small onion, thinly sliced (1 cup)

2 cloves garlic, minced

1 teaspoon smoked paprika

1½ teaspoons black pepper

1 teaspoon salt

2 tablespoons plus 2 teaspoons extra-virgin olive oil

4 cod or halibut fillets (5 to 6 ounces each)

IN a large bowl, combine the green beans, bell peppers, onion, garlic, smoked paprika, 1 teaspoon of the pepper, and ½ teaspoon of the salt. Drizzle with 2 tablespoons of the olive oil and toss to combine. Cut four 15-inch squares of parchment paper. Divide the vegetable mixture into 4 portions and place one in the center of each piece of parchment.

LIGHTLY drizzle the fish with the remaining 2 teaspoons olive oil and season with the remaining ½ teaspoon each salt and pepper. Place the fillets over the vegetable mixture on the parchment. Bring up two opposite edges of paper and fold several times over the fish. Fold in the ends.

PLACE the packets in a 6-quart oval slow cooker. Cover and cook on high for 2 to 3 hours, or until the fish flakes easily with a fork.

SHRIMP AND GARDEN VEGGIE SAUCE OVER SPAGHETTI SQUASH

SERVES 6

PREP: 35 minutes

SLOW COOK: 6 hours (low) or 3 hours (high), plus 30 minutes (high)

TOTAL: 7 hours 5 minutes

Overcooked shrimp can be rubbery and tough. Adding the shrimp to the slow cooker just 30 minutes before the end of the cooking time ensures that they stay tender.

1½ pounds Roma (plum) tomatoes, peeled (if desired) and chopped

1 medium red bell pepper, coarsely chopped

1 cup sliced cremini or button mushrooms

1 cup chopped peeled eggplant

⅓ cup Whole30-compliant tomato paste

6 cloves garlic, minced

2 teaspoons dried oregano

1½ teaspoons coarse salt

¼ to ½ teaspoon red pepper flakes

1½ pounds fresh or thawed frozen peeled and deveined extra-jumbo shrimp

½ cup chopped fresh basil

1 spaghetti squash (2½ pounds)

2 tablespoons extra-virgin olive oil

¼ teaspoon black pepper

½ cup chopped Whole30-compliant Kalamata olives

⅓ cup pine nuts, toasted if desired (see Tip)

IN a 4-quart slow cooker, stir together the tomatoes, bell pepper, mushrooms, eggplant, tomato paste, garlic, oregano, 1 teaspoon of the salt, and the red pepper flakes.

COVER and cook on low for 6 to 7 hours or on high for 3 to 3½ hours.

TURN the slow cooker to high if using the low setting. Add the shrimp. Cover and cook for 30 minutes, or until the shrimp are pink and opaque. Stir in ¼ cup of the basil.

MEANWHILE, cut the squash lengthwise in half and scrape out the seeds and strings. Place the squash halves, cut sides down, in a 2-quart rectangular microwave-safe baking dish and add ½ cup water. Microwave on high, uncovered, until the squash is tender, 14 to 16 minutes. Let the squash stand until cool enough to handle. Use a fork to scrape the flesh into a medium bowl. Drizzle with the olive oil and sprinkle with the remaining ½ teaspoon salt and the black pepper.

SERVE the shrimp and vegetable sauce over the squash. Sprinkle with olives, pine nuts, and remaining ¼ cup basil.

TIP *To toast pine nuts, heat in a dry skillet over medium heat, stirring, until fragrant and lightly browned, about 2 minutes.*

SALMON WITH LEMON AND DILL

SERVES 4

PREP: 25 minutes

SLOW COOK: 1 hour (high)

TOTAL: 1 hour 25 minutes

A preparation for salmon doesn't get any more classic than this—flavored with lemon and dill and served on a crisp cucumber salad. Meyer lemons are thought to be a cross between a regular lemon and a Mandarin orange. They're smaller, sweeter, and rounder than regular lemons, with golden-yellow flesh. If you can't find them, regular lemons work just as well.

4 salmon fillets (4 to 6 ounces each), skin removed

½ teaspoon salt

½ teaspoon black pepper

2 Meyer lemons or regular lemons, sliced and seeded, plus additional lemon wedges for serving

1 tablespoon chopped fresh dill, plus more for serving

1 cup diced English cucumber

1 medium red bell pepper, diced

2 teaspoons cider vinegar

1 garlic clove, minced

LINE a 6-quart slow cooker with parchment paper. Sprinkle the salmon with the salt and pepper and place on the parchment. Top with the lemon slices and dill.

COVER and cook on high for 1 hour.

MEANWHILE, in a small bowl, combine the cucumber, bell pepper, vinegar, and garlic. Cover and refrigerate until serving.

REMOVE the salmon from the slow cooker; discard the lemon slices. Top the salmon with the cucumber salad and additional chopped dill and serve with lemon wedges.

SALMON WITH SMOKY VEGETABLE HASH

SERVES 4

PREP: 15 minutes

SLOW COOK: 5 hours (low) or 2½ hours (high), plus 25 minutes (high)

TOTAL: 5 hours 40 minutes

How do you get a smoky flavor in the slow cooker? With the magic of smoked paprika—made from Spanish chiles that have been dried over a wood fire. Smoked paprika—also called pimenton—can be mild or hot, but most of what's on supermarket shelves is of the mild variety.

2 teaspoons grated lemon zest

½ teaspoon smoked paprika

½ teaspoon garlic powder

1¼ teaspoons salt

¾ teaspoon black pepper

12 ounces baby Yukon Gold potatoes, quartered

1 small head cauliflower (about 1½ pounds), cut into large florets

1 large yellow onion, cut into quarters

2 tablespoons extra-virgin olive oil

½ cup Whole30-compliant chicken broth or Chicken Bone Broth (page 294)

1 tablespoon fresh lemon juice

4 salmon fillets (4 ounces each), skin removed

4 slices Whole30-compliant bacon, crisp-cooked and crumbled

Fresh chopped parsley

IN a small bowl, stir together the lemon zest, paprika, garlic powder, ¾ teaspoon of the salt, and ½ teaspoon of the pepper. In a 6-quart slow cooker, combine the potatoes, cauliflower, and onion. Drizzle the vegetables with the olive oil and sprinkle with the seasoning. Toss to combine. Add the broth and lemon juice.

COVER and cook on low for 5 to 6 hours or on high for 2½ to 3 hours.

SPRINKLE the salmon with the remaining ½ teaspoon salt and remaining ¼ teaspoon pepper. Place the salmon on the vegetables. Turn the cooker to high if using the low setting. Cover and cook for 25 minutes, or until the salmon just starts to flake with a fork.

SERVE the salmon with the potatoes and vegetables. Top servings with crumbled bacon and parsley.

CIOPPINO

SERVES 4

PREP: 25 minutes

SLOW COOK: 6 hours (low) or 3 hours (high), plus 30 minutes (low)

TOTAL: 6 hours 55 minutes

This chunky, tomatoey fish stew was created by Italian immigrant fishermen in San Francisco who made it with whatever fish and shellfish they caught that day. It's similar to French bouillabaisse, but simpler and more rustic. A squeeze of fresh lemon right before serving brightens the flavor.

1 can (28 ounces) Whole30-compliant diced tomatoes, undrained

1 medium onion, chopped

¾ cup Whole30-compliant chicken broth or Chicken Bone Broth (page 294)

¼ cup Whole30-compliant tomato paste

2 stalks celery, chopped

3 cloves garlic, minced

¼ teaspoon salt

1 bay leaf

1 pound firm white fish (such as cod, halibut, or pollock), cut into 1-inch pieces

¾ pound peeled and deveined medium shrimp

1 can (6 ounces) Whole30-compliant crabmeat, drained

Fresh chopped parsley

1 lemon, cut into wedges

IN a 6-quart slow cooker, combine the tomatoes, onion, broth, tomato paste, celery, garlic, salt, and bay leaf.

COVER and cook on low for 6 to 8 hours or on high for 3 to 4 hours.

STIR the fish, shrimp, and crabmeat into the slow cooker. Turn to low if cooking on high. Cover and cook until the fish just starts to flake with a fork and shrimp are pink, 30 minutes. Remove and discard the bay leaf. Stir in parsley and serve with lemon wedges.

INSTANT POT VARIATION *Follow the directions in the first two steps using a 6-quart Instant Pot. Lock the lid in place. Select Manual, adjust to Less/Low, and cook for 3 minutes. Use natural release for 2 minutes, then quick release. In the third step, add the seafood, select Sauté, and adjust to Less/Low. Simmer, uncovered, until the fish just barely starts to flake when pulled apart with a fork, 3 to 5 minutes. Continue with the remaining directions to serve.*

🔒 SHRIMP BOIL

SERVES 6

PREP: 15 minutes

SLOW COOK: 5 hours (low) or 2½ hours (high), plus 30 minutes (high)

TOTAL: 5 hours 45 minutes

With a generous dose of Old Bay seasoning and kielbasa sausage, this Southern seafood dish is a tad on the salty side—but that's kind of the nature of a shrimp boil. The long soak in the seasoned broth gives the potatoes lots of flavor.

1½ pounds small red potatoes, halved

1 onion, peeled and quartered

3 cloves garlic, minced

½ cup Old Bay seasoning

2 cups Whole30-compliant chicken broth or Chicken Bone Broth (page 294)

1½ pounds fresh or thawed frozen large shell-on deveined shrimp

1 pound Whole30-compliant kielbasa sausage, cut into 1-inch pieces

1 tablespoon fresh lemon juice

Chopped fresh parsley

1 lemon, cut into wedges

IN a 6-quart slow cooker, combine the potatoes, onion, and garlic. Sprinkle with the Old Bay and toss to coat. Add 2 cups water and the broth.

COVER and cook on low for 5 to 6 hours or on high for 2½ to 3 hours.

TURN the slow cooker to high if using the low setting. Stir in the shrimp and sausage. Cover and cook until the shrimp are pink and opaque and the sausage is heated through, 30 minutes.

USE a slotted spoon to transfer the shrimp, sausage, potatoes, and onion to a large serving platter; drizzle with the lemon juice. Top with parsley and serve with lemon wedges.

INSTANT POT VARIATION *Follow the directions of the first two steps using a 6-quart Instant Pot. Lock the lid in place. Select Manual, adjust to Less/Low, and cook for 5 minutes. Use natural release for 3 minutes, then quick release. In the third step, add the shrimp and sausage and lock the lid in place. Select Manual, adjust to Less/Low, and cook for 1 minute. Use quick release. Follow the remaining directions to serve.*

SOLE EN PAPILLOTE WITH OLIVES, PISTACHIOS, AND TARRAGON

SERVES 4

PREP: 30 minutes

SLOW COOK: 2 hours (low) or 1 hour (high)

TOTAL: 2 hours 30 minutes

The olive-pistachio relish for this fish is so incredibly delicious, you will find yourself looking for other ways to use it. While it's especially good with fish, it's also fantastic with beef or chicken.

FOR THE FISH

8 sole fillets (3 to 4 ounces each), thawed if frozen

4 teaspoons extra-virgin olive oil

½ teaspoon salt

¼ teaspoon black pepper

FOR THE RELISH

1 cup Whole30-compliant Castelvetrano olives or other green olives, pitted and sliced lengthwise into quarters

¼ cup finely chopped salted toasted pistachios

2 tablespoons extra-virgin olive oil

1 tablespoon grated lemon zest

1 tablespoon chopped fresh tarragon

1 clove garlic, minced

FOR THE VINAIGRETTE

3 tablespoons extra-virgin olive oil

1 tablespoon fresh lemon juice or cider vinegar

1 teaspoon Whole30-compliant Dijon mustard

⅛ teaspoon salt

⅛ teaspoon black pepper

1 package (5 ounces) mixed salad greens

1 small fennel bulb, thinly sliced (see Tip)

MAKE THE FISH: Cut four 15-inch squares of parchment paper. Place 2 fillets, stacked on top of each other, on each of the four squares. Drizzle each stack with 1 teaspoon of the olive oil and season with the salt and pepper. Bring up two opposite edges of the paper and fold several times over the fish. Fold in the ends. Place the packets in a 6-quart slow cooker.

COVER and cook on low for 2 to 2¼ hours or on high for 1 to 1½ hours, or until the fish just starts to flake with a fork.

MEANWHILE, MAKE THE RELISH: In a small bowl, combine the olives, pistachios, olive oil, lemon zest, tarragon, and garlic; set aside.

MAKE THE VINAIGRETTE: In a small jar, combine the olive oil, lemon juice, mustard, salt, and pepper; shake until well combined.

IN a large bowl, combine the greens and fennel; drizzle with the vinaigrette and toss to coat.

SERVE the fish on the salad, spooning the relish on top of the fish.

> **TIP** *To trim a fennel bulb, cut off the stalk about 1 inch from the bulb. Cut a thin slice from the root end and discard. Remove any wilted outer layers. Stand the bulb upright and cut in half. Cut away and discard the tough core from each half. Slice the fennel according to the recipe.*

THAI FISH CURRY WITH CASHEWS, MANGO, AND CILANTRO

FROM SIMON HALL OF SIMON HALL PRIVATE CHEF

SERVES 6

PREP: 45 minutes

SLOW COOK: 2½ hours (high)

TOTAL: 3 hours 20 minutes

As a single parent, I seem to always be busy. But it's always amazing when I can share new and inspiring foods with my family, and a meal in one pot is a lifesaver! My kids love cauliflower rice, fish, and spicy foods, so they immediately took to this curry. It's packed full of subtle flavors and served with fun accoutrements exploding with different flavors.

1 cup Whole30-compliant vegetable or fish broth

1 can (13.6 ounces) Whole30-compliant coconut cream

3 tablespoons Whole30-compliant Thai green curry paste

2 tablespoons Clarified Butter (page 296) or ghee

1 medium yellow onion, chopped

2 cups chopped celery

½ head cauliflower, chopped (2½ cups)

½ pound turnips, peeled and chopped (2 cups)

2 medium carrots, peeled and chopped

3 cloves garlic, crushed

1 piece (2 inches) fresh ginger, peeled and grated

Grated zest and juice of 2 limes

2 pounds cod or other firm white fish, cut into 1-inch pieces

1 tablespoon coconut aminos

2 tablespoons Whole30-compliant fish sauce

1 cup broccoli florets

1 medium chopped bell pepper

1 cup snow peas

(continued)

IN a 6-quart slow cooker, stir together the broth, coconut cream, curry paste, butter, onion, celery, cauliflower, turnips, carrots, garlic, ginger, and lime zest and juice.

COVER and cook on high for 2 hours.

ADD the fish, coconut aminos, fish sauce, broccoli, and bell pepper. Cover and cook on high for 30 minutes, or until the fish just starts to flake with a fork. Stir in the snow peas, cilantro, salt, and black pepper. Let stand for 5 minutes.

MEANWHILE, if using, prepare the cauliflower rice according to the package directions.

IF desired, serve the curry over the cauliflower rice. Top with cashews, mango, and additional cilantro, if desired. Serve with lime wedges.

(continued)

1 bunch cilantro, coarsely chopped, plus more for garnishing, if desired

¼ teaspoon salt

¼ teaspoon black pepper

1 package (12 ounces) frozen riced cauliflower or 3 cups raw cauliflower rice (see page 60), optional

¼ cup chopped raw cashews

1 small ripe mango, diced (about 1½ cups) (see Tip)

1 lime, cut into wedges

TIP *To cut a mango, use a "Y" peeler to peel it, then use a sharp knife to trim the stem. Set the mango on one of its narrow sides and, holding it in one hand with a knife in the other, slice through the flesh slightly off center to avoid the pit. Repeat with the other side. Dice or cut as desired.*

SIMON HALL, SIMON HALL PRIVATE CHEF

Simon Hall is the owner of Simon Hall Private Chef, a Whole30 Approved catering, personal chef, and meal prep service based in Knoxville, Tennessee. Simon's personal health journey inspired him to share the benefits of eating real, clean food in a unique way with his community. The Whole30 program changed his life in many ways, so now he offers a path for others to begin their Whole30 journeys through his meal prep and catering services. Simon loves the community surrounding the Whole30 lifestyle and strives to provide more opportunities for others to join in on the real food movement.

INSTANT POT RECIPES

INSTANT POT
CHICKEN CACCIATORE WITH ZUCCHINI NOODLES

SERVES 4

PREP: 25 minutes

CLOSED POT: 25 minutes

TOTAL: 50 minutes

Cacciatore means "hunter" in Italian and refers to a dish cooked with onions, mushrooms, tomatoes, herbs, and sometimes wine. This Whole30 version doesn't contain any wine and subs zucchini noodles for the standard wheat pasta or rice that is usually served with the chicken, but it still has amazingly rich flavor.

8 boneless, skinless chicken thighs (about 2¼ pounds)

1 teaspoon dried oregano

1 teaspoon salt

¼ teaspoon black pepper

1 tablespoon coconut oil

1 medium onion, chopped

1 red bell pepper, cut into 1-inch pieces

1 package (8 ounces) sliced mushrooms

1 can (14.5 ounces) Whole30-compliant diced tomatoes, undrained

½ cup Whole30-compliant chicken broth or Chicken Bone Broth (page 294)

2 tablespoons Whole30-compliant tomato paste

2 cloves garlic, minced

1 package (10.7 ounces) zucchini noodles or 2 small zucchini, spiralized

Fresh chopped parsley (optional)

SEASON the chicken with the oregano, ½ teaspoon of the salt, and the pepper. Add the coconut oil to a 6-quart Instant Pot. Select Sauté and adjust to Normal/Medium. When the oil is hot, add half of the chicken and cook, turning once, until browned on both sides, 4 to 8 minutes. Repeat with the remaining chicken. Select Cancel. Transfer the chicken to a plate.

ADD the onion, bell pepper, mushrooms, tomatoes, broth, tomato paste, garlic, and remaining ½ teaspoon salt to the pot. Add the chicken. Lock the lid in place.

SELECT Manual and cook on high pressure for 12 minutes. Use quick release.

TRANSFER the chicken to a plate; cover to keep warm. Select Sauté and adjust to Normal/Medium. When the sauce is simmering, add the zucchini noodles. Cook, stirring frequently, until the sauce is thickened and the zucchini is crisp-tender, about 2 minutes. Select Cancel. Serve, topped with parsley if desired.

⬡ INSTANT POT
BBQ CHICKEN
FROM MICHELE ROSEN OF PALEO RUNNING MOMMA

SERVES 4

PREP: 45 minutes

CLOSED POT: 20 minutes

TOTAL: 1 hour 5 minutes

A few dates give this barbecue sauce the requisite sweetness you expect, while smoked paprika contributes smokiness without a grill. The recipe makes about 3 cups of the sauce—you'll have about a cup or so left over. Use it on burgers or for dipping roasted root vegetable fries or wedges.

FOR THE BARBECUE SAUCE

3 pitted Medjool dates

½ cup hot water

1 can (15 ounces) Whole30-compliant tomato sauce, preferably no salt added

½ cup cider vinegar

1 tablespoon smoked paprika

2 teaspoons Whole30-compliant brown mustard

2 teaspoons onion powder

1 teaspoon garlic powder

½ teaspoon salt (omit if tomato sauce contains salt)

FOR THE CHICKEN

1 tablespoon extra-virgin olive or avocado oil

1 medium red onion, sliced

2 cloves garlic, minced

1½ to 2 pounds boneless, skinless chicken breasts or thighs

2 teaspoons Whole30-compliant BBQ rub

4 small sweet potatoes or white potatoes

2 green onions, thinly sliced

MAKE THE BARBECUE SAUCE: Soak the dates in the hot water until softened, about 2 minutes. Place the dates and water in a food processor or high speed blender. Add the tomato sauce, vinegar, paprika, mustard, onion powder, garlic powder, and salt (if using). Cover and process or blend until smooth; set aside.

MAKE THE CHICKEN: Select Sauté on a 6-quart Instant Pot and adjust to Normal/Medium. Add the olive oil to the pot. When it's hot, add the onion and cook, stirring, for 1 minute. Add the garlic and cook, stirring, until just softened, 30 to 60 seconds. Select Cancel. Season both sides of the chicken with the BBQ rub and add to the pot. Add 2 cups of the barbecue sauce and stir to combine. Lock the lid in place.

SELECT Manual and cook on high pressure for 12 minutes. Use quick release. Transfer the chicken to a plate; cover to keep warm. Select Sauté. Cook the sauce, stirring, until thickened, about 5 minutes. Select Cancel.

MEANWHILE, prick the sweet potatoes all over with a fork. Microwave on high, turning once, until tender, 8 to 10 minutes. Use two forks to shred the chicken. Return the chicken to the pot and toss with the sauce. Slice the potatoes open. Serve the chicken over the potatoes and top with green onions.

MICHELE ROSEN, PALEO RUNNING MOMMA

Michele Rosen is the face behind *Paleo Running Momma*, a real-food blog sharing clean-eating family favorites that you'll be excited to share with your loved ones. She's also a wife, the mom of three school-aged kids, and a long-distance runner. Michele began her real food journey in 2013 with the Whole30 and hasn't looked back! Her goal is to introduce people to Whole30 and Paleo home cooking they'll love just as much (if not more) than their old favorites, and help families wholeheartedly embrace a Paleo lifestyle.

INSTANT POT CHICKEN TINGA

SERVES 6

PREP: 20 minutes

CLOSED POT: 45 minutes

TOTAL: 1 hour 5 minutes

This classic Mexican shredded chicken tostada topping/taco filling gets smoky heat from chipotle powder. A small amount of cinnamon adds just a hint of sweetness.

1 medium yellow onion, chopped

1 can (14.5 ounces) Whole30-compliant fire-roasted tomatoes, undrained

1 cup Whole30-compliant chicken broth or Chicken Bone Broth (page 294)

2 cloves garlic

1½ teaspoons chipotle powder

1 teaspoon dried oregano

1 teaspoon salt

½ teaspoon ground cumin

¼ teaspoon ground cinnamon

2 ½ pounds bone-in chicken thighs, skin removed (see Tip, page 169)

2 packages (12 ounces each) frozen riced cauliflower and sweet potato

1 avocado, halved, pitted, peeled, and sliced

1 lime, cut into wedges

FOR the sauce, in a blender, combine the onion, tomatoes, broth, garlic, chipotle powder, oregano, salt, cumin, and cinnamon. Cover and blend until smooth. Add the sauce to a 6-quart Instant Pot. Add the chicken to the sauce. Lock the lid in place.

SELECT Manual and cook on high pressure for 10 minutes. Use natural release.

MEANWHILE, prepare the riced cauliflower and sweet potato according to the package directions.

TRANSFER the chicken to a plate; let cool slightly. Remove and discard the bones. Use two forks to shred the chicken. Return the chicken to the pot and stir to coat.

SERVE the chicken and sauce in shallow bowls with the cauliflower–sweet potato mixture. Serve with the avocado slices and lime wedges.

INSTANT POT
CHICKEN WITH 40 CLOVES OF GARLIC
FROM HAYLEY AND BILL STALEY OF PRIMAL PALATE

SERVES 4

PREP: 35 minutes

CLOSED POT: 30 minutes

TOTAL: 1 hour 5 minutes

Chicken with 40 Cloves of Garlic is one of our favorite ways to prepare a bone-in chicken, and it couldn't be easier with the help of the Instant Pot. Get ready for some of the most tender chicken you've ever had, plus delightful little cloves of garlic that are mild enough to eat whole!

3 to 3½ pounds meaty chicken pieces (breast halves, drumsticks, and thighs)

½ teaspoon salt

1 tablespoon Clarified Butter (page 296), ghee, or other Whole30-compliant fat

40 cloves garlic (about 2 heads), peeled

2 teaspoons Whole30-compliant Italian seasoning

1 cup Whole30-compliant chicken broth or Chicken Bone Broth (page 294)

2 sprigs fresh rosemary (optional)

2 sprigs fresh thyme (optional)

1 package (5 ounces) mixed salad greens (optional)

Whole30-compliant Italian dressing (optional)

SPRINKLE the chicken with the salt. On a 6-quart Instant Pot, select Sauté and adjust to Normal/Medium. Add the butter. When it's melted, add half the chicken, skin sides down, and cook, turning once, until browned on both sides, about 8 minutes. Transfer to a plate. Repeat with the remaining chicken.

ADD the garlic to the pot. Cook, stirring frequently, 1 to 2 minutes. Add half the chicken and season with half the Italian seasoning. Repeat with the remaining chicken and seasoning. Add the broth. Lock the lid in place.

SELECT Manual and cook on high pressure for 15 minutes. Use natural release for 10 minutes, then quick release.

SERVE the garlic with the chicken. If desired, top with fresh rosemary and thyme, and serve with greens drizzled with dressing.

HAYLEY AND BILL STALEY, PRIMAL PALATE

Hayley and Bill are the founders of *Primal Palate*, one of the premier online destinations for Paleo and Whole30-compliant recipes and meal planning. With the goal of helping to make healthy eating easier for people, Hayley and Bill launched Primal Palate Organic Spices in 2015, bringing to life a line of Whole30 Approved spice blends.

INSTANT POT
RICH AND SAUCY BEEF TACOS
FROM CHARLOTTE SMYTHE OF CONFESSIONS OF A CLEAN FOODIE

SERVES 4

PREP: 30 minutes

CLOSED POT: 25 minutes

TOTAL: 55 minutes

Generously seasoned with garlic, chiles, and warm spices, this versatile beef mixture can be used in a variety of ways. In addition to wrapping it in a lettuce leaf for tacos, you can spoon it over a baked potato or serve it alongside a crunchy slaw.

1 tablespoon Clarified Butter (page 296) or ghee

1 pound lean ground beef

½ teaspoon salt

½ teaspoon black pepper

1 large onion, diced (about 1 cup)

1 medium red bell pepper, diced

2 cloves garlic, minced

1 jalapeño, diced

1 teaspoon smoked paprika

1 teaspoon chili powder

½ teaspoon Korean pepper flakes (optional)

½ teaspoon ground coriander

¼ teaspoon ground cumin

1 tablespoon coconut aminos

1 cup Whole30-compliant canned crushed tomatoes

12 Boston or Bibb lettuce leaves

1 avocado, halved, pitted, peeled, and sliced

Chopped fresh cilantro

ON a 6-quart Instant Pot, select Sauté and adjust to More/High. Add the butter to the pot. When it's hot, add the beef and cook, stirring to break up with a wooden spoon, until browned, about 5 minutes. Season with the salt and pepper. Add the onion, bell pepper, garlic, and jalapeño. Cook, stirring occasionally, until the vegetables are tender, about 5 minutes. Stir in the paprika, chili powder, Korean pepper flakes, coriander, and cumin. Add the coconut aminos and crushed tomatoes. Stir, scraping the browned bits on the bottom of the pot. Lock the lid in place.

SELECT Meat/Stew and cook for 10 minutes. Use natural release for 10 minutes, then use quick release.

SERVE the meat mixture in the lettuce leaves. Top with avocado slices and cilantro.

INSTANT POT
BACON, EGG, AND SWEET POTATO SALAD

SERVES 4

PREP: 40 minutes

CLOSED POT: 15 minutes

TOTAL: 55 minutes

The flavors of this colorful salad balance so beautifully—the sweetness of the potatoes, smokiness of the bacon, and richness of the eggs are all wrapped up in a vinegary mustard dressing and served on peppery arugula with the crunch of toasted walnuts. The salad is best served just slightly warm or at room temperature.

½ cup slivered red onion

⅓ cup cider vinegar

½ teaspoon coarse salt

6 strips Whole30-compliant bacon, chopped

1 to 1¼ pounds sweet potatoes, peeled and cut into 1-inch cubes

8 large eggs

2 teaspoons Whole30-compliant coarse-grain mustard

½ cup avocado oil or walnut oil

6 cups arugula, tough stems trimmed

½ cup chopped walnuts, toasted (see Tip)

IN a small bowl, toss together the onion, vinegar, and ¼ teaspoon of the salt. Cover and let stand at room temperature while preparing the salad.

ON a 6-quart Instant Pot, select Sauté and adjust to Normal/Medium. Add the bacon. Cook, stirring occasionally, until the bacon is crisp, about 8 minutes. Press Cancel. Use a slotted spoon to transfer the bacon to paper towels to drain. Crumble the bacon when cool enough to handle.

CAREFULLY pour 1 cup water into the bacon grease in the pot. Add the sweet potatoes and place the eggs on the potatoes (the eggs should not touch each other). Lock the lid in place.

SELECT Manual and cook on high pressure for 5 minutes. Use quick release.

MEANWHILE, combine water and ice in a large bowl to fill halfway. Carefully transfer the eggs to the ice water to cool, about 10 minutes. Use a slotted spoon to transfer the sweet potatoes to another large bowl; set aside. Peel the eggs and thinly slice or cut into halves or quarters.

DRAIN the onion, reserving the vinegar. In a medium bowl, whisk together ¼ cup of the vinegar, the mustard, and remaining ¼ teaspoon salt. Slowly whisk in the oil until the dressing is well combined and thickened. Drizzle the potatoes with about ¼ cup of the dressing. Toss gently to coat.

TO serve, divide the arugula among four serving plates. Top with the sweet potatoes, eggs, drained onion, and bacon. Drizzle with the remaining dressing. Sprinkle with the walnuts.

TIP *To toast walnuts, heat in a skillet over medium heat, stirring, until fragrant and lightly browned, about 2 minutes.*

INSTANT POT
BRAZILIAN SEAFOOD STEW

SERVES 4

PREP: 20 minutes

CLOSED POT: 25 minutes

TOTAL: 45 minutes

You'll need a firm, thick white fish such as cod, halibut, or red snapper to stand up to the other ingredients—shrimp, sweet potatoes, red bell pepper, diced tomatoes—in this chunky sweet and spicy coconut-infused stew

FOR THE SEASONING AND SEAFOOD

1 teaspoon smoked paprika

½ teaspoon salt

½ teaspoon garlic powder

½ teaspoon ground cumin

¼ teaspoon ground coriander

1 pound red snapper, halibut, or cod fillets, cut into 1-inch pieces

1 pound peeled and deveined medium shrimp

FOR THE STEW

2 tablespoons extra-virgin olive oil

1 medium yellow onion, chopped

2 cloves garlic, minced

1 red bell pepper, sliced into matchsticks

1 package (10 ounces) frozen sweet potatoes

1 can (14 ounces) Whole30-compliant fire-roasted diced tomatoes, undrained

1 can (13.6 ounces) Whole30-compliant coconut milk

½ teaspoon red pepper flakes

2 teaspoons sweet paprika

1 lime, cut into wedges

SEASON THE SEAFOOD: In a small bowl, combine the smoked paprika, salt, garlic powder, cumin, and coriander. Place the cod and shrimp in a large bowl and sprinkle with the seasoning. Set aside.

MAKE THE STEW: On a 6-quart Instant Pot, select Sauté and adjust to Normal/Medium. Add the olive oil to the pot. When it's hot, add the onion and garlic and cook, stirring occasionally, until the onion is softened, about 2 minutes. Press Cancel.

ADD the bell pepper, sweet potatoes, tomatoes, coconut milk, red pepper flakes, and sweet paprika; stir. Add the fish and shrimp to the pot. Stir gently. Lock the lid in place.

SELECT Manual and cook on high pressure for 2 minutes. Use quick release.

SERVE the stew with lime wedges.

INSTANT POT
COFFEE-BRAISED CUMIN-CRUSTED POT ROAST TACOS WITH JALAPEÑO-LIME GUACAMOLE

SERVES 4

PREP: 15 minutes

CLOSED POT: 1 hour 30 minutes

TOTAL: 1 hour 45 minutes

The braising liquid for this hearty dish is coffee. Make sure it's a blend you like and that it's freshly brewed.

2 teaspoons cumin seeds

1 teaspoon garlic powder

1½ teaspoons salt

1 teaspoon black pepper

1 boneless beef chuck pot roast (2 to 2½ pounds), trimmed

1 tablespoon olive oil

1 cup brewed coffee

1 medium yellow onion, cut into thin wedges

2 avocados, halved, peeled, seeded, and coarsely chopped

Grated zest and juice of ½ lime

1 jalapeño, seeded and minced

1 head iceberg or butter lettuce

4 medium radishes, sliced

¼ cup chopped fresh cilantro

IN a small bowl, combine the cumin seeds, garlic powder, 1 teaspoon of the salt, and the pepper. Rub the spice mixture over the roast. Select Sauté on a 6-quart Instant Pot. Add the olive oil. When the oil is hot, add the roast. Cook until browned on all sides, about 10 minutes. Press Cancel. Add the coffee and onion to the pot. Lock the lid in place.

SELECT Manual and cook on high pressure for 60 minutes. Use natural release.

MEANWHILE, for the guacamole, in a medium bowl combine the avocado, lime zest and juice, and jalapeño. Season with the remaining ½ teaspoon salt.

USE a slotted spoon to transfer the beef and onions to a large bowl or platter. Discard the cooking liquid. Use two forks to shred the beef. Serve the beef and onion in lettuce leaves with the guacamole, radishes, and cilantro.

⊕ INSTANT POT
GARLIC-SAGE SAUSAGE LOAF WITH ORANGE-WALNUT GREMOLATA

SERVES 6

PREP: 25 minutes

CLOSED POT: 30 minutes

TOTAL: 55 minutes

When the meatloaf is done cooking, it's allowed to rest for just a few minutes while cubed butternut squash cooks for a mashed-veggie side. A sprinkling of the gremolata—a mixture of chopped toasted walnuts, orange zest, and chopped parsley—adds texture and a spark of fresh flavor to the finished dish.

1 large egg, lightly beaten

1 stalk celery, finely chopped

½ cup finely chopped onion

⅓ cup finely chopped dried apricots

3 cloves garlic, minced

1 teaspoon dried sage, crushed

½ teaspoon fennel seeds, crushed

⅛ teaspoon ground cloves

1 teaspoon salt

¾ teaspoon black pepper

1½ pounds ground pork

1 butternut squash (2¼ to 2½ pounds), peeled, halved, seeded, and cut into 1-inch cubes

1 tablespoon Clarified Butter (page 296) or ghee

½ cup chopped walnuts, toasted (see Tip)

½ cup chopped fresh parsley

1½ teaspoons grated orange zest

IN a large bowl, combine the egg, celery, onion, apricots, garlic, sage, fennel seeds, cloves, ½ teaspoon of the salt, and ½ teaspoon of the pepper. Add the pork; mix well. On a 12 x 18-inch piece of foil, shape the meat mixture into an 8-inch-long loaf. Place in the center of the foil. Wrap the foil around the loaf to enclose. Poke several holes on the top of the foil to allow steam to escape.

PLACE the rack in a 6-quart Instant Pot. Add 1 cup water to the pot. Place the foil packet on the rack. Lock the lid in place.

SELECT Manual and cook on high pressure for 25 minutes. Use natural release.

CAREFULLY remove the foil packet and rack. Pour the water out of the pot. Return the rack to the pot. Add ¾ cup water to the pot. Place the squash on the rack. Lock the lid in place.

SELECT Manual and cook on high pressure for 4 minutes. Use quick release. Transfer the squash to a large bowl. Add the butter, remaining ½ teaspoon salt, and remaining ¼ teaspoon pepper. Use a potato masher or fork to mash the squash.

IN a small bowl, combine the walnuts, parsley, and orange zest. Unwrap the sausage loaf and cut into 6 slices. Serve the mashed squash alongside the slices, sprinkled with the gremolata.

TIP *To toast walnuts, heat in a skillet over medium heat, stirring, until fragrant and lightly browned, about 2 minutes.*

INSTANT POT PORK CHAR SIU

FROM JOSH KATT OF KITCHFIX

SERVES 4

PREP: 45 minutes

CLOSED POT: 40 minutes

TOTAL: 1 hour 25 minutes

Char siu is similar to barbecued pork, but with an Asian twist. In typical recipes, there are usually a lot of preservative-filled ingredients, so I decided to create a healthy version that still delivers on flavor! I love to make a large batch of char siu and enjoy it throughout the week. It's great on cauliflower rice, in lettuce wraps, or served with sautéed cabbage and onions.

FOR THE PORK CHAR SIU

2 tablespoons toasted sesame oil

2 pounds Whole30-compliant pork tenderloin, cut into 4-inch pieces

2 teaspoons salt

1 cup minced white onion

8 cloves garlic, minced

1 tablespoon Whole30-compliant tomato paste

1 tablespoon Whole30-compliant five-spice powder

1 cup pineapple juice

½ cup apple juice concentrate

¼ cup coconut aminos

1 tablespoon Whole30-compliant fish sauce

1 tablespoon red wine vinegar

FOR THE VEGETABLE MEDLEY

1 tablespoon toasted sesame oil

1 tablespoon minced garlic

1 piece (1 inch) fresh ginger, peeled and minced

2 green onions, sliced

1 cup shredded cabbage

1 cup broccoli florets

4 cups cauliflower florets

2 tablespoons coconut aminos

½ teaspoon salt

2 large eggs, lightly beaten

MAKE THE CHAR SIU: On a 6-quart Instant Pot, select Sauté and adjust to Normal/Medium. Add the sesame oil to the pot. When it's hot, add the pork and salt. Cook, stirring occasionally, until browned on all sides, about 5 minutes. Transfer the pork to a medium bowl; set aside. Add the onion and garlic to the pot. Cook, stirring occasionally, until lightly golden, about 5 minutes. Add the tomato paste and five-spice powder. Cook, stirring, for 1 minute. Press Cancel. Add the pineapple juice, apple juice concentrate, coconut aminos, fish sauce, and vinegar. Return the pork to the pot.

LOCK the lid in place. Select Manual and cook on high pressure for 15 minutes. Use quick release. Transfer the pork to a platter; cover to keep warm.

ON the Instant Pot, select Sauté and adjust to Normal/Medium. Bring the sauce to a simmer. Cook, stirring occasionally, until the sauce is reduced by half, 15 to 20 minutes.

MAKE THE VEGETABLE MEDLEY: Meanwhile, heat the sesame oil in an extra-large skillet over medium-high heat. Add the garlic, ginger, and green onions. Cook, stirring, until the garlic is lightly browned, about 30 seconds. Add the cabbage, broccoli, and cauliflower and cook, stirring, for 8 to 10 minutes. Add the coconut aminos, salt, and 2 tablespoons water. When the water has evaporated, move the vegetables to one side of the pan. Add the eggs to the empty side and cook, stirring frequently, to scramble the eggs, 1 to 2 minutes. Stir the eggs into the vegetables.

SERVE the sauce over the pork with the vegetable medley alongside.

INSTANT POT
GREEN CURRY PORK AND NOODLE BOWLS

SERVES 4

PREP: 35 minutes

CLOSED POT: 50 minutes

TOTAL: 1 hour 25 minutes

Thankfully, most of the green (and red) curry pastes that are widely available in grocery stores are Whole30 compliant—ready to give Thai-style curries such as this coconut-sauced dish complex and authentic flavor in one fell swoop!

2½ pounds Whole30-compliant boneless pork shoulder, trimmed and cut into 1-inch pieces

¾ teaspoon salt

½ teaspoon black pepper

2 tablespoons coconut oil

1 can (13.6 ounces) Whole30-compliant coconut milk

¼ cup Whole30-compliant green curry paste

1 small onion, chopped

2 medium red, yellow, or green bell peppers, chopped

1 piece (1 inch) fresh ginger, peeled and grated

3 cloves garlic, minced

1 package (12 ounces) frozen carrot spirals or 4 large carrots, spiralized, long noodles snipped (4 cups)

¼ cup unsweetened shredded coconut, lightly toasted (see Tip)

¼ cup chopped fresh cilantro or basil

1 lime, cut into wedges

SPRINKLE the pork with the salt and pepper. In a 6-quart Instant Pot, use the Sauté setting and heat 1 tablespoon of the coconut oil. Add half the pork and cook until browned, about 5 minutes. Transfer the pork to a plate. Repeat with the remaining 1 tablespoon oil and pork. Return all the pork to the pot. Add the coconut milk, curry paste, onion, bell pepper, ginger, and garlic.

LOCK the lid in place. Select Manual and cook for 10 minutes on high pressure. Use natural release. Stir in the carrot noodles. Cover and let sit for 5 minutes to soften the noodles.

SPOON the curry into bowls, top with lightly toasted coconut and cilantro or basil, and serve with lime wedges.

TIP *To toast coconut, heat in a skillet over medium heat, stirring, until golden brown, about 2 minutes.*

INSTANT POT
CHINESE FIVE-SPICE RIBS
FROM HAYLEY AND BILL STALEY OF PRIMAL PALATE

SERVES 4

PREP: 30 minutes

CLOSED POT: 40 minutes

BAKE: 10 minutes

TOTAL: 1 hour 20 minutes

This recipe has been a family favorite for years, though we streamlined it using our amazing Instant Pot. If you like sweet and savory fall-off-the-bone ribs, then this recipe is for you! It's both easy to make and delicious.

2 tablespoons coconut oil

3 pounds pork baby back ribs, cut into 3 portions

1 tablespoon Whole30-compliant five-spice powder

½ teaspoon paprika

½ teaspoon ground coriander

1 teaspoon Primal Palate curry powder or other Whole30-compliant curry powder

2 cups water or Whole30-compliant chicken broth or Chicken Bone Broth (page 294)

1 package (10 ounces) frozen roasted cauliflower or about 4 cups cauliflower florets, roasted (see Tip)

⅓ cup coconut aminos

2 teaspoons toasted sesame oil

½ teaspoon ground ginger

¼ teaspoon granulated garlic

½ teaspoon Himalayan pink salt

Chopped fresh parsley

IN a large cast-iron skillet, heat the coconut oil over medium-high heat. Add the ribs, meaty sides down, and cook until browned, about 4 minutes. Season the ribs with the five-spice powder, paprika, coriander, and curry powder.

MEANWHILE, place the rack in a 6-quart Instant Pot. Add the water or broth.

PLACE the ribs on the rack. Lock the lid in place. Select Manual and cook on high pressure for 20 minutes. Use natural release for 10 minutes, then quick release.

MEANWHILE, prepare the cauliflower according to the package directions. Preheat the oven to 400°F.

IN a small bowl, stir together the coconut aminos, sesame oil, ginger, and granulated garlic. Place the ribs on a foil-lined rimmed baking sheet and brush with the some of the sauce. Sprinkle with the salt. Bake for 10 minutes, brushing with the remaining sauce after the first 5 minutes. Cut into the ribs and sprinkle with parsley. Serve with the cauliflower.

TIP *If using fresh cauliflower florets, spread them in a shallow baking pan and drizzle with 1 tablespoon olive oil. Bake at 425°F until tender, about 20 minutes.*

INSTANT POT
HERBED CHICKEN WITH FENNEL-CELERY SALAD

SERVES 4

PREP: 20 minutes

CLOSED POT: 55 minutes

TOTAL: 1 hour 15 minutes

The lemony salad that accompanies this tender herbed chicken is so incredibly delicious, and has all kinds of fresh and crunchy going on! Try it as a side with just about any grilled or roasted meat, chicken or fish.

FOR THE CHICKEN

¼ cup Clarified Butter (page 296) or ghee

1½ teaspoons salt

1 teaspoon smoked paprika

1 teaspoon dried thyme

½ teaspoon dried rosemary

½ teaspoon garlic powder

½ teaspoon black pepper

1 whole chicken (3 to 3½ pounds), giblets removed

1 lemon, cut in half

FOR THE SALAD

1 large fennel bulb, trimmed (see Tips) and very thinly sliced

3 stalks celery, very thinly sliced

¼ cup sliced almonds, toasted (see Tips)

¼ cup packed fresh flat-leaf parsley leaves

3 tablespoons extra-virgin olive oil

2 tablespoons fresh lemon juice

¼ teaspoon salt

⅛ to ¼ teaspoon black pepper

MAKE THE CHICKEN: Place the rack in a 6-quart Instant Pot. Add 1½ cups water to the pot.

IN a small bowl, combine the butter, salt, paprika, thyme, rosemary, garlic powder, and black pepper. Distribute half of the butter mixture under the skin of the chicken and rub the other half on the outside. Place the lemon halves in the cavity. Place the chicken, breast side up, on the rack. Lock the lid in place.

SELECT Manual and cook on high pressure for 30 minutes. Use natural release.

MAKE THE SALAD: Meanwhile, in a large bowl, combine the fennel, celery, almonds, parsley, olive oil, and lemon juice. Sprinkle with the salt and pepper; toss to combine.

CAREFULLY transfer the chicken to a serving platter. Discard the cooking liquid. Serve the chicken with the salad.

TIP *To trim a fennel bulb, cut off the stalk about 1 inch from the bulb. Cut a thin slice from the root end and discard. Remove any wilted outer layers. Stand the bulb upright then cut it in half. Cut away and discard the tough core from each half. Slice the fennel according to the recipe.*

TIP *To toast almonds, heat in a skillet over medium heat, stirring, until fragrant and lightly browned, about 2 minutes.*

INSTANT POT SLOPPY JOE–STUFFED MUSHROOMS

SERVES 4

PREP: 30 minutes

CLOSED POT: 25 minutes

TOTAL: 55 minutes

No buns? No big deal! Our saucy, slightly sweet meat mixture is just as yummy spooned over juicy portobello mushroom caps—and is actually much easier to eat with a knife and fork!

4 medium portobello mushrooms (3 to 4 ounces each)

3 green onions

1 pound ground beef

1 small red bell pepper, chopped

1 small stalk celery, thinly sliced

½ cup Whole30-compliant beef broth or Beef Bone Broth (page 294)

⅓ cup Whole30-compliant tomato paste

2 to 3 tablespoons balsamic vinegar

2 cloves garlic, minced

1 teaspoon dried oregano

½ teaspoon salt

½ teaspoon black pepper

¼ cup chopped fresh parsley

USE a damp cloth or paper towel to wipe the mushrooms. Remove the stems from the mushrooms and chop; set aside. Using a small spoon, scrape the gills from the mushroom caps and discard. Set the mushrooms aside. Thinly slice the green onions; separate the white and green parts.

ON a 6-quart Instant Pot, select Sauté and adjust to Normal/Medium. Add the chopped mushroom stems, white parts of the green onions, the ground beef, bell pepper, and celery. Cook, stirring with a wooden spoon to break up the meat, until the meat is browned, about 10 minutes. Press Cancel. Drain any fat.

ADD the broth, tomato paste, 2 tablespoons of the vinegar, the garlic, oregano, salt, and pepper to the meat mixture. Stir until well combined. Place the mushroom caps, stemmed sides down, over the meat mixture, overlapping them slightly, if needed. Lock the lid in place.

SELECT Manual and cook on high pressure for 3 minutes. Use natural release.

TRANSFER the mushrooms to serving plates, stemmed sides up. Stir the meat mixture. If desired, stir in the remaining 1 tablespoon vinegar. Spoon the meat mixture on the mushrooms. Sprinkle with the reserved green onion green parts and the parsley.

INSTANT POT
HOT-AND-SOUR SALMON SALAD

SERVES 4

PREP: 10 minutes

CLOSED POT: 10 minutes

TOTAL: 20 minutes

The contrast of warm salmon with cool greens and crunchy quick-pickled veggies is really nice, but this salad is equally as good when the fish is cooked ahead and chilled so that the whole salad is served cold. Try it with tuna instead of salmon as well.

1 cup cider vinegar

½ cup thinly sliced radishes

½ cup matchstick carrots

½ cup thinly sliced cucumber

½ teaspoon salt

4 skinless salmon fillets (4 ounces each)

Cracked black pepper

2 tablespoons avocado oil

2 tablespoons fresh lemon juice

3 tablespoons Whole30-compliant hot sauce

1 package (5 ounces) mixed salad greens

2 tablespoons chopped fresh chives

IN a small bowl, combine the vinegar, radishes, carrots, cucumber, and ¼ teaspoon of the salt. Let sit while preparing the salmon.

ADD the rack and 1 cup water to a 6-quart Instant Pot. Season the salmon with remaining ¼ teaspoon salt and the pepper. Place the salmon on the rack. Lock the lid in place.

SELECT Manual and cook on high pressure for 3 minutes. Use quick release. Remove the salmon.

FOR the dressing, whisk together the oil, lemon juice, and hot sauce in another small bowl. Drain the vegetables; discard the vinegar. Arrange the greens on serving plates and top with the vegetables. Use a fork to break the salmon into chunks. Add the salmon to the salads. Drizzle with the dressing and sprinkle with the chives.

INSTANT POT
POTATO-JALAPEÑO FRITTATA WITH BACON

SERVES 4

PREP: 15 minutes

CLOSED POT: 1 hour 5 minutes

COOL: 10 minutes

TOTAL: 1 hour 30 minutes

The trio of bacon, eggs, and potatoes is classic hearty break-fast food. Here, they're spiced up with pickled jalapeños and a topping of salsa and hot sauce (if you like).

1½ pounds small red or gold potatoes

8 large eggs

½ cup thinly sliced green onions, plus more for serving

4 slices Whole30-compliant bacon, crisp-cooked and crumbled

¼ cup Whole30-compliant pickled jalapeños, chopped

¼ cup chopped fresh parsley

½ teaspoon salt

½ teaspoon black pepper

Clarified Butter (page 296) or ghee, for greasing

½ teaspoon paprika

Whole30-compliant salsa

Whole30 Sriracha (page 179) or Whole30-compliant hot sauce (optional)

PLACE the potatoes in a 6-quart Instant Pot. Add ½ cup water. Lock the lid in place.

SELECT Manual and cook on high pressure for 5 minutes. Use natural release. Discard water. Let the potatoes cool until easy to handle.

MEANWHILE, combine the eggs, green onions, bacon, pickled jala-peños, parsley, salt, and black pepper. Slice the potatoes. Carefully stir into the egg mixture.

PLACE the rack in the pot. Add 1½ cups water. Grease a 1-quart soufflé dish with butter or ghee. Pour the egg mixture into the prepared dish. Sprinkle with the paprika. Place the dish on the rack. Lock the lid in place.

SELECT Manual and cook on high pressure for 20 minutes. Use natural release. Carefully remove the dish. Let the frittata cool on a wire rack for at least 10 minutes before slicing.

SPOON salsa on servings, top with additional sliced green onions, and serve with sriracha or hot sauce if desired.

INSTANT POT
CHINESE SESAME CHICKEN
FROM ALEX SNODGRASS OF THE DEFINED DISH

SERVES 4

PREP: 30 minutes

CLOSED POT: 15 minutes

TOTAL: 45 minutes

Here is my Whole30 take on the Chinese takeout staple. It's clean, absolutely delicious, and will leave you oh-so satisfied. The best part? It's one of my kids' favorites!

2 pounds boneless, skinless chicken breasts, sliced into thin strips

½ teaspoon black pepper

1 tablespoon plus 1 teaspoon arrowroot powder

3 tablespoons avocado oil

½ cup Whole30-compliant chicken broth or Chicken Bone Broth (page 294)

¼ cup coconut aminos

1 tablespoon rice vinegar

2 teaspoons toasted sesame oil

½ teaspoon Whole30-compliant fish sauce

¼ teaspoon red pepper flakes (optional)

1 package (10.8 ounces) frozen broccoli florets, or 4 cups broccoli florets, steamed (see Tips)

2 tablespoons sesame seeds, toasted (see Tips)

2 green onions, sliced

PLACE the chicken in a medium bowl and sprinkle with the pepper. Add 1 tablespoon of the arrowroot and toss to coat.

ON a 6-quart Instant Pot, select Sauté and adjust to Normal/Medium. Add the avocado oil. When it's hot, add half the chicken and cook, stirring once, until golden brown, about 6 minutes. Transfer to a plate. Repeat with the remaining chicken. Select Cancel.

MEANWHILE, in a small bowl, whisk together the broth, coconut aminos, vinegar, sesame oil, fish sauce, and remaining 1 teaspoon arrowroot until the arrowroot is dissolved. Add red pepper flakes (if using).

RETURN all of the chicken to the pot. Pour the sauce over the chicken. Lock the lid in place. Select Manual and cook for 6 minutes. Use quick release. Stir the chicken. Let stand until slightly thickened, 5 to 10 minutes. Meanwhile, cook the broccoli according to package directions.

SERVE the chicken over the broccoli. Sprinkle with the sesame seeds and green onions.

TIP *To toast sesame seeds, heat in a skillet over medium heat, stirring, until fragrant and lightly browned, about 2 minutes.*

TIP *To steam fresh broccoli florets, combine in a microwave-safe bowl with 3 tablespoons water. Cover and microwave on high for 3 minutes or until crisp-tender.*

INSTANT POT
SCALLOPS AND POTATOES WITH GARLIC-SAFFRON AIOLI

SERVES 4

PREP: 40 minutes

CLOSED POT: 25 minutes

TOTAL: 1 hour 5 minutes

Although the saffron in the garlic mayonnaise is optional, it does give the aioli a beautiful sunny yellow color and infuses it with a distinctive floral, slightly pungent flavor. Saffron—the stamens of a type of crocus that have to be hand-harvested—is not cheap, but thankfully, a very little goes a long way.

1 teaspoon ground coriander

¾ teaspoon black pepper

⅛ teaspoon ground nutmeg

1 pound fresh or thawed frozen sea scallops

3 tablespoons extra-virgin olive oil

12 ounces small round red potatoes, quartered

2 medium parsnips, peeled and cut crosswise into ½-inch-thick slices

1 medium shallot, cut into wedges

1 teaspoon coarse salt

1 medium zucchini or yellow summer squash, cut into 1½-inch pieces

½ cup Whole30-compliant avocado mayonnaise

2 tablespoons fresh lemon juice

1 small clove garlic, minced

Pinch saffron threads, crushed (optional)

Dash coarse salt

½ cup fresh basil leaves

IN a small bowl, combine the coriander, ¼ teaspoon of the pepper, and the nutmeg. Sprinkle the seasoning on the scallops.

ON a 6-quart Instant Pot, select Sauté and adjust to Normal/Medium. Add 1 tablespoon of the olive oil to the pot. When it's hot, add half the scallops and cook, turning once, just until browned, 2 to 3 minutes. Transfer the scallops to a plate; cover to keep warm. Repeat with 1 tablespoon of the oil and the remaining scallops.

IN a large bowl, combine the potatoes, parsnips, and shallot. Drizzle with the remaining 1 tablespoon oil and sprinkle with the salt and remaining ½ teaspoon pepper. Toss to coat.

ADD ¾ cup water to the pot. Place the rack in the bottom of the pot. Add the potato mixture to the rack. Lock the lid in place.

SELECT Manual and cook on high pressure for 9 minutes. Use quick release. Arrange the scallops and zucchini in an even layer on the potato mixture. Lock the lid in place.

SELECT Manual and cook on high pressure for 1 minute. Use quick release.

IN a small bowl, stir together the mayonnaise, lemon juice, garlic, saffron (if using), and the dash salt.

SPRINKLE the scallops and vegetables with the basil and serve with the aioli.

INSTANT POT
CHICKEN AND VEGETABLE SOUP

SERVES 4

PREP: 20 minutes

CLOSED POT: 25 minutes

TOTAL: 45 minutes

It's important to use a quick release when making this Italian-style chicken soup so that the zucchini doesn't get overcooked and mushy sitting in the hot broth during a natural release, but stays bright green and pleasantly crisp-tender.

2 tablespoons Clarified Butter (page 296) or ghee

1½ pounds boneless, skinless chicken breasts, cut into 1-inch pieces

1 large yellow onion, chopped

1 teaspoon salt

¼ teaspoon red pepper flakes

4 cups Whole30-compliant chicken broth or Chicken Bone Broth (page 294)

1 can (14.5 ounces) Whole30-compliant diced tomatoes, undrained

1 medium zucchini, halved lengthwise and sliced ½ inch thick

2 cloves garlic, minced

1½ teaspoons Whole30-compliant Italian seasoning

2 tablespoons chopped fresh basil

ON a 6-quart Instant Pot, select Sauté and adjust to Normal/Medium. Add the butter, chicken, onion, salt, and red pepper flakes. Cook, stirring occasionally, until the chicken is opaque, 4 to 5 minutes. Select Cancel. Stir in the broth, tomatoes, zucchini, garlic, and Italian seasoning. Lock the lid in place.

SELECT Manual and cook on high pressure for 5 minutes. Use quick release.

SERVE the soup topped with the basil.

INSTANT POT
SMOKY BEEF AND BACON CHILI

SERVES 4

PREP: 40 minutes

CLOSED POT: 40 minutes

TOTAL: 1 hour 20 minutes

The beef for this chili is cooked in bacon drippings, which is where all of the great smoky flavor comes from. It's got a generous dose of chili powder—2 whole tablespoons! If you like your chili with some serious heat, use a hot chili powder or 1 tablespoon each of mild and hot.

1 pound Whole30-compliant bacon, chopped

1 pound lean ground beef

2 tablespoons mild chili powder

½ teaspoon salt

1 can (28 ounces) Whole30-compliant diced tomatoes, undrained

1 cup Whole30-compliant beef broth or Beef Bone Broth (page 294)

1 medium onion, chopped

1 medium red bell pepper, chopped

1 medium jalapeño, seeded and chopped

2 cloves garlic, minced

Chopped fresh cilantro (optional)

ON a 6-quart Instant Pot, select Sauté and adjust to Normal/Medium. Add the bacon and cook, stirring occasionally, until crisp, about 10 minutes. Transfer the bacon to paper towels.

ADD the ground beef to the bacon drippings in the pot. Cook, stirring frequently, until browned, 8 to 10 minutes. Drain off the fat, if needed. Return three-fourths of the bacon to the pot. Stir in the chili powder and salt. Stir in the tomatoes, broth, onion, bell pepper, jalapeño, and garlic. Lock the lid in place.

SELECT Manual and cook on high pressure for 20 minutes. Use quick release.

SERVE the chili topped with the remaining bacon, and cilantro if desired.

INSTANT POT
SPARERIBS WITH WHITE BBQ SAUCE AND COLLARD GREENS

SERVES 4

PREP: 15 minutes

CLOSED POT: 1 hour

TOTAL: 1 hour 20 minutes

Never heard of white barbecue sauce? You will be spreading the good word—and making this dish again and again—after tasting it. The vinegary mayo-based sauce is a specialty of northern Alabama and tastes not unlike the ever-popular ranch dressing.

FOR THE RIBS

1½ teaspoons salt

1 teaspoon black pepper

1 teaspoon garlic powder

1 teaspoon onion powder

1 rack pork spareribs or baby back ribs (about 4 pounds), membrane removed (see Tip) and cut into 4 portions

¼ cup cider vinegar

FOR THE SAUCE

½ cup Whole30-compliant avocado mayonnaise or Basic Mayonnaise (page 295)

2 tablespoons cider vinegar

½ teaspoon Whole30-compliant hot sauce

½ teaspoon coconut aminos

¼ teaspoon onion powder

¼ teaspoon garlic powder

⅛ teaspoon salt

⅛ teaspoon black pepper

FOR THE COLLARD GREENS

2 tablespoons extra-virgin olive oil

2 cloves garlic, minced

1 bag (1 pound) cleaned and chopped collard greens or 2 bunches collard greens, stemmed and chopped

1 tablespoon cider vinegar

½ teaspoon salt

¼ teaspoon red pepper flakes

MAKE THE RIBS: In a small bowl, combine the salt, pepper, garlic powder, and onion powder. Sprinkle over the ribs. In a 6-quart Instant Pot, combine 1 cup water and the vinegar. Add the rack and place the ribs on the rack. Lock the lid in place.

SELECT Manual and cook on high pressure for 20 minutes. Use natural pressure for 10 minutes, then quick release the remaining pressure. Remove the rack and discard the cooking liquid.

MAKE THE SAUCE: Meanwhile, in a small bowl, whisk together the mayonnaise, vinegar, hot sauce, coconut aminos, onion powder, garlic powder, salt, and pepper.

PREHEAT the broiler. Place the ribs on a foil-lined large rimmed baking sheet, meaty sides up. Spoon the sauce on the ribs. Broil until bubbly and starting to brown, about 3 minutes.

MAKE THE COLLARD GREENS: On the Instant Pot, select Sauté and adjust to Normal/Medium. Add the olive oil. When it's hot, add the garlic and cook, stirring, for 30 seconds. Add the collard greens. Use tongs to toss the greens with the oil and garlic. Press Cancel. Add 1 cup of water to the pot. Lock the lid in place.

SELECT Manual and cook on high pressure for 3 minutes. Use quick release. Drain and discard the liquid. Use tongs to transfer the collard greens to a bowl. Toss with the vinegar, salt, and red pepper flakes. Serve the ribs with the collard greens.

TIP *To remove the membrane (silver skin) from the back of the ribs, start at one end of the rack and slide a table knife under the membrane. Lift and loosen the membrane. Use a paper towel to grab the edge of the membrane and pull it off. Or you can ask your butcher to do this for you.*

INSTANT POT
SPICED SHREDDED PORK WITH APPLE-BROCCOLI SLAW

SERVES 8

PREP: 20 minutes

CLOSED POT: 1 hour 30 minutes

TOTAL: 1 hour 50 minutes

This classic Mexican-spiced pork shoulder is delicious served with the crunchy apple-broccoli salad, but it's also just the thing to tuck into a lettuce wrap and top with your favorite salsa and/or guacamole.

3 pounds Whole30-compliant boneless pork shoulder, trimmed and cut into 3 portions

1¼ teaspoons salt

½ teaspoon black pepper

2 tablespoons olive oil

1 cup Whole30-compliant chicken broth or Chicken Bone Broth (page 294)

4 cloves garlic, minced

1 tablespoon chili powder

1 teaspoon ground coriander

1 teaspoon ground cumin

¾ cup Whole30-compliant avocado mayonnaise or Basic Mayonnaise (page 295)

3 tablespoons cider vinegar

1 package (14 ounces) broccoli slaw mix

1 large tart apple, cored and cut into matchsticks

1 tablespoon fresh lime juice

SEASON the pork with 1 teaspoon of the salt and the pepper. On a 6-quart Instant Pot, select Sauté and adjust to Normal/Medium. Add the oil to the pot. When it's hot, add the pork and cook, turning occasionally, until browned, about 10 minutes. Transfer the pork to a bowl. Add the broth and garlic to the pot, stirring to scrape any browned bits from the bottom. Select Cancel.

SEASON the browned pork with the chili powder, coriander, and cumin. Return the pork to the pot. Lock the lid in place.

SELECT Manual and cook on high pressure for 60 minutes. Use natural release. Transfer to a bowl.

MEANWHILE for the slaw, in a medium bowl, stir together the mayonnaise, vinegar, and remaining ¼ teaspoon salt. Stir in the broccoli slaw mix and apple. Cover and refrigerate until serving.

USE two forks to shred the pork. Drizzle the pork with 1 cup of the cooking liquid and the lime juice and toss to combine. Serve the pork with the slaw.

INSTANT POT
SPICED COCONUT CHICKEN WITH CUMIN CAULIFLOWER RICE

SERVES 4

PREP: 30 minutes

CLOSED POT: 10 minutes

TOTAL: 40 minutes

You will be amazed at the difference lightly crushing and toasting cumin seeds makes to the intensity of their flavor. It's just so much fresher and more interesting. Crushing them in a mortar and pestle is the easiest way, but if you don't have one, place the seeds in a small plastic bag and roll over them lightly with a rolling pin.

4 tablespoons coconut oil

4 skinless, boneless chicken breast halves (1½ pounds total)

1 cup chopped cored fresh tomatoes

¼ cup Whole30-compliant chicken broth or Chicken Bone Broth (page 294)

1 to 2 pitted dates

1 tablespoon Whole30-compliant red curry paste

4 cloves garlic, minced

½ teaspoon ground ginger

½ teaspoon ground coriander

¾ teaspoon salt

¾ cup Whole30-compliant canned coconut milk (see Tip)

2 tablespoons Clarified Butter (page 296) or ghee

1 package (16 ounces) fresh cauliflower crumbles or 4 cups raw cauliflower crumbles (see page 60)

1 teaspoon cumin seeds, crushed

⅓ cup chopped fresh cilantro

¼ cup thinly sliced green onion tops

ON a 6-quart Instant Pot, select Sauté and adjust to Normal/Medium. Add 1 tablespoon of the oil to the pot. When it's hot, add half the chicken. Cook, turning once, until browned, 4 to 6 minutes. Transfer the chicken to a bowl. Repeat with 1 tablespoon oil and the remaining chicken. Return all the chicken to the pot.

IN a medium bowl, combine the tomatoes, broth, dates, curry paste, garlic, ginger, coriander, and ½ teaspoon of the salt. Add to the pot with the chicken. Lock the lid in place.

SELECT Manual and cook on high pressure for 4 minutes. Use quick release. Transfer the chicken to a cutting board and cut into bite-size pieces. Set aside.

ADD the coconut milk and butter to the tomato mixture in the pot. Use an immersion blender to blend until smooth. (Or, transfer the tomato mixture to a regular blender; cover and blend until smooth.) Add the chicken to the sauce in the pot. Select Sauté and adjust to Normal/Medium. Cook, stirring occasionally, until slightly thickened, 3 to 5 minutes.

MEANWHILE, in a large skillet, heat the remaining 2 tablespoons oil over medium heat. When it's hot, add the cauliflower, cumin seeds, and remaining ¼ teaspoon salt. Cook, stirring occasionally, until the cauliflower is crisp-tender and starting to brown, 4 to 6 minutes.

SERVE the chicken and sauce on the cauliflower and sprinkle with the cilantro and green onion tops.

> **TIP** *Canned coconut milk separates in the can with the cream rising to the top. Make sure to whisk the coconut milk well before measuring.*

INSTANT POT
INDIAN BUTTER CHICKEN
FROM CRISTINA CURP OF THE CASTAWAY KITCHEN

SERVES 4

PREP: 30 minutes

CLOSED POT: 30 minutes

TOTAL: 1 hour 10 minutes

We like using ghee to make butter chicken without, well, the butter! Creamy and rich, finished off with fresh cilantro and crunchy almonds, this anti-inflammatory comfort dish really hits the spot.

3 tablespoons Clarified Butter (page 296) or ghee

1 large sweet onion, diced

1 piece (2 inches) fresh ginger, peeled and minced

3 cloves garlic, minced

2 bay leaves

8 boneless, skinless chicken thighs (2 to 2½ pounds)

1 tablespoon Whole30-compliant garam masala

1½ tablespoons ground turmeric

1 tablespoon ground cumin

1 teaspoon fine sea salt

1½ teaspoons black pepper

2 tablespoons fresh lemon juice

1 teaspoon cider vinegar

1 cinnamon stick

1 cup Whole30-compliant coconut milk (see Tip)

1 tablespoon grass-fed beef gelatin

½ cup chopped almonds

1 package (12 ounces) frozen riced cauliflower or 3 cups raw cauliflower rice (see page 60)

⅓ cup chopped fresh cilantro

ON a 6-quart Instant Pot, select Sauté and adjust to Normal/Medium. Add the butter. When it's hot, add the onion, ginger, garlic, and bay leaves. Cook until the onion is tender, 5 to 6 minutes. Add the chicken, garam masala, turmeric, cumin, salt, and pepper and stir to combine. Cook, stirring occasionally, until the chicken is lightly browned, about 10 minutes. Add the lemon juice, vinegar, and cinnamon stick. Stir, scraping up any browned bits from the bottom of the pot. Stir in the coconut milk. Bring to a simmer. Select Cancel. Stir in the gelatin until dissolved. Lock the lid in place.

SELECT Manual and cook on high pressure for 20 minutes. Use quick release.

SELECT Sauté and adjust to Normal/Medium. Stir in the almonds. Simmer until the liquid is reduced by one-third, about 10 minutes.

MEANWHILE, prepare the cauliflower rice.

REMOVE and discard the bay leaves and cinnamon stick. Serve the chicken mixture over the cauliflower and top with the cilantro.

TIP *Canned coconut milk separates in the can with the cream rising to the top. Make sure to whisk the coconut milk well before measuring.*

CRISTINA CURP, THE CASTAWAY KITCHEN

Cristina Curp is a Miami native, published author, and the creative mind behind *The Castaway Kitchen*, a blog dedicated to delicious, healing recipes. Two years post-partum, she found herself at rock bottom, physically and emotionally. Cristina turned her life around with the Whole30! Learning she could manage her autoimmune conditions, including Hidradenitis Suppurativa, with food and lifestyle changes ignited a fire. She now uses her chef skills and infectious positivity to help and inspire others to find health and wellness.

⊕ INSTANT POT TURKEY CHILI

SERVES 4

PREP: 20 minutes

CLOSED POT: 20 minutes

TOTAL: 40 minutes

On a cool fall night when you're craving a bowl of classic chili, turn to this recipe, which can be done—start to finish—in just about 40 minutes. A topping of cubed avocado provides a cooling, creamy contrast to the spicy chili.

1 tablespoon extra-virgin olive oil

1 package (19.2 ounces) lean ground turkey

1 large yellow onion, chopped

2 cloves garlic, minced

1 teaspoon salt

1 can (28 ounces) Whole30-compliant crushed tomatoes

1 medium yellow bell pepper, chopped

1 medium jalapeño, seeded and chopped

1 tablespoon chili powder

1 medium avocado, halved, pitted, peeled, and diced

2 tablespoons chopped fresh cilantro

ON a 6-quart Instant Pot, select Sauté and adjust to Normal/Medium. Add the oil to the pot. When it's hot, add the turkey, onion, garlic, and salt. Cook, stirring occasionally with a wooden spoon to break up the meat, until browned, 8 to 10 minutes. Select Cancel.

STIR in ½ cup water, the tomatoes, bell pepper, jalapeño, and chili powder. Lock the lid in place. Select Manual and cook on high pressure for 5 minutes. Use quick release.

TOP servings with the avocado and cilantro.

INSTANT POT
POLISH SAUSAGE AND CABBAGE SOUP

SERVES 6

PREP: 20 minutes

CLOSED POT: 1 hour 10 minutes

TOTAL: 1 hour 30 minutes

Once you put all of the ingredients into the pot and push the button, you have more than an hour to do other things while the pot comes to pressure, the soup cooks, and the pot releases—and then this warming, comforting one-dish dinner is ready!

---

4 slices Whole30-compliant bacon, chopped

1 medium yellow onion, chopped

½ cup chopped celery

6 cups Whole30-compliant chicken or Chicken Bone Broth (page 294)

1 package (10 ounces) shredded cabbage

3 medium carrots, peeled and chopped

1 large russet potato, peeled and cubed

½ teaspoon dried thyme

¼ teaspoon salt

¼ teaspoon white pepper

1 bay leaf

2 tablespoons cider vinegar

1 package (12 to 14 ounces) Whole30-compliant kielbasa, sliced

Fresh dill

ON a 6-quart Instant Pot, select Sauté and adjust to Normal/Medium. Add the bacon and cook until crisp, about 5 minutes. Use a slotted spoon to transfer the bacon to paper towels. Add the onion and celery to the bacon drippings in the pot. Cook, stirring occasionally, until softened, 2 to 3 minutes. Add the broth, cabbage, carrots, potato, thyme, salt, pepper, bay leaf, and vinegar. Lock the lid in place.

SELECT Manual and cook on high pressure for 20 minutes. Use natural release.

REMOVE and discard the bay leaf. Add the kielbasa. Cover and let stand until heated through, about 5 minutes. Sprinkle servings with the crumbled bacon and fresh dill.

INSTANT POT
ZA'ATAR PULLED PORK WITH SPICED BROCCOLI-CAULIFLOWER RICE

SERVES 6

PREP: 20 minutes

CLOSED POT: 1 hour 30 minutes

TOTAL: 2 hours

Za'atar is a Middle Eastern spice blend with a nutty flavor from toasted sesame seeds and a delightful tanginess from sumac, the dried and ground vibrantly red berries of a bush native to the region. Za'atar is becoming increasingly available commercially, but if you can't find it at your regular supermarket, look in a Middle Eastern market or online.

FOR THE PORK

2 tablespoons Whole30-compliant za'atar seasoning

1 pork shoulder (3 to 4 pounds), trimmed

1 tablespoon extra-virgin olive oil

1 medium yellow onion, chopped

1 serrano chile pepper, seeded and finely chopped

4 Roma (plum) tomatoes, cored and chopped

FOR THE SPICED BROCCOLI-CAULIFLOWER RICE

2 packages (10 ounces each) frozen riced cauliflower and broccoli

1 tablespoon Clarified Butter (page 296) or ghee

½ teaspoon ground turmeric

½ teaspoon ground coriander

½ teaspoon ground cumin

¼ teaspoon salt

¼ teaspoon black pepper

MAKE THE PORK: Rub the za'atar on all sides of the pork. On a 6-quart Instant Pot, select Sauté and adjust to Normal/Medium. Add the olive oil. When it's hot, add the roast and cook until browned on all sides, about 10 minutes. Remove the roast from the pot. Add the onion and serrano pepper and cook just until softened, about 2 minutes. Add the tomatoes and cook just until softened, about 3 minutes. Return the roast to the pot. Spoon some of the tomato mixture over the roast. Lock the lid in place.

SELECT Manual and cook on high pressure for 60 minutes. Use natural release.

MAKE THE BROCCOLI-CAULIFLOWER RICE: Prepare the riced broccoli and cauliflower according to the package directions. Stir in the butter, turmeric, coriander, and cumin. Sprinkle with the salt and pepper.

REMOVE the pork from the pot. Discard any fat and place the pork in a large bowl. Strain the cooking liquid through a fine-mesh sieve; add the solids to the pork and discard the cooking liquid. Use two forks to shred the pork.

SERVE the shredded pork over the broccoli-cauliflower rice.

INSTANT POT
PICADILLO-STYLE BEEF

SERVES 6

PREP: 20 minutes

CLOSED POT: 1 hour 15 minutes

TOTAL: 1 hour 35 minutes

Picadillo, beef or pork in a well-seasoned tomato sauce, is popular in many Latin American countries. In Cuba it's usually served with beans and rice, in Mexico it's used as a filling, and in this recipe it is served with potatoes. It usually contains both golden raisins and olives and/or capers. The sweetness of the raisins contrasted with the briny, salty olives adds interest and complexity to the dish.

2 tablespoons extra-virgin olive oil

1 medium yellow onion, finely chopped

1 medium red bell pepper, finely chopped

4 cloves garlic, minced

1 boneless beef chuck roast (2 to 2½ pounds), cut into 3 or 4 pieces

1 can (8 ounces) Whole30-compliant tomato sauce

1 tablespoon red wine vinegar

2 teaspoons ground cumin

2 teaspoons dried oregano

1 teaspoon salt

¼ teaspoon black pepper

6 medium Yukon Gold potatoes, quartered

½ cup quartered pitted Whole30-compliant manzanilla olives or other green olives

⅓ cup unsulfured golden raisins

¼ cup Whole30-compliant capers, drained

ON a 6-quart Instant Pot, select Sauté and adjust to Normal/Medium. Add the olive oil. When it's hot, add the onion, bell pepper, and garlic and cook, stirring occasionally, until softened, 3 to 5 minutes. Add the beef and cook until browned, about 5 minutes. Press Cancel. Add the tomato sauce, vinegar, cumin, oregano, salt, and pepper; stir to combine. Lock the lid in place.

SELECT Manual and cook on high pressure for 50 minutes. Use quick release.

ADD the potatoes, olives, raisins, and capers. Lock the lid in place. Select Manual and cook on high pressure for 8 minutes. Use quick release.

USE a slotted spoon to remove the potatoes, vegetables, and beef. Use two forks to shred the beef. Serve the beef and vegetables over the potatoes.

⬤ INSTANT POT PORCHETTA

SERVES 4

PREP: 15 minutes

CLOSED POT: 30 minutes

TOTAL: 45 minutes

Traditional Italian porchetta is a laborious dish of pork shoulder or loin that is slathered with seasonings, wrapped in bacon, marinated overnight, and slow roasted. This recipe uses the same seasonings—garlic, fennel, rosemary, and thyme—but the pork cooks in just 15 minutes in the Instant Pot. Cooking under pressure helps the meat absorb the flavors in the same way long marinating does.

3 tablespoons extra-virgin olive oil

4 cloves garlic, minced

1 tablespoon fennel seeds

½ teaspoon dried thyme

½ teaspoon dried rosemary

1¼ teaspoons salt

1 Whole30-compliant pork tenderloin (1½ pounds), fat trimmed

6 slices Whole30-compliant bacon

1 package (9 ounces) shaved Brussels sprouts (or see Tip)

2 medium shallots, sliced

¼ teaspoon coarse black pepper

PLACE the rack in a 6-quart Instant Pot. Add 1 cup water to the pot.

USING a mortar and pestle, combine 1 tablespoon of the olive oil, the garlic, fennel seeds, thyme, rosemary, and 1 teaspoon of the salt until a paste forms. Rub the paste all over the pork. Tuck the small end under. Wrap the bacon around the tenderloin. Place the tenderloin on the rack. Lock the lid in place.

SELECT Manual and cook on high pressure for 15 minutes. Use natural release. Remove the pork from the pot; cover with foil to keep warm. Discard the cooking liquid.

ON the Instant Pot, select Sauté and adjust to More/High. Add the remaining 2 tablespoons olive oil. When it's hot, add the Brussels sprouts, shallots, and remaining ¼ teaspoon salt. Cook until tender, 4 to 6 minutes. Sprinkle with coarse black pepper.

SLICE the tenderloin and serve with the Brussels sprouts.

> **TIP** *To shave your own Brussels sprouts, use a food processor to shave about 10 ounces trimmed Brussels sprouts. You should have about 5 cups shaved sprouts.*

INSTANT POT
MUSHROOM PORK CHOPS

SERVES 4

PREP: 30 minutes

CLOSED POT: 15 minutes

TOTAL: 45 minutes

Mushroom lovers, make this dish! Tender, juicy pork chops are topped with a mountain of saucy mushrooms and crisp-cooked bacon—and served with a side of fresh, lemony, bright-green broccoli.

4 tablespoons Clarified Butter (page 296) or ghee

2 packages (8 ounces each) sliced cremini mushrooms

½ cup sliced yellow onion

2 cloves garlic, minced

¾ teaspoon salt

1¼ cups Whole30-compliant chicken broth or Chicken Bone Broth (page 294)

4 Whole30-compliant bone-in, 1-inch-thick pork loin chops (2 pounds total)

½ teaspoon dried thyme

¼ teaspoon black pepper

2 tablespoons arrowroot powder

1 pound broccoli florets

1 teaspoon fresh lemon juice

4 slices Whole30-compliant bacon, crisp-cooked and crumbled

ON a 6-quart Instant Pot, select Sauté and adjust to Normal/Medium. Add 2 tablespoons of the butter to the pot. When it's hot, add the mushrooms, onion, garlic, and ½ teaspoon of the salt and cook, stirring occasionally, until the vegetables are browned and tender, 6 to 8 minutes. Select Cancel. Stir in 1 cup of the broth. Sprinkle the pork chops with the thyme and pepper; add to the pot. Lock the lid in place.

SELECT Manual and cook on high pressure for 4 minutes. Use quick release. Transfer the pork chops to a serving platter; cover to keep warm.

IN a small bowl, whisk together the arrowroot and remaining ¼ cup broth. Add the arrowroot mixture to the pot. Select Sauté and adjust to Normal/Medium. Cook until the sauce comes to a simmer. Select Cancel.

PLACE the broccoli florets in a microwave-safe dish and add 3 tablespoons water. Cover and microwave, stirring once, until tender, about 5 minutes. Stir in the lemon juice, remaining 2 tablespoons butter, and remaining ¼ teaspoon salt.

SERVE the mushroom sauce over the pork chops and top with the bacon. Serve the broccoli alongside.

> **TIP** *Here's an easy, neat way to quickly cook bacon when you don't need the drippings: Place the slices of bacon between two paper towels on a microwave-safe plate. Microwave on high for 1 minute. Change the paper towels and microwave in 15-second increments until the bacon is the desired doneness.*

INSTANT POT
JERK CHICKEN WITH PEPPERS AND PINEAPPLE

SERVES 4

PREP: 20 minutes

CLOSED POT: 25 minutes

TOTAL: 45 minutes

Although jerk seasoning relies on a blend of flavors, it's the allspice that is the most distinctive. In fact, in Jamaica, real jerk chicken is cooked over smoky fires made with pimento wood (from the tree that produces allspice berries). If you like your jerk chicken on the spicier side, simply increase the cayenne pepper a bit or serve with hot sauce.

½ cup Whole30-compliant chicken broth or Chicken Bone Broth (page 294)

2 medium red onions, cut into large wedges

2 red bell peppers, cut into 1-inch pieces

2 cups 1-inch cubes pineapple

1 jalapeño, seeded and chopped

¾ teaspoon salt

½ teaspoon ground allspice

½ teaspoon garlic powder

¼ teaspoon ground cinnamon

⅛ teaspoon cayenne pepper

4 boneless, skinless chicken breasts (1½ pounds)

1 package (12 ounces) frozen riced cauliflower or 3 cups raw cauliflower rice (see page 60)

Chopped fresh cilantro (optional)

IN a 6-quart Instant Pot, stir together the broth, onions, bell peppers, pineapple, and jalapeño.

IN a small bowl, stir together the salt, allspice, garlic powder, cinnamon, and cayenne pepper. Sprinkle the chicken with the seasoning. Place the chicken in a single layer on top of the onion mixture. Lock the lid in place.

SELECT Manual and cook on high pressure for 9 minutes. Use quick release.

MEANWHILE, prepare the cauliflower rice according to the package directions.

SERVE the chicken and vegetables over the cauliflower rice; drizzle with some of the cooking juices. If desired, top with cilantro.

INSTANT POT
WHOLE CAULIFLOWER IN SPICED TOMATO-MEAT SAUCE

SERVES 4

PREP: 20 minutes

CLOSED POT: 1 hour

TOTAL: 1 hour 20 minutes

This tomato sauce, infused with the traditional Greek flavors of garlic, onion, chile, oregano, cinnamon, and bay leaf, tastes especially authentic made with lamb—but ground beef is delicious too!

1 pound ground lamb or beef

1 medium yellow onion, chopped

3 cloves garlic, minced

2 teaspoons ancho chile powder

1 teaspoon dried oregano, crushed

½ teaspoon salt

1 stick (3 inches) cinnamon

1 bay leaf

¼ cup Whole30-compliant tomato paste

1 can (14.5 ounces) Whole30-compliant beef broth or 1¾ cups Beef Bone Broth (page 294)

1 can (14.5 ounces) Whole30-compliant diced tomatoes, undrained

1 medium head cauliflower

¼ cup chopped fresh parsley

ON a 6-quart Instant Pot, select Sauté and adjust to Normal/Medium. Add the lamb and onion. Cook, stirring occasionally with a wooden spoon to break up the meat, until browned, 8 to 10 minutes. Add the garlic, chile powder, oregano, salt, cinnamon stick, and bay leaf. Cook for 1 minute. Add the tomato paste and cook for 1 minute. Stir in the broth and tomatoes. Remove the leaves from the cauliflower. Trim the stem so the cauliflower stands upright. Add the cauliflower, stem side down, to the pot. Lock the lid in place.

SELECT Manual and cook on high pressure for 10 minutes. Use quick release.

CAREFULLY remove the cauliflower from the pot. Cut into 4 wedges. Discard the cinnamon stick and bay leaf. Stir the parsley into the sauce. Serve the sauce with the cauliflower.

BASICS

⬤ INSTANT POT
CHICKEN BONE BROTH

MAKES 8 CUPS

PREP: 15 minutes

CLOSED POT: 1 hour 40 minutes

TOTAL: 1 hour 55 minutes

Carcass from a roasted 3- to 4-pound chicken

2 carrots, roughly chopped

3 stalks celery, roughly chopped

2 onions, roughly chopped

5 or 6 sprigs fresh parsley

1 sprig fresh thyme

2 tablespoons cider vinegar

10 whole black peppercorns

1 teaspoon salt

IN a 6-quart Instant Pot, place the carcass, carrots, celery, onions, parsley, thyme, vinegar, peppercorns, and salt. Add enough water to reach 1 inch below the maximum fill line. Lock the lid in place.

SELECT Soup/Broth. Use natural release.

STRAIN the broth through a fine-mesh strainer set over a large bowl or clean pot. Discard the solids. Transfer the broth to multiple containers to speed up cooling—don't freeze or refrigerate it while it's hot! Allow the broth to sit in the fridge, uncovered, for several hours, until the fat rises to the top and hardens. Scrape off the fat with a spoon and discard it.

REFRIGERATE the broth in airtight containers for 3 to 4 days or freeze for up to 6 months.

> **TIP** *A properly prepared bone broth might look a little jiggly when cold. That's just the gelatin from the collagen in the bones. When ready to use the broth, gently heat it and it will return to a liquid state.*

⬤ INSTANT POT
BEEF BONE BROTH

MAKES 9 CUPS

PREP: 10 minutes

ROAST: 35 minutes

CLOSED POT: 3 hours 20 minutes

TOTAL: 4 hours 5 minutes

3 to 4 pounds beef bones

2 carrots, roughly chopped

3 stalks celery, roughly chopped

2 onions, roughly chopped

5 or 6 fresh sprigs parsley

1 sprig fresh thyme

2 tablespoons cider vinegar

10 whole black peppercorns

1 teaspoon salt

PREHEAT the oven to 400°F. Place the bones in a shallow roasting pan or rimmed baking sheet. Roast until the bones are golden-brown, about 35 minutes.

IN a 6-quart Instant Pot, place the bones, carrots, celery, onions, parsley, thyme, vinegar, peppercorns, and salt. Add enough water to reach 1 inch below the maximum fill line. Lock the lid in place.

SELECT Manual and adjust to high pressure for 120 minutes. Use natural release.

STRAIN the broth through a fine-mesh strainer set over a large bowl or clean pot. Discard the solids. Transfer the broth to multiple containers to speed up cooling—don't freeze or refrigerate it while it's hot! Allow the broth sit in the fridge, uncovered, for several hours, until the fat rises to the top and hardens. Scrape off the fat with a spoon and discard it.

REFRIGERATE the broth in airtight containers for 3 to 4 days or freeze for up to 6 months.

BASIC MAYONNAISE

MAKES 1½ CUPS

PREP: 10 minutes

TOTAL: 10 minutes

1¼ cups light olive oil

1 large egg (see Tip)

½ teaspoon dry mustard

½ teaspoon salt

Juice of ½ lemon

PLACE ¼ cup of the olive oil, the egg, dry mustard, and salt in a blender, food processor, or mixing bowl. Blend, process, or mix thoroughly. While the food processor or blender is running (or while mixing in a bowl with an immersion blender), slowly drizzle in the remaining 1 cup olive oil until the mayonnaise has emulsified. Add the lemon juice and blend on low or stir to incorporate.

TIP *The key to this emulsion is making sure all the ingredients are at room temperature. Leave your egg out on the counter for an hour, or let it sit in a bowl of hot water for 5 minutes before mixing. Keep one lemon on the counter at all times for the express purpose of making mayo—trust us, you'll be making a lot of this. The slower you add the oil, the thicker and creamer the emulsion will be. You can slowly pour the oil by hand out of a spouted measuring cup, or use a plastic squeeze bottle to slowly drizzle it into the bowl, food processor, or blender. If you're using an immersion blender, pump the stick up and down a few times toward the end to whip some air into the mixture, making it even fluffier.*

EGG-FREE MAYONNAISE

MAKES 1¼ CUPS

PREP: 10 minutes

TOTAL: 10 minutes

½ cup coconut butter, slightly warmed

½ cup warm water

¼ cup light olive oil

2 cloves garlic, peeled

1 tablespoon fresh lemon juice (optional; see Tip)

¼ teaspoon salt

PLACE all the ingredients in a food processor or blender and blend on high until the mixture thickens, 1 to 2 minutes.

TIP *If you plan on using this egg-free mayo as a base for dressings and sauces, skip the lemon juice. You then have a neutral flavor base to which you can add any kind of acid (like a citrus juice or vinegar) based on the dressing or sauce you select.*

CLARIFIED BUTTER

Plain old butter isn't allowed on the Whole30 because it contains traces of milk proteins, which may be problematic for dairy-sensitive individuals. Clarifying butter is the technique of simmering butter slowly at a low temperature to separate the milk solids from the pure butterfat. The end result is a delicious, pure, dairy-free fat, perfect for flavoring dishes or cooking (even on high heat).

MAKES 1½ CUPS

PREP: 5 minutes

COOK: 20 minutes

TOTAL: 25 minutes

1 pound (4 sticks) unsalted butter

CUT the butter into 1-inch cubes. In a small pot or saucepan, melt the butter over medium-low heat and let it come to a simmer without stirring. As the butter simmers, foamy white dairy solids will rise to the surface. With a spoon or ladle, gently skim the dairy solids off the top and discard, leaving just the pure clarified butter in the pan.

ONCE you've removed the majority of the milk solids, strain the butter through cheesecloth into a glass storage jar, discarding the milk solids and cheesecloth when you are done. Allow the butter to cool before storing.

CLARIFIED butter can be stored in the refrigerator for up to 6 months or at room temperature for up to 3 months. (With the milk solids removed, clarified butter is shelf-stable for a longer period of time than regular butter.)

GHEE

You'll also see ghee suggested in the recipes—ghee is just a different form of clarified butter. To make ghee, simply simmer the butter longer, until the milk proteins begin to brown, clump, and drift to the bottom of the pan. Ghee has a sweeter, nuttier flavor than clarified butter. You can also purchase pastured organic ghee online.

While it's not part of our official Whole30 rules, we always encourage you to look for pastured organic butter when making your own clarified butter or ghee. Common brands available at health food stores nationwide include Straus, Kerrygold, Kalona SuperNatural, and Organic Valley.

BBQ SAUCE

MAKES 2 CUPS

PREP TIME: 15 minutes

COOK TIME: 1 hour 10 minutes

TOTAL TIME: 1 hour 25 minutes

2 tablespoons ghee or clarified butter

1 small onion, diced

3 cloves roasted garlic (see Tip)

1 large sweet potato, peeled and cut into 1-inch dice

½ cup apple cider

1 can (3 ounces) tomato paste

1 tablespoon apple cider vinegar

1 teaspoon paprika

1 teaspoon salt

½ teaspoon chipotle powder

HEAT the ghee in a medium skillet over medium heat. When the ghee is hot, add the onion and cook, stirring occasionally, until it starts to brown and caramelize, 15 to 20 minutes.

MEANWHILE, combine the roasted garlic, sweet potato, and apple cider in a medium saucepan. Add enough water to just barely cover the sweet potato—do not over-cover. Bring to a boil, then reduce the heat to a simmer and cook until the sweet potato is fork-tender, about 15 minutes. Strain and reserve the liquid from the pan.

COMBINE the sautéed onion and sweet potato mixture in a food processor or blender. Add the tomato paste, vinegar, paprika, salt, and chipotle powder. Add ¼ cup of the reserved cooking liquid and blend on low to medium speed. If the mixture is still too thick, add more liquid, ¼ cup at a time, while blending until you arrive at the desired consistency. (The sauce should pour like ketchup.)

STORE in the refrigerator for up to 2 to 3 days.

TIP *If you roast an entire head of garlic at once, you'll have leftovers to use in other recipes. Remove the skin from the leftover roasted cloves and place the garlic in an airtight container. Pour in enough extra-virgin olive oil to cover the cloves completely, and store in the refrigerator for up to 1 week. No need to reheat the cloves before adding them to a recipe—just toss them into the pot or pan cold and let them reheat with your dish.*

ROASTED GARLIC

To roast garlic in the oven, preheat the oven to 400°F. Peel the loose outer skin from a large head of garlic and wrap in foil, closing off the top. Place on a baking sheet and roast for 45 minutes, until the bulb is lightly browned at the top and feels soft when you squeeze it. Remove the garlic bulb from the foil carefully, and set aside until it's cool to the touch. Peel each clove of garlic carefully, using the sharp tip of a paring knife to break open each individual clove—it may be easier to squeeze the garlic out.

WHOLE30 RESOURCES

This first part of this resources section includes websites, cookbooks, and social media feeds we really like, from people with whom I have developed a close personal and professional relationship. They're smart, talented people who are Whole30 experts in their own right. They've done the program, offer specific resources for your Whole30 success, and really get the spirit and intention of the program.

Not *everything* in these websites, cookbooks, and social media feeds is Whole30 compliant, but you already knew that, right? They don't eat Whole30 all the time, and as I explain in *Food Freedom Forever*, neither will you. I'm just pointing this out because you have to read website content, recipes, and social media hashtags just as carefully as you have to read labels. Anybody on the Internet can say a meal or ingredient is "#Whole30" or "Whole30 compliant," but it's your job to determine whether that's actually true.

Unless it's coming from me (the Whole30 website, my books, or our social media feeds), one of our Whole30 Certified Coaches, or one of our Whole30 Endorsed cookbooks, don't take any label of "Whole30 compliant" at face value. Use your critical thinking skills, read your labels/ingredients/recipes carefully, and make your own educated decision about whether the item in question really is Whole30.

WEBSITES

WHOLE30

whole30.com

The official home of the Whole30 program. This is where you'll find our free Whole30 forum, all our free downloads, Whole30 Approved partners, our Certified Coaches, and more Whole30-related articles than you could possibly hope to read in thirty days.

FACEBOOK: whole30
INSTAGRAM: @whole30, @whole30recipes, @whole30approved
TWITTER: @whole30
ZIING: Whole30
YOUTUBE: whole30
PINTEREST: @whole30

THE WHOLE SMITHS: MICHELLE SMITH

thewholesmiths.com

Michelle Smith is passionate about eating real food and creating a sustainable food system that everyone can enjoy for many years to come. Her recipes focus on minimally processed and sustainable foods that are easy to prepare, taste great, and make us feel good again.

FACEBOOK: thewholesmiths
INSTAGRAM: @thewholesmiths
TWITTER: @thewholesmiths
SNAPCHAT: @thewholesmiths
PINTEREST: thewholesmiths

NOM NOM PALEO: MICHELLE TAM

nomnompaleo.com

Since 2010, Michelle Tam has been religiously taking pictures of her Whole30 meals and sharing her Whole30 meal plans and recipes. She also penned the *New York Times* best-selling cookbook *Nom Nom Paleo* and the new *Ready or Not*, both of which feature a large number of Whole30-friendly meals.

FACEBOOK: nomnompaleo
INSTAGRAM: @nomnompaleo
TWITTER: @nomnompaleo
PINTEREST: nomnompaleo
SNAPCHAT: michitam

DANIELLE WALKER'S AGAINST ALL GRAIN

againstallgrain.com

Danielle Walker is a *New York Times* best-selling author and photographer who shares her grain-free and gluten-free recipes on her blog and in her cookbooks, *Against All Grain*, *Meals Made Simple*, and *Celebrations*. With her acquired culinary skills, love for food, and deeply touching personal story, she is a go-to source for those suffering from all types of diseases and allergies.

FACEBOOK: AgainstAllGrain
INSTAGRAM: @againstallgrain
TWITTER: @againstallgrain
YOUTUBE: AgainstAllGrain
PINTEREST: @Againstallgrain

WELL FED: MELISSA JOULWAN

meljoulwan.com

Not only is Melissa Joulwan the author of three Whole30-friendly cookbooks (*Well Fed*, *Well Fed 2*, and *Well Fed Weeknights*) and a Whole30 Certified Coach, she's also a brilliant food, fitness, health, and lifestyle blogger with hundreds of Whole30-compliant recipes, meal plans, and resources freely available on her site.

FACEBOOK: MelJoulwan
INSTAGRAM: @meljoulwan
TWITTER: @meljoulwan
PINTEREST: meljoulwan

SUSTAINABLE DISH: DIANA RODGERS

sustainabledish.com

Diana Rodgers, RD, LDN, NTP, is a real-food registered dietitian and Whole30 Certified Coach living on a working organic farm. She is the author of *The Homegrown Paleo Cookbook* and *Paleo Lunches and Breakfasts on the Go* and hosts the *Sustainable Dish* podcast. She speaks internationally about nutrition, the environmental impact of our food choices, and animal welfare, and fully embraces the Whole30 philosophy in her practice.

FACEBOOK: sustainabledish
INSTAGRAM: @sustainabledish
TWITTER: @sustainabledish

COOKBOOKS

There are only a handful of books in which 100 percent of the recipes featured are officially Whole30 Approved. You're reading one of them right now—the others are *The Whole30: The 30-Day Guide to Total Health and Food Freedom*, *The Whole30 Cookbook*, and *The Whole30 Fast and Easy*.

THE "HOW-TO" FOR THE WHOLE30

Although *The Whole30* features more than 100 delicious and totally compliant recipes, it's more than just a cookbook—it's a complete Whole30 handbook, start to finish, including planning and preparation tips, an extensive FAQ, and Whole30 kitchen basics. If you're loving the recipes in *The Whole30 Slow Cooker* but want a game plan to help you maximize your Whole30 success, *The Whole30* is all you'll need.

However, there are other cookbooks that feature delicious, Whole30-compliant recipes or Whole30-friendly recipes that could easily be adapted for compliance. You'll still need to be on the lookout for noncompliant ingredients, however, and save the baked goods, desserts, and treats sections for life after your Whole30.

THE WHOLE SMITHS GOOD FOOD COOKBOOK

BY MICHELLE SMITH

The first ever Whole30 Endorsed cookbook features 150 recipes (80 of which are Whole30-compliant) to help you prepare delicious, healthy meals during your Whole30 and in your food freedom.

WELL FED, WELL FED 2, and WELL FED WEEKNIGHTS

BY MELISSA JOULWAN

Hundreds of mouth-watering recipes and meal ideas from every corner of the world, plus time-saving meal prep and cooking tutorials.

NOM NOM PALEO: FOOD FOR HUMANS and READY OR NOT: 150+ MAKE-AHEAD, MAKE-OVER, AND MAKE-NOW RECIPES

BY MICHELLE TAM AND HENRY FONG

Whether you're a planner or an improviser, these cookbooks feature family-friendly recipes and step-by-step instructional photographs for everything from make-ahead feasts to lightning-fast leftover makeovers.

AGAINST ALL GRAIN, MEALS MADE SIMPLE, CELEBRATIONS, and EAT WHAT YOU LIKE (December 2018)

BY DANIELLE WALKER

Grain-free, dairy-free, and Whole30-friendly, Danielle provides family-friendly meals, quick and easy dinners, and complete holiday and special event menus in her best-selling cookbooks.

PALEO BREAKFASTS AND LUNCHES ON THE GO and THE HOMEGROWN PALEO COOKBOOK

BY DIANA RODGERS

You'll find healthy "on-the-go" packable meals (no sandwiches in sight) in *Paleo Breakfasts and Lunches on the Go*; and 100 delicious farm-to-table recipes and a complete guide to growing your own healthy food in *The Homegrown Paleo Cookbook*.

WHOLE30 CERTIFIED COACHES

coach.whole30.com/coaches

Our Whole30 Certified Coaches are a wealth of Whole30 knowledge and expertise. Some have professional credentials (like R.D., M.D., and Ph.D.) that allow them to incorporate the Whole30 into their healthcare practices, while others specialize in Whole30 for families; Whole30 in conjunction with yoga or fitness programs; meal planning and grocery shopping; Whole30 on a budget; and more. Connect with a Certified Coach in your area for in-person social support, accountability, and resources.

WHOLE30 INSPIRATION

Our special guest contributors to *The Whole30 Slow Cooker* have gorgeous websites and social media feeds with hundreds of Whole30-compliant recipes, meal planning strategies, kitchen tips, and lifestyle guidance to keep you happy and healthy long after your Whole30 journey is over. Note, not everything they create is Whole30-friendly; read your recipes carefully, and save sweets and treats for your food freedom.

TRU PROVISIONS: GRACE BRINTON

truprovisions.com

Grace Brinton is the founder and head chef of Tru Provisions, a Whole30 Approved meal delivery company in Boston, MA.

FACEBOOK: truprovisions
INSTAGRAM: @truprovisions
TWITTER: @truprovisions

THE CASTAWAY KITCHEN: CRISTINA CURP

thecastawaykitchen.com

Cristina is a chef, mom, and author who loves creating delicious, healing recipes and spreading good vibes.

FACEBOOK: thecastawaykitchen
INSTAGRAM: @thecastawaykitchen
TWITTER: @castawaykitchen
PINTEREST: castawaykitchen
YOUTUBE: The Castaway Kitchen

SIMON HALL PRIVATE CHEF: SIMON HALL

simonhallprivatechef.com

Simon Hall Private Chef offers Whole30 Approved private chef, catering, and meal prep services across the southeast.

FACEBOOK: chefsimonhall
INSTAGRAM: @simonhallprivatechef

KITCHFIX: JOSH KATT

Kitchfix.com

Josh Katt is the founder/CEO of Kitchfix, a company offering prepared meals throughout Chicagoland, and Paleo goods in groceries nationwide.

FACEBOOK: kitchfix
INSTAGRAM: @kitchfix
TWITTER: @kitchfix
YOUTUBE: Kitchfix

BAZAARLAZARR:
CHRISTI LAZAR

bazaarlazarr.com

Christi Lazar is a New York-based digital marketer, and food writer, photographer, and creator of the popular blog *BazaarLazarr*.

FACEBOOK: bazaarlazarr
INSTAGRAM: @bazaarlazarr
TWITTER: @bazaarlazarr

PALEO RUNNING MOMMA:
MICHELE ROSEN

paleorunningmomma.com

Michele Rosen is the recipe creator, runner, and blogger behind *Paleo Running Momma*, a real food website featuring clean-eating family favorites.

FACEBOOK: paleorunningmomma
INSTAGRAM: @paleorunningmomma
TWITTER: @paleorunmomma
PINTEREST: paleorunmomma

CONFESSIONS OF A CLEAN FOODIE:
CHARLOTTE SMYTHE

confessionsofacleanfoodie.com

Charlotte Smythe is Minneapolis based blogger and real food advocate.

FACEBOOK: confessionsofacleanfoodie
INSTAGRAM: @confessionsofacleanfoodie
TWITTER: @foodiconfession
PINTEREST: thecleanfoodie1

THE DEFINED DISH:
ALEX SNODGRASS

thedefineddish.com

Alex Snodgrass is a Dallas-based food blogger, focusing on mostly Whole30 and Paleo recipes.

FACEBOOK: thedefinedish
INSTAGRAM: @thedefineddish
PINTEREST: thedefineddish
YOUTUBE: The Defined Dish

PRIMAL PALATE:
HAYLEY AND BILL STALEY

primalpalate.com

Primal Palate hosts over 750 Whole30 compliant recipes on their website, and offers a line of Whole30 Approved organic spice blends.

FACEBOOK: thefoodlovers
INSTAGRAM: @primalpalate
TWITTER: @primalpalate
PINTEREST: thefoodlovers
YOUTUBE: Primal Palate

MEAL PLANNING

REAL PLANS

w30.co/w30realplans

Delicious, totally compliant Whole30 meals in a weekly plan to fit your taste and schedule. Fully customizable; choose which days of the week and meals to plan, exclude ingredients to which you are allergic or just don't like, prioritize recipes using specific kitchen gadgets like a slow cooker or Instant Pot, and generate an automated shopping list and meal prep instructions for each week. Features more than 1,000 Whole30-compliant recipes to build into your family's perfect weekly meal plan.

WHOLE30 APPROVED

This is a list of our official Whole30 Approved partners, with the addition of some Whole30-friendly products from companies we love. These companies make a variety of products to support your Whole30 journey, but in many cases, not every product they make fits our guidelines. Read your labels, or look for the official Whole30 Approved logo on their website or packaging. We add to our list of official Whole30 Approved partners every week, so visit whole30.com/whole30-approved for the full roster.

WHOLE30 CURATED KITS

THRIVE MARKET WHOLE30 CURATED KITS (thrivemarket.com/whole30): Whole30 Approved curated kits, "Melissa's Picks" featuring her favorite Whole30 products, and more than 100+ compliant pantry staples delivered to your door. New members save 25 percent and free shipping on their first order.

BAREFOOT PROVISIONS WHOLE30 KITS (w30.co/w30bpkits): Whole30 Approved curated kits for emergency foods, healthy fats, and pregnancy nutrition, shipped throughout the world, no membership required.

NATURA MARKET CANADA WHOLE30 KITS (w30.co/w30natura): Your Canadian source for Whole30 Approved curated kits and over 100 compliant and Approved items delivered to your door.

ON-THE-GO AND TRAVEL FOOD

RXBAR (rxbar.com): Egg white protein–based bars. Most flavors are Whole30 compliant; read your labels and don't use these as treats, please. Use the discount code "whole30" online to save 10 percent.

DNXBAR (dnxbar.com/whole30): Six delicious flavors of grass-fed meat bars packed with organic ingredients to fuel your on-the-go lifestyle.

EPIC (epicbar.com): Grass-fed/pastured jerky bars, bits, and strips, and bacon bites for salads and soups. Most varieties are Whole30 compliant (read your labels).

CHOMPS SNACK STICKS (gochomps.com): Grass-fed and free-range beef, venison, and turkey snack sticks.

WILD ZORA (wildzora.com): Natural and grass-fed meat and veggie bars.

BROOKLYN BILTONG (brooklynbiltong.com): Seasoned, all-natural dried beef snacks.

NICK'S STICKS (nicks-sticks.com): 100% grass-fed beef and free range turkey meat snack sticks.

SERENITY KIDS BABY FOOD (myserenitykids.com): Puréed organic vegetables and pastured-raised meat from small American family farms.

SEASNAX (seasnax.com): Nutrient-packed roasted seaweed sheets in a variety of flavors.

FRESH FOODS (Meat and Produce)

APPLEGATE FARMS (applegate.com/whole30): More than twenty Approved natural and organic humanely raised meat products. No antibiotics and no GMO ingredients ever.

BUTCHERBOX (butcherbox.com/whole30): 100-percent grass-fed, grass-finished beef, organic chicken, and heritage breed pork, delivered to your door CSA-style for less than $6.50 per meal.

HUNGRY HARVEST (hungryharvest.net): Recovered farm-fresh produce and organic produce, delivered to your door CSA-style in the mid-Atlantic (and rapidly growing).

U.S. WELLNESS MEATS (grasslandbeef.com): Grass-fed and free-range meats from family farmers, including the first-ever Whole30 Approved sugar-free bacon.

PANORAMA (panoramameats.com): Grass-fed beef from certified organic family farmers.

VERDE FARMS (verdefarms.com): Pasture-raised grass-fed beef raised according to strict animal welfare protocols.

THE HONEST BISON (honestbison.com): Grass-fed and humanely raised bison offerings, including soup bones.

PEDERSON'S NATURAL FARMS (thesimplegrocer.com): Certified humane and sugar-free bacon, sausages, hot dogs, and ham.

NATURE'S RANCHER (naturesrancher.com): Certified humane, all natural, nitrate/nitrite free pork, beef, poultry, and lamb.

NAKED BACON (nakedbaconco.com): Sugar-free, nitrite-/nitrate-free, all-natural bacon and breakfast sausage.

SIZZLEFISH (sizzlefish.com): Online seafood market for hand-selected and perfectly portioned seafood.

CECE'S VEGGIE NOODLE CO. (cecesveggieco.com): Fresh, riced veggies from cauliflower and broccoli, and raw spiralized veggie noodles made from zucchini, butternut squash, sweet potatoes, and beets.

HEALTHY FATS

PRIMAL KITCHEN AVOCADO OIL AND MAYO (primalkitchen.com): Heart-healthy avocado oil and avocado oil–based sugar-free mayonnaise, in original and chipotle flavors.

FATWORKS (fatworksfoods.com): Traditional handcrafted cooking fats, including tallow (beef, buffalo, and lamb), lard, leaf lard, duck fat, goose fat, and chicken schmaltz.

TIN STAR GHEE (tinstarfoods.com): Cultured, handmade pastured ghee and brown butter ghee made from the milk of grass-fed cows.

PURE INDIAN FOODS GHEE (pureindianfoods.com): Grass-fed, organic, non-GMO ghee and cooking oils.

GEORGIA GRINDERS (georgiagrinders.com): Handcrafted, premium almond, cashew, and pecan nut butters made out of simple, all natural ingredients.

OMGHEE (omghee.com): Small-batch, grass-fed, organic, non-GMO ghee.

MEENUT BUTTER (meeeatpaleo.com): Handmade, small-batch sugar- and peanut-free nut butter blends.

PANTRY STAPLES

SAFE CATCH (safecatch.com): Wild-caught tuna in cans and pouches, featuring the lowest mercury content of any brand—safe even for pregnant women.

CUCINA ANTICA PASTA SAUCES (cucina-antica.com): Cooking sauces made with imported Italian San Marzano tomatoes.

MONTE BENE (montebene.com): Pasta sauces made without preservatives, added sugar, gluten, water, or tomato paste.

ORGANICO BELLO (organicobello.com): USDA Organic and Non-GMO Verified pasta sauces, salsas and canned tomatoes made with 100% imported organic Italian tomatoes.

BIG TREE FARMS COCONUT AMINOS (bigtreefarms.com): A soy sauce substitute made from brewed and naturally fermented coconut blossom nectar and sea salt.

RED BOAT FISH SAUCE (redboatfishsauce.com): All-natural, first-press, "extra-virgin" Vietnamese fish sauce made without MSG or preservatives.

EPIC (epicbar.com): The first-ever ready-to-heat pasture-raised and grass-fed beef, chicken, and turkey broth, from their Whole Animal Project.

BARE BONES (barebonesbroth.com): Nutritious, pasture-raised and grass-fed, organic chicken and beef bone broths.

BONAFIDE PROVISIONS (bonafideprovisions.com): Organic, grass-fed, pasture-raised chicken and beef bone broth.

KETTLE & FIRE (kettleandfire.com): Grass-fed, organic beef and chicken bone broth in shelf-stable packaging.

OSSO GOOD (ossogoodbones.com): Pasture-raised and grass-fed, all-natural chicken and beef sippable, organic bone broths and soups.

VITAL PROTEINS BROTH (vitalproteins.com): Powdered bone broth from 100% grass-fed beef; just add hot water.

PRIMAL PALATE ORGANIC SPICES (primalpalate.com): Organic, gluten-free, non-GMO, non-irradiated high-quality spices and spice blends, including an AIP-friendly spice pack.

SPICE CAVE ORGANIC SPICE BLENDS (thespicecave.com): All-natural spice blends to pair with your protein choices: Land, Sea, and Wind.

PALEO POWDER SEASONINGS (paleopowderseasoning.com): All-purpose Paleo, MSG-free, and gluten-free seasonings.

FREEZER AND FRIDGE STAPLES

ZÜPA NOMA SOUPS (drinkzupa.com): Ready-to-sip nutrient-dense soups containing over four servings of whole, organic vegetables per bottle.

TIO GAZPACHO (tiogazpacho.com): Chef-crafted drinkable soups made with super clean non-GMO ingredients.

BONAFIDE PROVISIONS (bonafideprovisions.com): Organic, grass-fed, pasture-raised Drinkable Veggie bone broth beverages.

FARMHOUSE CULTURE (farmhouseculture.com):
Organic, probiotic-rich krauts, Gut Shots, and vegetables with zingy, zesty flavors.

TRIBALÍ FOODS (tribalifoods.com): Organic 100% grass fed beef and chicken patties, made with only real ingredients.

GRANDCESTORS MEALS (grandcestors.com):
Individual serving sizes of prepared frozen meals with hearty portions.

PRIMITIVE FEAST (primitivefeast.com): Clean and flavorful frozen entrees, shipped nationwide.

DRESSINGS AND SAUCES

NOBLE MADE MARINADES AND COOKING SAUCES (newprimal.com): Classic, citrus herb, and spicy marinades; plus five varieties of Buffalo and BBQ sauces for meat and veggies, from The New Primal.

PRIMAL KITCHEN DRESSINGS (primalkitchen.com): Extensive variety of avocado oil–based, sugar-free dressings and marinades.

TESSEMAE'S ALL NATURAL (tessemaes.com): All-natural and certified organic dressings, sauces, condiments, and marinades from their family to yours.

YAI'S THAI SAUCES (yaisthai.com): Thai-inspired, hand-crafted salsas, sauces, almond sauce, and curry sauces.

MESA DE VIDA COOKING SAUCES (mesadevida.com): Healthy cooking sauce & flavor bases inspired by vibrant cuisines from around the globe.

BEVERAGES

SPINDRIFT (spindriftfresh.com): Sparkling water made with only real squeezed fruit, water, and bubbles.

HINT WATER (drinkhint.com): Pure, unsweetened water infused with truly natural fruit flavors. Available in more than 25 refreshing flavors, in still and sparkling.

LACROIX WATER (lacroixwater.com): Sugar- and calorie-free naturally flavored sparkling waters.

RETHINK WATER (rethinkwater.com): The first ever zero-sugar, zero-sweetener, zero-calorie, USDA-certified-organic, flavored water for kids.

NUTPODS (nutpods.com): Unsweetened, carrageenan-free almond and coconut milk coffee creamers in four delicious varieties and seasonal offerings.

NEW BARN ALMOND MILK (thenewbarn.com):
The first Whole30 Approved almond milk, with only four simple, organic ingredients.

FOUR SIGMATIC (foursigmatic.com): Functional mushroom powders to help you relax, be well, energize, and support productivity.

CRIO BRU COFFEE ALTERNATIVE (criobru.com): All-natural 99-percent caffeine-free coffee alternative made from Fair Trade cocoa beans, roasted, ground, and brewed just like coffee.

CHOFFY BREWED CHOCOLATE (choffy.com): Artisan quality 100-percent premium ground cacao beans, brews just like coffee.

KLIO HERBAL TEA (kliotea.com): Unique herbal teas imported from Greece.

LIFESTYLE

VITAL PROTEINS (vitalproteins.com): Pasture-raised collagen peptides and gelatin for healthier skin, nails, and hair; to promote joint and bone health and aid in athletic performance.

DOC PARSLEY'S SLEEP REMEDY (docparsley.com): Developed by sleep expert Dr. Kirk Parsley, Sleep Remedy aims to lay the foundation for the best sleep possible.

LYTELINE ELECTROLYTES (lyteline.com): Healthier hydration products, including a sports drink, electrolytes, and trace minerals.

RESTAURANTS AND MEAL DELIVERY

ZOËS KITCHEN (zoeskitchen.com): Fresh-made Mediterranean with a robust Whole30 Approved menu in more than 250 locations nationwide.

SNAP KITCHEN (snapkitchen.com): Fresh, prepared meals from scratch, with dozens of Whole30 Approved options. Pick-up, deliver, or subscribe to weekly Whole30 meal plans.

TRUE FARE (truefare.com): Chef-prepared, seasonal, and organic breakfasts, lunches, dinners, and snacks shipped frozen across the United States.

Visit whole30.com/whole30-approved for dozens of catering, meal delivery, and restaurant options in every region of the U.S.

WHOLE30 SUPPORT

Resources to give you Whole30 support, motivation, and accountability.

WHOLE30 DAY BY DAY: YOUR DAILY GUIDE TO WHOLE30 SUCCESS

whole30.com/daybyday

Advice, tips, hacks, and inspiration to guide you through every day of your Whole30, with guided reflections, dedicated space to track your non-scale victories and Whole30 meals, and daily check-ins to keep you motivated.

WHOLESOME

whole30.com/wholesome

Our free weekly newsletter filled with Whole30-related advice, tips, recipes, reader stories, discounts, giveaways, and more.

THE WHOLE30 FORUM

forum.whole30.com

If you have a question, we can almost guarantee it's been answered. Find those answers, solicit expert advice from our moderators, and get support from fellow Whole30ers on our free forum.

WHOLE30 RESOURCES

whole30.com/pdf-downloads

Home to a host of helpful PDF downloads (including our shopping list, meal template, label-reading guide, pantry-stocking guide, and more).

DEAR MELISSA

whole30.com/category/dear-melissa

My own Whole30 (and life after) advice column, where I answer your questions and share from my own experience.

CONNECT WITH MELISSA

I love hearing your stories, answering your questions, giving you my best Whole30 and food freedom advice . . . and tough-loving you when you need it.

FACEBOOK: hartwig.melissa
INSTAGRAM: @melissa_hartwig
TWITTER: @melissahartwig_
ZIING: #melissahartwigwhole30

COOKING CONVERSIONS

Metric weights listed here have been slightly rounded to make measuring easier.

VOLUME

U.S.	METRIC	IMPERIAL
¼ tsp	1.2 ml	
½ tsp	2.5 ml	
1 tsp	5 ml	
½ Tbsp (1½ tsp)	7.5 ml	
1 Tbsp (3 tsp)	15 ml	
¼ cup (4 Tbsp)	60 ml	2 fl oz
⅓ cup (5 Tbsp)	75 ml	2½ fl oz
½ cup (8 Tbsp)	125 ml	4 fl oz
⅔ cup (10 Tbsp)	150 ml	5 fl oz
¾ cup (12 Tbsp)	175 ml	6 fl oz
1 cup (16 Tbsp)	250 ml	8 fl oz
1¼ cups	300 ml	10 fl oz (½ pint)
1½ cups	350 ml	12 fl oz
2 cups (1 pint)	500 ml	16 fl oz
2½ cups	625 ml	20 fl oz (1 pint)
1 quart	1 liter	32 fl oz

WEIGHT

U.S.	METRIC
¼ oz	7 grams
½ oz	15 g
¾ oz	20 g
1 oz	30 g
8 oz (½ lb)	225 g
12 oz (¾ lb)	340 g
16 oz (1 lb)	455 g
2 lb	900 g
2¼ lb	1 kg

INDEX

NOTE: *Page references in italics indicate photographs.*

INDEX

CHANGE YOUR LIFE WITH
THE BEST-SELLING BOOKS FROM

WHOLE30®

OVER 1 MILLION COPIES SOLD

THE WHOLE30®

The 30-DAY Guide to TOTAL HEALTH and FOOD FREEDOM

From the best-selling authors of *IT STARTS WITH FOOD*

Melissa Hartwig and Dallas Hartwig

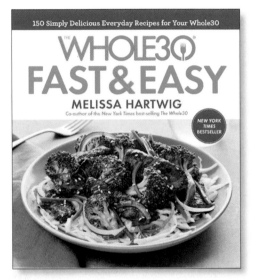

150 Simply Delicious Everyday Recipes for Your Whole30

THE WHOLE30®
FAST & EASY

MELISSA HARTWIG

Co-author of the *New York Times* best-selling *The Whole30*

NEW YORK TIMES BESTSELLER

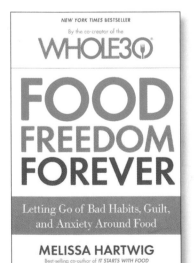

NEW YORK TIMES BESTSELLER

By the co-creator of the

WHOLE30®

FOOD
FREEDOM
FOREVER

Letting Go of Bad Habits, Guilt,
and Anxiety Around Food

MELISSA HARTWIG

Best-selling co-author of *IT STARTS WITH FOOD*

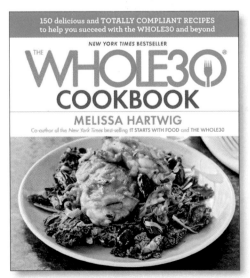

150 delicious and TOTALLY COMPLIANT RECIPES
to help you succeed with the WHOLE30 and beyond

NEW YORK TIMES BESTSELLER

THE WHOLE30®
COOKBOOK

MELISSA HARTWIG

Co-author of the *New York Times* best-selling *IT STARTS WITH FOOD* and *THE WHOLE30*

THE WHOLE30®
DAY
BY
DAY

ADVICE   TIPS   HACKS   INSPIRATION

Your Daily Guide to
Whole30 Success

MELISSA HARTWIG

Best-selling co-author of *The Whole30*

HMH hmhco.com